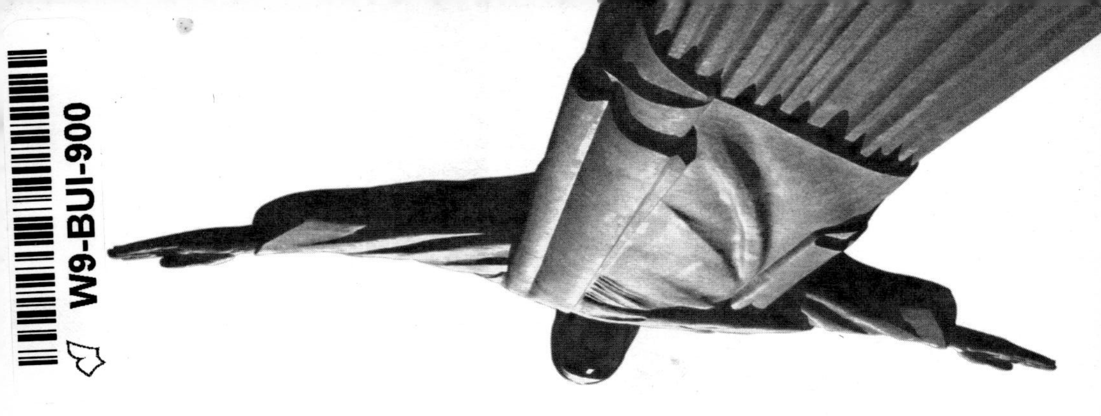

Footprint

Rio de Janeiro

Alex Robinson

Contents

About the author

A first degree in Religious Literature and a Masters in Divinity left Alex Robinson still wondering what to do when he grew up. While he tried to reach a decision he decided to become a journalist and see the world. Since then he has worked in television for the BBC, Channel 4, Carlton and Discovery Channel on programmes like Dispatches, Equinox, Everyman and the Money Programme, and has wandered around 60 or so countries. He fell in love with India, with South America and then with Gardênia who took him to São Paulo where he now lives with her and their son, Raphael. He has written or photographed for magazines and newspapers from *Marie Claire* and *Conde Nast Traveller* to the *Financial Times* and *Independent on Sunday* and for all the major UK guide book companies. And he is still wondering what to do when he grows up.

Acknowledgements

Alex would like to thank Gardênia and Raphael for their hard work, patience and company, Ben Box and Mick Day for the firm foundation of the previous Rio de Janeiro book, Alan Murphy for the commission and patience, Sarah Sorensen for her care with the maps and Nicola Jones for all her very hard work and thoroughness. In Rio Alex would like to thank Danielle for all her time and the use so often of her flat, Alê Santos for all those fashion and shopping tips, Maria Eliza, Stephen Thompson, Richard Dye and Aragão for company and help in Rio, Mick Day for his rundown of Rio's surf spots, all at Regua for their inspiring work; Aidan at Body and Soul Adventures on Ilha Grande, Toca do Vinícius for the Vinícius de Moraes CD, Grupo Afro Reggae for their time and inspiring music and the people of Rio; especially the poorest from whom all the city's great things come.

Introducing Rio de Janeiro

There is no urban view more beautiful than that from the Corcovado Christ figure at sunset. Rainforest surrounds you on all sides. In front, the gentle curves of the Sugar Loaf and a myriad of other mountains rise from the Atlantic, flanked by endless beaches. Immediately below, the lights of the city twinkle in the orange and violet of the tropical twilight. It is no wonder Brazilians call Rio "A Cidade Maravilhosa"; the wonderful city.

Even before they arrive here, most visitors are familiar with this view, just as they are familiar with the mythology of Carnival, its beautiful people and brilliant costumes; its frenetic parades, its mythical *bacchanale*... They may know the gentle, eternally sunny, eternally feminine lilt of bossa nova as immortalized by *The Girl from Ipanema* or the husky electronica of Bebel Gilberto. And they'll know of the football played in enormous stadiums to the ecstatic beat of scores of samba drums. Rio won't disappoint. It really does have all of these, and a good deal more which is less well-known but equally captivating. For better. And for worse.

Beaches

Peter Fleming, the author of one of the best travel books about Brazil, once said that 'a man in a hurry will be miserable in Brazil.' And this is certainly true of Rio. At times it seems that the city's raison d'être is to do nothing. And there is nowhere better to do nothing than on the beach. Rio crumbles. Its social problems are insurmountable. But people here are always looking at the beach and don't notice. If Nero had been a Brazilian he would have left his fiddle at home and gone surfing in Ipanema. The perfect crescents, like Flamengo and Botafogo, which huddle around the Sugar Loaf, are now sadly too dirty for safe swimming. Copacabana can be decidedly suspect, but Ipanema, Leblon, Vidigal, São Conrado, Barra da Tijuca, Recreio dos Bandeirantes, Prainha, Macumba... there are enough perfect stretches of sand in Rio for all of the city's problems and more. And beyond the urban area there are even more; near Paraty are beaches so wild that fresh jaguar prints can be seen on them in the morning. And Ilha Grande, a steep-sided, forest-swathed island in an emerald bay, is fringed with countless more.

Carnival and beyond

To say that Cariocas, as Rio residents are called, like to do nothing is perhaps unfair. They love to party. At least half of the year is spent in frenetic social activity. Carnival is no mere Mardi Gras celebration; it is the culmination of months of free parties which begin in December and reach a peak over New Year, when millions gather on Copacabana beach for a spectacular firework display. Free concerts continue throughout January – on the beaches in Flamengo and Copacabana; on the promenades and pavements in Ipanema and Leblon. And then in February comes Carnival week itself. Over the rest of the year there is always something going on any day of the week – from street parties in Gávea to all-night clubbing in Leblon. At the weekend, Lapa, once the seediest area in central Rio, bursts with Bohemian life and its streets throb with samba, *frevo*, *forró* and a hundred other frenetic Brazilian beats.

At a glance

Rio is divided physically and culturally by the steep mountains of the Serra da Carioca. To the south are the city's fashionable suburbs and beaches, to the north lives most of Rio's massive underclass. The two zones converge at the foot of the mountains in the city centre, where most of the city's museums and historic buildings can be found.

Central Rio

Praça 15 de Novembro and around

This little square lies in the crowded centre of Rio on the edge of Guanabara Bay. It contains many of Rio's baroque palaces, historic buildings and museums. Just north of the *praça*, the Travessa do Comércio is one of the most enchanting colonial streets in the city.

Largo da Misericórdia and the museums

The city was born here, just south of Praça 15, on a hill crowned with a splendid monastery. Now only remnants of the former beauty remain, some pretty churches and a cluster of the city's best museums.

Cinelândia

Just south of the centre, this area was once the Bohemian heart of belle-époque Rio. It looks fairly undistinguished today but preserves the once glorious Theatro Municipal and one of Brazil's most important art galleries, the Museu Nacional de Belas-Artes.

Largo da Carioca and around

Great for a wander, this higgledy piggledy street of colonial churches and modern buildings just north of Cinelândia hosts a variety of interesting sights within a very small area.

Praça Tiradentes and the cathedral

Southwest of Praça 15, this square was an important site in the establishment of Brazil's independence. Just to its south is Rio's modernist cathedral, the 18th-century Arcos de Lapa and the starting point for one of Rio's best-kept secrets – the tram ride to Santa Teresa.

Lapa

As tawdry as Dickensian Whitechapel, with a weekend nightlife to rival Madrid's Malasaña, this huddle of grubby colonial streets dotted with surprisingly smart clubs is *the* place to samba in Rio at the weekend.

Central station and Praça da República

Made famous by Walter Salles's eponymous film, Rio's railway station is a hotchpotch of shady parks, huge thoroughfares and office blocks. To the west is the Sambódromo; purpose-built to host Rio's Carnival.

Candelária

North of the centre, Rio's best-loved church of high-society sits in an island surrounded by traffic and skyscrapers. A handful of interesting cultural centres host exhibitions nearby.

Praça Mauá and the port area

Southern Brazil's largest and most opulent colonial monastery sits on the edge of a string of abandoned warehouses which look like a gangster hideaway from a Hollywood heist movie.

The southern suburbs

Glória, Catete and Flamengo

Though now a little frayed, Glória and Catete retain crumbling vestiges of their glorious past. These were once the favourite seaside residential areas of the fashionable set. Now popular bases for backpackers.

Santa Teresa

Situated up on a ridge behind Glória, the steep, winding, cobbled streets clanking with 19th-century trams, colonial mansion houses and restaurants with sweeping views of the bay would be a charming place to stay were it not for its reputation for occasional muggings.

Pão de Açúcar, Botafogo and Urca

One of Rio's most captivating views: a perfect wine-glass bay watched over by the granite dome of the Pão de Açucar, or the Sugar Loaf, its flanks shrouded in the remnants of a forest.

Copacabana and Leme

The world's most famous urban beach is a magnificent crescent of broad white sand backed by skyscrapers. Great for people watching.

Ipanema, Arpoador and Leblon

One beach, three names. This playground of the city's fashionable elite is watched over by shanty towns, which twinkle like stars on the sides of the dramatic Dois Irmãos mountains at the beach's far western end.

Gávea, Lagoa and Jardim Botânico

As fashionable for nightlife as Ipanema and Leblon are for beachlife; the wealthy and surgically-enhanced fill the restaurants of Lagoa and Jardim Botânico while their kids hang out in the bars of Gávea.

Corcovado and the Christ statue

Christ perpetually cradles Rio in his embrace from the top of Corcovado mountain, lit in brilliant xenon in the midst of lush forest.

South of Leblon and Tijuca National Park

Further south, Rio dissipates into surf beaches and mock-Miami suburbs and shopping malls; but the sea here is the cleanest within the city and there are great views back to the centre. Tijuca National Park, to the west, is the largest urban rainforest in the world.

Northern Rio

An area of vast sprawling *favelas*. Nestled on the edges of this urban, industrial wilderness is the Emperor's former palace and the largest football stadium in the world – Maracanã.

Best

Ten of the best

1 **Lapa** – a cluster of tawdry colonial streets whose samba clubs offer the most fevered, bohemian and frenetic weekend nightlife in the city, p47.

2 **Mosteiro de São Bento** – Rio's most impressive colonial building with an austere exterior and one of the finest baroque interiors in Brazil, p54.

3 **Santa Teresa tram** – Rio's best short journey winds up from the modernist cathedral, over the Lapa aqueduct in the city centre and into the hilly cobbles of pretty Santa Teresa, p62.

4 **Sugar Loaf** – a cable car floats over the city to this giant boulder sticking up out of the bay. The views from the top are second only to Corcovado, p64.

5 **Ipanema beach** – Latin America's great Vanity Fair is played out daily on this glorious stretch of white sand. Far away and close to the views are astounding, p70.

6 **Christ on Corcovado** – the most spectacular urban view in the world. Come for sunset, p76.

7 **Tijuca National Park** – the largest stretch of urban forest in the world and a cool, relaxing eyrie of epiphytes, mosses and little springs above the humid expanse of Rio, p82.

8 **Niterói Museum of Modern Art** – the exhibits are so-so, but the setting of Oscar Niemeyer's space age circular building on a peninsula looking out over Rio is inspired, p91.

9 **Paraty** – the facades of the state's prettiest colonial town look out over a bay of verdant islands in the midst of rainforest-clad hills and countless beaches, p104.

10 **Carnival** or **New Year's Eve** – two of the world's largest and most colourful parties. Prepare for delirious bewilderment, p179 and p186.

Trip planner

Rio is warm the whole year round, although hotels are busy and more expensive during the domestic high season (mid-December to mid-January) and around Carnival, which runs for five riotous days from the Friday afternoon before Shrove Tuesday to the morning hangover of Ash Wednesday.

The Rio summer, which lasts from November to May, is hot and sweaty with temperatures ranging between 25°C and 35°C and occasionally reaching up to 40°C. The mountains are considerably cooler. There are often heavy rains between November and early March, which tend to come in bursts of a few days – associated with cold fronts sweeping up from Argentina.

Conditions in Rio during the winter (May to September) are like those of a North European summer – bright blue sky with sporadic rain, and overcast skies, with temperatures ranging from 14°C (when there is a cold front) to the high 20s. It can reach freezing at an altitude of 1,200 m or above; warm clothes are needed on high ground like Itatiaia or Petrópolis.

A weekend

If you are only in Rio for a weekend, then make it a long one from Friday to Monday, and consider hiring a car and driver or private guide (see pages 217 and 221). **Friday night**: ease into Rio. Eat out in one of the Zona Sul's funky casual dining spots in Ipanema or Leblon before walking along Rua Dias Ferreira and the surrounding streets in search of a bar which takes your fancy. **Saturday**: breakfast in your hotel before leaving early to catch the first cable car up the Sugar Loaf. Spend the rest of the morning lazing on the beach in Ipanema, sightseeing in central Rio or on the Ilha de Paquetá. Be sure not to miss the Lapa antiques market in the afternoon – one of the best places for people watching in Rio and a real Carioca experience, with live music and street dancing. In the evening treat yourself to a meal in one of Copacabana's best restaurants before going out to dance at a club in

Lapa. **Sunday**: spend the morning on the beach and lunchtime at the Aprazível restaurant in Santa Teresa, where they have a live *choro* show. In the afternoon head for Tijuca National Park and arrive at Corcovado at around 1600 – making Rio's most magnificent view a spectacular finale to your stay.

One week

A week gives ample time both to see Rio well and to take an excursion. Plan to spend at least one weekend in Rio itself, taking advantage of the lively nightlife. **Friday**: arrive in Rio and spend the rest of the day orientating yourself or relaxing on Ipanema beach before eating in a restaurant close to your hotel. **Saturday**: spend the morning and early afternoon sightseeing in central Rio, taking lunch at the Confeitaria Colombo or taking it easy in Ipanema and Copacabana. Visit Lapa antiques market in the afternoon and go out at night to one of Lapa's samba clubs. **Sunday**: relax on the beach to recover from the previous night, take a long lunch at the Aprazível restaurant and head to Tijuca and Corcovado at around 1600, staying at the Christ statue to watch the sunset. **Monday**: Go up the Sugar Loaf in the morning and leave after an early lunch for Itatiaia, Ilha Grande or Paraty. **Tuesday/Wednesday**: take a boat trip in Paraty, go walking in Itatiaia, or enjoy the beaches of Ilha Grande, returning to Rio on Wednesday afternoon. **Thursday**: Visit the Sugar Loaf in the early morning and spend the afternoon sightseeing in the centre, shopping in Ipanema or São Conrado, or visiting the Museum of Modern Art and nearby beaches in Niterói. Alternatively or take a full- or half-day city tour. Treat yourself to a final meal in one of Rio's fine-dining restaurants.

More than a week

Take Monday to Thursday from the one-week itinerary and add a trip to Búzios and/or Petrópolis and the Serra dos Órgãos, or combine Paraty and Ilha Grande, or Paraty and Itatiaia.

Contemporary Rio de Janeiro

There are two great themes underscoring life in Rio and Brazil as a whole: contradiction and exaggeration. Almost everything which is interesting about Rio comes from its subterranean depths. Brazilian football was born in the poorest parts of Rio with Leônidas da Silva, the first great black footballing star and the inventor of the bicycle kick. Others like Garrincha and more recently Ronaldo and Romario followed. Pelé, too, although not from Rio was born poor and marginalized. Samba, funk, and Carnival itself are products of Rio's poorest, and even the cultural elite – Di Cavalcanti, Villa-Lobos, Tom Jobim, Chico Buraque and Vinícius de Moraes drew and continue to draw on the poor of Rio for the raw material of their artistic output. And yet, except for these artists and a few concerned charity workers, Rio's poor are utterly ignored by Rio's rich establishment, and although they live in each other's pockets, they rarely, if ever, truly meet.

This enormous contradiction is the key to understanding Rio, and perhaps Brazil. There are contradictions everywhere. The plush and tidy Zona Sul – the southern half of the city where Corcovado and Ipanema lie, contrasts sharply with the Zona Norte whose low hills are covered with breeze-block houses and open sewers as far as the eye can see. One of the world's most privileged and wealthiest beach areas, São Conrado, whose apartment blocks have half-Olympic-sized pools, tennis courts and private helipads, sits literally a stone's throw from the world's largest slum. Brazil is, in fact, the most unequal society in the world. And Rio is its most unequal city. According to World Bank figures the richest 20% have an income 27.3 times greater than the poorest 20%. This compares to 5.1 times greater in India.

Contradiction is an essential part of the Carioca and Brazilian national character. These statistics are sobering, yet a few hours in Rio are enough for anyone to see that Brazil is a country with a sunny self-confidence; people, whether poor or rich, are so pleasant and positive that, as one writer once remarked, 'anyone who does not get along with them had better examine himself; the fault is his.' Confidence is expressed in the national mottoes 'Order and Progress', 'Brazil; the country of the future'. But this sunny exterior masks a far more private, hidden Brazil. Brazilians can be frighteningly self-deprecating, referring to their country as 'the land where tomorrow never comes' or 'Brazil, land of unlimited impossibilities'. This is a country of manic mood changes – great enthusiasm and great desperation; the former expressed publicly on the streets and in celebrations; and the latter glimpsed only occasionally and kept very, very private and behind closed doors.

Rio's city centre, too, is a product of contradiction. A trip around the National Historical Museum quickly shows that it once was as magnificent as that of Buenos Aires. Yet only a few relics of that magnificence still remain. At the time when the city was investing more in the arts than it ever had done previously, it was knocking vast areas of its centre down in the name of Order and Progress. As a result, central Rio is a messy melange of glorious colonial monasteries, frayed Mervyn Peake palaces, mock-French neo-classical follies and Le Corbusier-indebted post-modernism; all interspersed with totalitarian 20th-century blocks and broad avenues. Little bars and clubs sit inside crumbling baroque; grand opera houses decay gradually in the tropical heat; toytown trams wind over scuffed white viaducts up into the steep hills of the surrounding suburbs.

Against this backdrop, and on the higgledy piggledy dragon's-tooth pavements and broad beaches that make up Rio's stage, the bizarre tragicomedy of contradictory Brazilian life is played out daily. And if the physical and psychological backdrop of this tragicomedy is contradiction, its day-to-day action is characterized by the second great Brazilian national trait, exaggeration. The Brazilian form of stoicism is celebration and their greatest celebration – Carnival. The opulent, incredible costumes and floats, the fever of dance and rhythm and the liberality that characterize the festival are all born of and created in the poorest parts of Rio. They are an exaggeration born of the extremes of life. In the words of the most famous Carnival organizer, Joãozinho; 'these people are poor all year long. Why would they want to parade as wretches?' But it is not just the festival which is exaggerated; the people themselves are, too.

The Argentinian writer, Luiza Valenzuela, once observed that Cariocas love to dress up, to create caricature and regard what they wear at Carnival as indicative of their true selves. Watch the Vanity Fair of Ipanema and Leblon on any early morning or late afternoon, with its parade of strutting pectorals and Armani shades, identical, perfectly tanned blondes with white poodles and Louis Vuitton. Grab a table in Lapa on a Saturday afternoon, or watch the street action in Copacabana from the safety of a cab or hotel room, and you will see characters that seem to have fallen from the pages of Dickens or Dostoyevsky; pantomime dame transvestites, Shakespearean drunks and itinerant preachers with megaphones.

Indeed Cariocas are people who have quite literally invented their own caricatures and who celebrate them. One national travel guide even includes a cartoon directory of types: *Mauricinhos* and *Patricinhas* from Ipanema are immaculately, if scantily, dressed rich kids with open-topped cars and a large bank roll. The *Pitbulls* are lower-middle-class young men who spend hours practising jiu-jitsu and who strut around with dogs on chains, their boardshorts exposing the top of their buttocks. And the *Malandros* – the spivs and petty criminals you see in Lapa and Copacabana, who are so beloved in Rio that the city's most famous poet wrote an opera about one of them.

One of the great pleasures of a visit to Rio is spending time with these Cariocas whose celebratory, costumed, energetic lives at times seem so much fuller and more colourful than sensible English reality. There are no other people who know how to enjoy themselves like Brazilians do, or who are more enthusiastic, who love more passionately, speak more sincerely, indulge more thoroughly, drive more recklessly or welcome more hospitably than Brazilians... and in all aspects but the political, Rio de Janeiro is their capital.

Travel essentials

Rio is well connected to the rest of the world by frequent flights from all of the major western European airports and the east and west coast of North America; flights can be less than £400 off peak. They rise steeply over the Christmas and Carnival period. Connections from Australia and New Zealand are easiest through Buenos Aires or Santiago. A number of cruise line operators call in on Rio. There are further international connections to Argentina, Paraguay, Uruguay and Bolivia via very long bus journeys on, thankfully, comfortable coaches. Car hire is readily available, although prices are some 20% higher than in Europe or North America.

The city has a decent public transport system with a clean, modern Metrô; which doesn't, however, reach the southern beaches of the Zona Sul. There are frequent, reasonably priced buses and yellow taxis, both of which are driven at high speed. Towns and beaches around Rio can be reached by bus and Niterói is connected to Rio by road or ferry.

Getting there

Air

From Europe Rio de Janeiro is connected to the principal European cities direct by **Aerolíneas Argentinas** (Amsterdam and Madrid), **Air France** (Paris), **Alitalia** (Rome), **British Airways** (London), **Iberia** (Barcelona and Madrid), **KLM** (Amsterdam), **LanChile** (Frankfurt and Madrid), **Lufthansa** (Frankfurt), **Pluna** (Madrid), **Swiss International Air Lines** (Zurich), **TAM** (Paris), **TAP Air Portugal** (Lisbon), **Varig** (Copenhagen, Frankfurt, London, Lisbon, Paris and Milan) and **Vasp** (Athens, Barcelona, Brussels, Frankfurt and Zurich).

Flights from the UK almost invariably leave from Heathrow. Standard fares start at around £460, although special offers are often available. **North South Travel** are usually cheaper (even than the internet operators) and their profits go towards community projects in developing countries; **Sunvil** and **Veloso** are always good value; **Journey Latin America** and **Trips Worldwide** can provide individual itineries and other services (see page 20). It is also worth looking at Ceefax and Oracle which have very cheap cancellation deals and www.lastminute.com.

From North America Rio de Janeiro is connected to the USA direct by **American Airlines** (Chicago, Dallas, Miami), **Continental** (New York), **Delta** (Atlanta), **TAM** (Miami), **United Airlines** (Chicago, Miami), **Varig** (Los Angeles, Miami and New York) and **Vasp**. Other US gateways are Boston, Cincinnati, Denver, Detroit and San Francisco. The cheapest routes are usually from Miami. There are many more connections via São Paulo, including **Air Canada**. Frequent deals can be found on www.cheapflights.com, www.expedia.com and www.brazilspecial.net.

! Departure tax for international flights is US$36 or equivalent in *reais*. National flights have a departure tax of US$2.50.

Airlines

Aerolineas Argentinas T 0845-6011915 (UK), www.aerolineas.com.ar
Air Canada T 1-888-2472262 (US), www.aircanada.ca
Air France T 0845-0845111 (UK), www.airfrance.com
Alitalia T 0870-5448259 (UK), www.alitalia.com
American Airlines T 1-800-4337300 (US), www.aa.com
British Airways T 0870-7733377 (UK), www.britishairways.com
Continental Airlines T 1-800-2310856 (US), www.continental.com
Delta Air Lines T 1-800-2211212 (US), www.delta.com
Iberia T 0845-6012854 (UK), www.iberia.com
KLM T 0870-5074074 (UK), www.klm.com
Lan Chile www.lanchile.com
Lufthansa T 0845-7737747 (UK), www.lufthansa.com
Pluna www.pluna.aero.ur
Swiss International Air Lines T 0845- 6010956 (UK), www.swiss.com
TAM T 0800-123100 (Brazil), www.tam.com.br
TAP Air Portugal www.tap.pt
United Airlines T 1-800-8648331 (US), www.united.com
Varig T 0870 120 3020 (UK), T 1-800-4682744 (US), www.varig.com
VASP T 0800-998277 (Brazil), www.vasp.com.br

Travel agents and companies

Journey Latin America 12-13 Heathfield Terrace, Chiswick, London W4 4JE, **T** 020-87473108, www.journeylatinamerica.co.uk
North South Travel Moulsham, Mill Centre, Parkway, Chelmsford CM2 7P T 01245-608291, www.northsouthtravel.co.uk
Sunvil Sunvil House, Upper Square, Old Isleworth, Middlesex, TW7 7BJ, T 020-87584774, www.sunvil.co.uk
Trips Worldwide, T 0117-3114400, www.tripsworldwide.co.uk.
Veloso Ground Floor, 34 Warple Way, London W3 0RG, **T** 020-87620616, www.veloso.com

Airport information There are two airports in Rio: the **Antônio Carlos Jobim International Airport** (**T** 021-33984526), still often referred to by its old name, **Galeão**, is about 15km outside the city centre; and the domestic airport, **Santos Dumont** (**T** 021-2102457), about 1 km south of the centre. There are banks with Visa ATMs and money-changing booths in both airports, together with tourist information (see page 28), left luggage, restaurants and a pharmacy.

The best way to reach the Zona Sul from the either airport is by the air-conditioned **bus** known locally as the *Frescão*. These operate from 0515 to 2400 and leave every 45 minutes from outside Terminal 1 of the international airport or the terminal building of Santos Dumont and run on two routes; one via the bus station and city centre through Santos Dumont airport (US$2); and the other via the bus station and city centre to all the beaches and main beachfront hotels of the Zona Sul (US$4).

There are also frequent non-air-conditioned buses between the two airports, the bus station, city centre and Copacabana. These are the least safe and least comfortable way of reaching the city from the airports, but are much cheaper.

If you take a **taxi** make sure the meter is reset and switched on. Expect to pay around US$20 from the airport to Ipanema.

Airpasses If you are travelling throughout Brazil, **TAM Airlines** and **Varig** offer airpasses of up to five flight coupons, valid for a maximum of 21 days from the date of the first domestic flight ($530). Check the airline websites for details of destinations offered and eligibility, see page 20.

Bus

International and long-distance buses arrive at the main bus station, **Rodoviária Novo Rio** (Av Rodrigues Alves, corner with Av Francisco Bicalho, just past the docks, **T** 021-22915151). There are good connections with Argentina, Paraguay, Uruguay and the southeast of Brazil. Most major destinations have *leito* (executive) buses, which are very comfortable. Tickets can be bought at ticket offices throughout the city and some travel agencies, including **Dantur Passagens e Turismo** (Av Rio Branco 156, loja 134, Centro, **T** 021-22623424), **Itapemirim Turismo** (R Uruguaiana 10, loja 24, Centro, **T** 021-25098543) and **Guanatur** (R Dias da Rocha 16A, Copacabana, **T** 021-22353275).

The *rodoviária* has a helpful information centre (see page 28), money exchange and left luggage (US$3). The local bus terminal is just outside on the right. The a/c *Real* bus (opposite the exit) goes along the beach to São Conrado. If you need a taxi collect a ticket from the office inside the entrance, this ensures against overcharging.

Boat

There is a frequent ferry service from Niterói which is much quicker than driving across the nine-mile bridge, especially during rush hour, when many people use it to commute to work. The ferry terminal in Niterói is located at Praça Araribóia; it arrives at Praça 15 de Novembro in Rio. See page 91, for further details.

Getting around

Rio's districts are connected by urban highways and tunnels heavy with traffic, if you don't have a car, you will need to take some form of public transport or taxis to get around.

Bus

Rio is laid out basically on a north-south axis, so almost any bus going south with '*Zona Sul*' written on it will stop in Ipanema or Copacabana and all have their destinations written on the side. The best buses to catch from the *rodoviária* (bus station) to Ipanema and Copacabana are 126, 127 or 128. Those heading for Flamengo or Botafogo can take 170. Rides cost less than US$1.

Buses are also occasional hunting grounds for pickpockets and should be treated with caution at night when taxis are a better bet.

Car

Foreign driving licences are acceptable in Brazil, although it may be worth taking an international licence as not all officials and rental companies are able to recognize foreign licences. A credit card is virtually essential for hiring a car. Car hire is easy and straightforward. The best way to hire is from the booths in the airport who have English-speaking staff. Prices are higher than in Europe or the USA – expect to pay upwards of $50 per day for a hatchback. For car hire companies, see page 217.

Service stations are closed in many places at the weekend. Road signs are misleading in Rio and you can end up in a *favela* (slum). Take special care if driving along the Estrada da Gávea to São Conrado as it is possible to unwittingly enter Rocinha, Rio's biggest slum.

Cycling

Rio is well-suited to cycling, both on and off-road and the city has some 74 km of cycle paths which run from the city centre through Zona Sul to Barra da Tijuca. On main roads it is important to be on the lookout for motor vehicles; cyclists are very much second-class citizens. Also note that when cycling on the coast you may encounter strong winds which will hamper your progress. See cycling tours, page27, for further information.

Metrô

Rio's Metrô system provides a good service; it is clean, fast and air conditioned. *Lihna 1* operates between the inner suburb of Tijuca (station Saens Peña) and Arcoverde (Copacabana), via the railway station (Central), Glória and Botafogo. *Linha 2* runs from Pavuna, passing Engenho da Rainha and the Maracanã stadium, to Estácio. It operates 0600-2300, Sunday 1400-2000; closed holidays. The fare is US$0.50 single; multi-tickets and integrated bus/Metrô tickets are available. Buses connecting with the Metrô have a blue-and-white symbol in the windscreen.

Taxi

Taxis have red number plates with white digits (yellow with black digits for private cars) and have meters. Smaller ones (mostly Volkswagen) are marked TAXI on the windscreen or roof. Make sure meters are cleared and on 'tariff 1', except between 2300 and 0600, Sundays and holidays when 'tariff 2' is used. Only use taxis with an official identification sticker on the windscreen. Don't hesitate to argue if the route is too long or the fare is too much. The fare between central Rio and Copacabana should be about US$7.

Radio Taxis are safer but almost twice as expensive. Some taxis can be hired for excursions or tours, but be sure to negotiate the price beforehand. For a list of reputable taxi firms see page 221.

Tram

The last remaining tram runs from near the Largo da Carioca across the old aqueduct (Arcos de Lapa) to the junction of Progresso and Eduardo Santos or to the junction of Alexandrino and Dr julio Otoni. It is a historical, scenic and interesting ride and is still the best way to reach Santa Teresa from central Rio. The tram can be caught from the terminus next to the cathedral or from Cinelândia. The fare is US$0.40. For more details, see Santa Teresa, page 62.

Walking

Walking is a good option for any of the regions during the daytime but should not be risked at night in the centre at any time, or in Lapa between Sunday and Thursday and on any of the beaches.

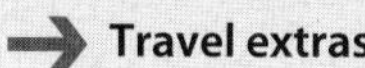

Travel extras

Money

The Brazilian currency is the *real* (R$); plural *reais*, which is divided into 100 centavos. Using an ATM is usually the most convenient and cheapest way of obtaining funds (see also Directory, page 216).

Tipping

In restaurants, tip 10% if no service charge is added. Taxi drivers are not tipped and airport porters are tipped about US$0.50 per item.

Health

No vaccinations are necessary for Rio. Tap water is not drinkable and be careful of ice cream sold on the street. Some rural areas have recorded cases of dengue fever, but it is relatively uncommon.

Safety

Rio has a reputation for being violent and unsafe. However, you are unlikely to encounter problems if you follow common sense and avoid attracting attention to yourself. Dress modestly and keep expensive jewellery, cameras and watches out of sight. Carry a photocopy of your passport and leave the original in the hotel safe. Carry ready-money in a pocket and the rest in a money belt. Be especially careful after dark in the city centre and on quiet areas of Copacabana beach. If you are mugged do not offer resistance; report the crime to the police immediately. Violence in Rio is mostly restricted to the Zona Norte between *favela* gangs and the police. The destinations listed outside of Rio are generally problem free.

Visas

Most citizens of EU countries do not need a visa, check with your embassy. US, Canadian, Australian, New Zealand and Japanese citizens do require a visa. 90-day visas are granted on arrival in Brazil.

Tours

Adventure tours

Rio Aventuras (**T** 021-91958462), abseiling, walking and hiking trips in Rio, including the Sugar Loaf . **Trilharte Ecoturismo** (**T** 021-22455626), adrenaline-filled abseiling, rock climbing and canyoning.

Boat tours

Antígona (**T/F** 024-33711165), daily schooner tours around Paraty and the islands, recommended. **Paraty Tours** (**T/F** 024-3711327), English and Spanish spoken. **Saveiros Tour** (**T** 021-22246990, www.saveiros.com.br), schooners around Guanabara Bay and down the coast. **Soberana da Costa**, (**T/F** 024-33711114), schooner trips from Paraty around the islands, recommended.

City tours

Most hotels will organize tours around Rio which take in the Christ on Corcovado, Sugar Loaf, Copacabana, the football stadium at Maracanã and sights in the city centre. Prices vary between $30 and $45. **Travel café** (R Cosme Velho 513, **T** 021-22858302), also offer rafting, skydiving, horse riding, and packages along the Costa Verde.

City tours by jeep

The tour operators listed below run tours throughout the country and will make reservations for flights and hotels. **Atlantic Forest Jeep Tour** (**T** 021-24959827), tours to Tijuca National Park and elsewhere. **Hanseatic** (**T** 021-22246672), German-run, recommended. **Jeep Tour Ecologies e Cultura** (**T/F** 021-5221620, www.jeeptour.com.br), city tours and trips to Tijuca National Park. **Marlin Tours** (**T** 021-25484433, bbm.robin@openlink.com.br), city tours. **Qualitours Jeep Tour in Rio** (**T/F** 021-2329710), city tours, tours to Tijuca and other destinations. **Rio by Jeep** (**T** 021-25758626), tours of Rio, including Tijuca National Park. Tandem hang-gliding also available.

Cycling tours

Cycling tours are run at weekends along the city's cycle paths, contact **Federação de Ciclismo** (**T** 021-2699994), tours are also available with **Rio Bikers**, R Domingos Ferreira 81 (**T** 021-2745872), bicycle hire available; and **Rio by Bike** (**T** 021-2595532, riobybike@travelrio. com), who will deliver and pick your bike up. **Ypê Amarelo Ecoturismo** (R Senador Dantas 117, Centro, **T** 021-5324395, ypeamarelo@uol. com.br), cycling, motocyling, trekking and more radical sports.

Cultural tours and walking tours

Cultural Rio (R Santa Clara 110/904, Copacabana, **T** 021-33224872), tours escorted personally by Professor Carlos Roquette. **Fábio Sombra** (**T** 021-22959220, fabiosombra@hotmail.com), private and tailor-made guided tours, particularly good on art and architecture.

Favela tours

Favela Tour (**T** 021-33222727, www.favelatour.com.br). Safe and interesting guided tours of Vila Canoa and Rochina *favelas*, US$25 (part of which helps fund a community school) with Marelo, the pioneer of *favela* tourism. He can also provide eco-tours and other excursions.

Helicopter sightseeing tours

Helisight (R Visconde de Pirajá 580, loja 107, Ipanema, **T** 021-35112141). Prices from US$43 to US$148 for up to 30 minutes over the city, including the Sugar Loaf and Corcovado. Wonderful.

Nature tours

Ecotourism in Brazil often fails to live up to its name. **Turismo Clássico**, (**T** 021-25233390, classico@infolink.com.br). **Metropol**, (**T** 021-25335010, www.metropolturismo.com.br), eco, adventure and cultural tours. Wildlife guides recommended for Itatiaia national park include: **Ralph Salgueiro**, (**T** 024-33511823, www.ecoralph.com); and **Edson Endrigo** (**T** 024-37428374, www.avesfoto.com.br),for birdwatching trips in Itatiaia and throughout Brazil.

Trips to samba shows

Although tacky and touristy but fun, for those looking for the stereotypes seen in Carmen Miranda films. Tickets cost around US$50, and are available through most hotels. **Fenician Tours** (**T** 021-22353843), are good value at US$30.

Tourist information

The city's official website, www.riodejaneiro-turismo.com.br, has an enormous and comprehensive range of information in English.

Tourist offices

Alo Rio, (**T** 0800-7071808, Mon-Fri 0800-2000) is a telephone service in English and Portuguese. **Embratur**, the Brazilian Tourist Board (R Uruguaiana 174, Centro, **T** 021-25096017, www.embratur.gov.br), provides information on the whole country. **Ibama**, the Brazilian Institute of Environmental Protection, (**T** 021-32246463, www.ibama.gov.br) provides information on national parks. **Riotur**'s main office (R Assembléia 10, Centro, **T** 021- 22177575, www.rio.rj.gov.br/riotur), is friendly and helpful, can book accommodation and provide a useful free brochure *RIO*; also in Copacabana (Av Princesa Isabel 183, **T** 021-25417522, Mon-Fri 0900-1800); the international airport (*0600-2400*), and the Novo Rio bus station (**T** 021-22634857, 0800-2000). **TurisRio** (R da Ajuda 5, **T** 021-22150011, www.turisrio.rj.gov.br), is helpful and has information for the state of Rio de Janeiro.

Maps

Guia Rex street guide, *Guia Schaeffer Rio de Janeiro* and *Geomapas* are good maps, available from **Touring Clube do Brasil** (Pres Antônio Carlos 130 and Av Brasil 4294), newsstands and hotels. **Cia de Comunicaçao** publishes a city map, good for orientation (US$2). The excellent *Guia Quatro Rodas do Rio*, is published each November.

Rio de Janeiro

Central Rio

Known as 'Centro', hot and sweaty central Rio spreads back from Guanabara Bay in a jumbled grid of streets between Santos Dumont Airport and the Mosteiro de São Bento. Much of its architectural heritage has been laid waste by successive waves of government intent on wiping out the past in favour of the dubious and grandiose visions of Order and Progress. But it remains the centre of Rio's history as well as the city, with some distinguished colonial buildings, Manueline follies and elaborate neoclassical facades huddled together under totalitarian blocks of flats and Le Corbusier-inspired concrete. All watch over a throng of cars and a bustle of people; business suits on lunch, beggars, skateboarders dressed in would-be New York oversized jeans and baseball caps, street performers, opportunists looking to snatch a purse. It can all feel a bit hectic and bewildering. But don't give up. There is plenty to explore here and a wealth of air-conditioned havens in which to escape for a coffee.

The greatest concentration of historic buildings is in the south of the centre, near Santos Dumont Airport, on and around **Praça 15 de Novembro**, from where Rio de Janeiro grew in its earliest days. Here you'll find the the bulk of the museums, some of the city's more beautiful little churches and older streets, and its grander colonial buildings like the **Paço Imperial** and the **Palácio Tiradentes**. To get here take the Metrô to Largo da Carioca in a sub-*bairro* of the centre known as **Cinelândia**, centred on Avenida Rio Branco and the wedding-cake, neoclassical **Theatro Municipal**. **Praça Quinze** is a stroll to the east along Avenida República do Chile. More colonial buildings lie at the centre's northern extremity around the Morro de São Bento, including the impressive **Mosteiro de São Bento**, and the city's most imposing church, **Nossa Senhora da Candelária**. These can be reached via Metrô Uruguaiana.

The city's main artery is the Avenida Presidente Vargas, at 4½ km long and over 90 m wide, it divides the northern and southern sections. This street begins at the waterfront, divides to embrace the Candelária church, then crosses the Avenida Rio Branco in a magnificent straight stretch past the **Central railway station**. Vargas is cut by two important arterial streets. Avenida Rio Branco, nearest to the sea, was once lined with splendid ornate buildings; these have largely been razed and replaced by monolithic modern blocks, but a few remain around **Cinelândia**. Avenida 31 de Março further to the west, beyond the railway station, leads to the Sambódromo and the Carnival district. Some of the better modern architecture is to be found along Avenida República do Chile, including the conical 1960's **Catedral de São Sebastião**, which looks like it should be by Niemeyer but isn't.

▸▸ *See Sleeping p112, Eating and drinking p135, Bars and clubs p157*

Praça 15 de Novembro and around

Originally an open space at the foot of the Morro do Castelo, the Praça 15 de Novembro (often called Praça Quinze) has always been one of the focal points in Rio de Janeiro. Today it has one of the greatest concentrations of historic buildings in the city. Having been through various phases of development in its history, it underwent major remodelling in the 1990s. The last vestiges of the original harbour, at the seaward end of the praça*, were restored. The steps no longer lead to the water, and the Avenida Alfredo Agache now goes through an underpass, creating an open space between the* praça *and the seafront and giving easy access to the ferry dock for Niterói. The area is well illuminated and moderately clean, and the municipality has started to stage shows, music and dancing in the* praça. *At weekends an antique, craft, stamp and coin fair (Feirarte II) is held from 0900-1900.*

! Opening times for churches, museums and public buildings change frequently. All museums close during Carnival.

Sights

Paço Imperial

Southeast corner of Praça 15 de Novembro, **T** 021-25334407.
Tue-Sun 1100-1830, free. Map 6, 5E, p256

The beautiful, colonial, and somewhat unkempt, Paço Imperial (former Royal Palace) was built in 1743 as the residence of the governor of the Capitania. It later became the king's storehouse and armoury (armazens), then the Casa da Moeda, before being made into the Paço Real when the Portuguese court moved to Brazil. After Independence it became the Imperial Palace and during the Republic was used as the post and telegraph office before gradually falling into decline. In the 1980s it was completely restored as a cultural centre and has several exhibition spaces, a theatre, arts cinema, library, a section showing the original construction, a superb model of the city and two respectable air-conditioned restaurants.

Palácio Tiradentes

Beside the Paço Imperial, across R da Assembléia, **T** 021-25881000.
Mon-Fri 1300-1900 by prior appointment, free. Map 6, 6E, p256

The Palácio Tiradentes was named in honour of the former dentist (*tiradentes* means 'teeth puller'), Joaquim José da Silva Xavier, who is often seen as the symbolic father of Brazilian independence. Tiradentes was a commoner from the state of Minas Gerais who dared to stand up to the Portuguese and their colonial administrators. But like all those who challenged the powerful elite, either during colonial or post-colonial times, he paid a heavy price. He was held prisoner in a building on this site and executed nearby. The current imperial, neoclassical edifice was built between 1922 and 1926. It is now the legislative assembly of Rio de Janeiro state and an exhibition space. A statue of Tiradentes, by Francisco de Andrade, stands in front.

Igreja do Glorioso Patriarca São José

R São José at Av Presidente Antônio Carlos, one block south of Praça 15. *Mon-Fri 0900-1200, 1400-1700, Sun 0900-1100.* *Map 6, F6, p256*

One of the oldest of the 16th-century churches, the Igreja do Glorioso Patriarca São José, has been considerably altered since its original construction. The rococo interior was mostly designed by Simeão de Nazaré – a pupil of Rio's most famous church sculptor, Mestre Valentim. See art and architecture, page 228.

Travessa do Comércio

Between Praça 15 de Novembro and R do Ouvidor. *Map 6, C/D5, p256*

This street is well worth exploring. It is always busy with no end of diverse activity. It can be reached through the **Arco do Teles**, (all that remains of an 18th-century construction, now incorporated into a modern building), on the northwest side of Praça 15 de Novembro. It's a narrow, twisting street, thick with neoclassical houses, wrought-iron arches and street lamps. This is how the whole city looked in the 19th century. Nowadays, it is crowded by the skyscrapers towering above. On Friday nights the Travessa and the numerous restaurants along its length, buzz with life. These include the Arco Imperial where Carmen Miranda lived between 1925-30 (her mother kept a boarding house).

Nossa Senhora da Lapa dos Mercadores

R do Ouvidor 35, at the northern end of the Travessa do Comércio. *Mon-Fri 0800-1400.* *Map 6, C5, p256*

This 18th-century church began life as a street oratory erected in a blind alley by market vendors who traditionally petitioned Our Lady of Lapa for help in hard times. It became a church in 1750, was remodelled in 1869-1872 and has now been fully restored.

Santa Cruz dos Militares

Entrance at R 1 de Março 36. *Map 6, C4, p256*

Across the street from Nossa Senhora da Lapa dos Mercadores is the church of Santa Cruz dos Militares, originally a Jesuit chapel next to a fort which stood here in the 17th century watching over the bay. It served as the city cathedral temporarily in the early 18th century when the church of São Sebastião became badly damaged, and was itself almost completely destroyed the following century. Its current interior by Mestre Antônio de Pádua e Castro dates almost entirely from post-World War I, but there are still a few rococo flourishes attributed to Mestre Valentim. The facade was inspired by the Templo dos Mártires in Lisbon.

The Carmelite churches

Map 6, D4/E4, p256

On Rua 1 de Março, across from Praça 15 de Novembro, there is a cluster of Carmelite buildings with a long history. The convent of the **Ordem Terceira do Monte do Carmo**, founded in 1611, is now a university building - the Faculdade Cândido Mendes. This was once a 'PR', meaning either property of the Prince Regent or Prédio Roubado (stolen building), depending on whether you were wealthy or poor. PRs were buildings appropriated by the imperial family – in this case to house mad Queen Maria who was locked up here in the 18th century for her and everyone else's safety. A covered bridge was built between the convent and the adjacent cathedral (see below) to prevent visiting royals and courtiers becoming sullied by mingling with the Rio hoi polloi.

Between the convent and the convent church, and separated from the Carmo Church by a passageway, is the old cathedral; **Nossa Senhora do Carmo da Antiga Sé**. It occupies the site of the original convent chapel, which stood here from 1590 until 1754 when this building replaced it. The new church became the

Superb mountains, rocks piled into columns, luxurious vegetation, bright and flowered islands, verdant beaches and all this combined with white housing, each hill crowned with its church or fortress, ships anchored or about to set off and many boats sailing about in a delicious climate all combine to make Rio de Janeiro the most enchanting setting that the mind can imagine.

Maria Graham 1821

designated royal chapel with the arrival of the Portuguese royal family in 1808, and subsequently the city's cathedral. The crypt allegedly holds the remains of Pedro Alvares Cabral, the European discoverer of Brazil; a claim disputed by the town of Santarém in Portugal, which also claims to be his last resting place.

The final church in the Carmelite group, and the order's present church, is the **Ordem Terceira do Carmo,** (*Mon-Fri 0800-1400, Sat 0800-1200*). Located just north of the old cathedral, it was built in 1754, consecrated in 1770 and rebuilt between 1797 and 1826, and has strikingly beautiful portals by Mestre Valentim, the son of a Portuguese nobleman and a slave girl. He also created the main altar of fine moulded silver, the throne and its chair and much else. The Chafariz do Mestre Valentim, or Chafariz do Pirâmide, a fountain designed by the same sculptor, stands in the *praça*.

● *At the rear of the old cathedral and the Igreja da Ordem Terceira do Carmo, on Rua do Carmo, is the* ***Oratório de Nossa Senhora do Cabo da Boa Esperança****; one of the few remaining public oratories from the colonial period in Rio.*

Largo da Misericórdia and the museums

There is a cluster of interesting museums between Praça 15 and Santos Dumont Airport. These can be reached via Largo da Misericórdia which runs immediately south of the Palácio Tiradentes. This was once the centre of the city, but is now dominated by the flow of countless buses whose terminus is nearby. Next to the Largo da Misericórdia is the oldest street in Rio, the Ladeira da Misericórdia now just a severed stump on the side of the grand Santa Casa da Misericórdia hospital. Yet until the early 20th century, it ran up a hill to Rio's original Jesuit monastery and to a fort which watched over the bay. The hill, fort and monastery no longer exist although the altar and nave of the latter are preserved in the little 16th-century chapel of ***Nossa Senhora do Bonsucesso*** *(open at irregular times for Mass).*

Museu da Imagem e do Som (MIS)

Praça Rui Barbosa 1, **T** 021-22620309. *Mon-Fri 1300-1800, US$1.50.* *Map 2, D12, p248*

The Sound and Image Museum, just north of the end of the *largo*, was founded to 'preserve the cultural memory of the city', and houses a collection of cinema images, photos of Carioca musicians, and recordings of popular music, including early *choro* by artists like Jacob do Bandolim. There are booths for listening to the music and a small cinema for watching the 16 mm and 35 mm film archives.

Museu Histórico Nacional

Praça Marechal Âncora, **T** 021-25509224. *Tue-Fri 1000-1730, Sat-Sun 1400-1800, US$2.* *Map 2, D13, p248*

Next door to the Sound and Image Museum, in a series of handsome buildings, is the National Historical Museum. This is one of the city's most distinguished museums, with a collection of historical treasures, colonial sculpture and furniture, maps, paintings, arms and armour, silver and porcelain. It also retains a rampart from that first fort which crowned the former Morro do Castelo hill from 1603 until the 20th century. The building was once the War Arsenal of the Empire, part of which was built in 1762 (this part is called the Casa do Trem). Two years later the Pátio de Minerva was added, and more significant expansion was undertaken in 1808 and again in 1922, when it was first inaugurated as a museum. Among the permanent exhibitions are: Colonization and Dependency, which has interesting exhibits on how Brazil has been economically dominated since Independence; Reminiscences of Imperial Times, with relics from the royal family and aristocracy; and The Age of the Carriage which is devoted to the evolution of transport within Brazil.

Museu Naval e Oceanográfico

R Dom Manuel 15, **T** 021-25337626. *Daily, 1200-1700, US$2.*
Map 6, F7, p256

The Naval and Maritime Museum is housed in a beautiful mock-palladian town house with eclectic flourishes. It has a collection of paintings and prints, as well as a display of weapons and figureheads, but most of the exhibits have been moved to the Espaço Cultural da Marinha (see page 53).

Cinelândia

The area around Praça Floriano was the liveliest part of the city in the 1920s and 1930s when Hollywood hit Brazil. All of the best cinemas were situated here and their popularity became so great that the praça *was rechristened after them. Today, Cinelândia remains lively, especially at the end of the week, owing to its proximity to the city's nightlife capital, Lapa (see page 47). The 30 m-wide Avenida Rio Branco, which bisects the area, is the financial heart of the city. Lined by a mish-mash of modernist and untidy art-deco skyscrapers, it was built at the turn of the 20th century under the 'tear it down' regime of Mayor Pereira Passos. Passos's obsession with progress and positivism is as Brazilian as samba, and contrasts markedly with the rest of Latin America. Rio and São Paulo once had long stately avenues that rivalled the best of Buenos Aires. Only clusters have survived the wrecking ball of Order and Progress, whose driving ideals are expressed on Eduardo Sá's ugly 1910* ***Monumento ao marechal Floriano Peixoto****, in the heart of Cinelândia in Praça Floriano. It is dedicated to the country's second president and inscribed with sentences like 'Love as a principle, founded on Order' and 'Progress for ever!' Three distinguished and predominantly neoclassical buildings sit close by, the* ***Theatro Municipal, Museu Nacional de Belas- Artes*** *and* ***Biblioteca Nacional****. These are built in a style known as 'eclectic' in Brazil, which, as its name suggests is a fusion of many styles in one (see Art and architecture, page 228).*

Sights

Praça Mahatma Gandhi

Map 2, G10, p248

Praça Mahatma Gandhi houses a 19th-century, cast-iron fountain, the **Chafariz do Monroe**. This is the largest ornamental fountain in the city and was built in France, though it originally sat in a square in Vienna. It was bought by Dom Pedro II in 1861 and features some respectable French baroque carving. The **Passero Público** gardens (*daily 0900-1700*), next to the *praça* were planted in 1779-83 by the artist Mestre Valentim, whose bust is near the old former gateway.

Theatro Municipal

Praça Floriano, **T** 021-22991633, www.theatromunicipal.rj.gov.br. *Mon-Fri 0900-1700. Tours available in English, **T** 021-22623501, book in advance, Mon-Fri 0900-1700, US$1.20. Map 2, F9, p248*

A luxuriously ornate temple built in homage to the Charles Garnier Opera House in Paris. Although it has seen better days it remains magnificent. On either side of the lavish, colonnaded facade are rotundas, surmounted by cupolas. The muses of poetry and music watch from above alongside an imperial eagle, wings outstretched and poised for flight. The interior is a mock-European fantasy of Carrara marble columns, crystal chandeliers and gilt ceilings, fronted by a vast sweeping staircase. The stage is one of the largest in the world. The theatre was designed by Franciso de Oliveira Passos, son of the contemporaneous city mayor, who won an ostensibly open architectural competition, together with French architect Albert Guilbert. The guided tour is worthwhile to see front and back stage, the decorations and the machine rooms. For performance information, see Arts and entertainment, page 174.

Museu Nacional de Belas-Artes

Av Rio Branco 199, **T** 021-22400068. *Tue-Fri 1000-1800, Sat-Sun 1400-1800, US$1.* *Map 2, E10, p248*

Fine art in Rio and in Brazil was stimulated by the arrival of the Portuguese royal family in 1808. Shortly after their arrival, in 1816, the Academia de Belas-Artes was founded by Joaquim Lebreton. This building, commissioned to house a national collection, was erected between 1906 and 1908 by Adolfo Morales de Los Rios. Its grand interior, with its covered cloisters lined with neoclassical statues and marble staircase, recalls Brazil's then aspiration to be French, and the building was indeed inspired by the Louvre. The collection comprises close to 20,000 pieces of decorative, popular and fine art. There is a gallery dedicated to works by Brazilian national and resident artists from the 17th century onwards, including paintings by Frans Janszoon Post, who painted Brazilian landscapes in classical Dutch style, and the Frenchmen Debret and Taunay. Another gallery charts the development of Brazilian art in the 20th century, including works by Cândido Portinari, Alberto da Veiga Guignard and others. A third gallery contains work by foreign artists. The temporary exhibition hall houses many of Rio de Janeiro's most important international exhibitions.

Biblioteca Nacional

Av Rio Branco 219/239, **T** 021-22628255. *Mon-Fri 0900-2000, Sat 0900-1500, US$1.* *Map 2, F10, p248*

An eclectic Carioca neoclassical building with a touch of art nouveau. The building is fronted by a stately portico supported by a Corinthian colonnade. Inside is a series of monumental staircases in Carrara marble. The stained glass in the windows is French. The first national library was brought to Brazil by the Prince Regent, Dom João, in 1808 from a collection from the Ajuda Palace in Lisbon. Today the library houses over nine million pieces, including a first edition of the *Lusiad of Camoes*, a 15th-century *Moguncia Bible* and *Book of Hours*, paintings donated by Pedro II, scores by Mozart and etchings by Dürer.

Palácio Capanema

Esplanada do Castelo, junction of Av Graça Aranha and R Araújo Porto Alegre, just off Av Rio Branco. *Tue-Fri 1000-1700, free.* *Map 2, E11, p248*

Those interested in contemporary art and Brazilian modernist architecture should visit the Palácio Capanema, the former Ministry of Education and Health building, then the Palácio da Cultura. Dating from 1937-45, it was designed by a team of architects led by Lúcio Costa and under the guidance of Le Corbusier. Inside are impressive murals by Cândido Portinari, one of Brazil's most famous artists. The gardens were laid out by Roberto Burle Marx.

Igreja da Santa Luiza

R de Santa Luiza. *Map 2, F11, p248*

Close to the Palácio Capanema, and overwhelmed by tall office buildings, is the attractive little church of Santa Luiza. When built in 1752 it had only one tower; the other was added late in the 19th century. Every year on 13 December, the church's feast day, devotees bathe their eyes with holy water, which is considered miraculous.

Largo da Carioca and around

This higgledy piggledy street of colonial churches, modern buildings, and street vending stalls, a minute's walk north of Cinelândia and sitting between Rua da Carioca and the Largo da Carioca Metrô station, is great for a wander. There is a whole variety of interesting sights here in a very small area. The Largo da Carioca itself, while not particularly interesting, is a useful landmark for navigating the area.

Sights

Convento de Santo Antônio

Largo da Carioca, **T** 021-2620129. *Mon, Wed and Fri 0800-1800, Tue 0600-1930, Sat-Sun 0800-1700, free.* *Map 2, E8, p248*

The convent of Santo Antônio, which is the second oldest convent in Rio, sits on a little hill off the Largo da Carioca. You will often see lots of single women gathered here praying earnestly; there are many more women than men in Brazil, and St Anthony is traditionally a provider of husbands. The first building constructed here was a small Franciscan hermitage. The church and convent were built in the 17th and 18th centuries, very much in the Portuguese style. Vicente do Salvador, who penned the first History of Brazil in 1627, lived here. The church interior is baroque around the chancel, main altars and two lateral altars. These are devoted, in turn, to St Anthony, St Francis and the Immaculate Conception. The beautiful sacristy is decorated with *azulejos* and adorned with paintings depicting scenes from St Anthony's life.

Ordem Terceira de São Francisco da Penitência

Largo da Carioca, **T** 021-22620197. *Tue-Fri 0900-1200, 1300-1600, free.* *Map 2, E8, p248*

Separated from the church (above) only by a fence of iron railings, the little church of the Ordem Terceira de São Francisco da Penitência is one of Rio's least known baroque jewels. It was built between 1653 and 1773, and has a splendid gilt interior with a fine panel painted by José de Oliveira. It houses an important collection of Franciscan relics and a small museum of sacred art.

São Francisco de Paula

Largo São Francisco de Paula, **T** 021-25090067. *Mon-Fri 0900-1300, free.* *Map 2, D8, p248*

Dominating the square which bears its name, is the twin-towered church of São Francisco de Paula. It was built very much in the Portuguese baroque style, between 1759 and 1801. Inside, in the main church and the Lady Chapel, are some fine examples of Carioca art: carvings by Mestre Valentim, paintings by Vítor Meireles and murals by Manuel da Cunha. The beautiful fountain at the back of the church is switched on only at night.

Nossa Senhora de Rosário e São Benedito dos Pretos

Corner of R Uruguiana and Ouvidor, across from the Largo São Francisco de Paula. *Free.* *Map 2, C8, p248*

Since the 17th century, this church has been at the centre of African Christian culture in Rio. During the 19th century it was the site of an elaborate festival recreating scenes from the courtly life of the King of Congo. A king and queen were crowned and they danced through the nearby streets, followed by long parades of courtiers in fancy dress – a precursor perhaps for Carnival. It was here that the announcements for the final abolition of slavery were prepared. The church once had a fabulous gilt interior, which was sadly destroyed in a fire in 1967. Next door to the church is a small museum devoted to slavery in Brazil and speaks starkly of life for black people in the last western country to abolish the slave trade.

● *The nearby belle-époque coffee house, Confeitaria Colombo,* (R Gonçalves Dias 32) *is an excellent stop for a break.*

Real Gabinete Português de Leitura

R Luís Camões 30, just to the north of Largo São Francisco de Paula, **T** 021-22213138. *Tue-Fri 1000-1745, Sat-Sun, 1400-1800, free.* *Map 2, D7, p248*

The Real Gabinete Português de Leitura is one of the city's hidden architectural treasures, and one of the best pieces of mock-Manueline architecture in Brazil. Manueline architecture is usually described as

Portuguese Gothic and takes its name from King Manuel I, who ruled Portugal between 1495 and 1521. But it is unlike any other European Gothic style, drawing strongly on Islamic and nautical themes – a lavish fusion of Islamic ornamentalism and sculpted seaweeds, anchors, ropes and corals. The modest exterior of the Real Gabinete, which was designed by Portuguese architect Rafael da Silva e Castro in 1880, was inspired by the lateral facade of Jerônimos. It is decorated with statues of Camões, Henry the Navigator, Vasco de Gama and Pedro Álvares Cabral, who claimed Brazil for Portugal. More interesting, however, is the magnificent reading hall built around the oldest central steel structure in Rio. Towering arches decorated with Islamic flourish ascend via coiled wooden ropes to an elaborate painted ceiling from which a massive iron chandelier hangs suspended. There are some 120,000 books in the library's collection.

Praça Tiradentes and the cathedral

One long block behind the Largo da Carioca and São Francisco de Paula is Praça Tiradentes, old and shady, with a ***statue to Dom Pedro I*** *carved in 1862 by Luís Rochet. The Emperor sits on horseback shouting his famous 1822 declaration of independence, the Grito de Ipiranga: 'Liberty or Death!' The* ***Teatro João Caetano*** *sits on the northeastern corner of the* praça *and is named after a famous 19th-century actor. Prince Dom Pedro first showed the green-and-yellow flag of Brazil in the original building, and it was an important venue for meetings discussing Brazilian independence. The current theatre was constructed in 1920 after the original had fallen into disrepair. There are two canvases on the second floor by the city's celebrated artist, Emiliano Di Cavalcanti .*

South of the praça, *bordering Cinelândia to the east and Lapa to the south, is a series of modernist buildings lining the busy thoroughfare of Avenida República do Chile. These include the* ***Petrobrás Headquarters*** *and the* ***Espaço Cultural da Caixa Econômica Federal*** *(which holds the Teatro Nelson Rodrigues,* *see page 176**). Most of these are brutal, untidy or both. Only the cathedral is remarkable.*

People watching spots

Best

- The coconut stands on the beach at Ipanema, p70
- Friday after 2000 at the bar in Gero restaurant in Ipanema, p144
- After 0100 at the Pizzaria Guanabara in Leblon, p146
- Rio Scenarium nightclub in Lapa, p158
- Lapa's Saturday antiques market, p194

Sights

Centro de Arte Hélio Oiticica

R Luís Camões 68, just north of Praça Tiradentes, **T** 021-22321104. *Tue-Fri 1400-2000, Sat-Sun 1100-1700. Metrô Largo da Carioca, buses 170/484 from the Zona Sul..* *Map 2, D7, p248*

Just north of the *praça,* in a handsome salmon pink colonial building, is the Hélio Oiticica centre for fine art, named after another famous Carioca artist and now a smart contemporary art exhibition space with six galleries, a good art bookshop and air-conditioned café. Important national and international artists exhibit here. Shops in nearby streets specialize in selling goods for Umbanda, the Afro-Brazilian religion.

Catedral de São Sebastião do Rio de Janeiro

Av República do Chile. **T** 021-22402669, www.catedral.com.br. *Daily 0800-1800, Mass Mon-Fri 1100, Sun 1000, free.* *Map 2, F7, p248*

The cathedral is a remarkable oblate concrete cone, fronted by a decorative ladder and resplendent with rich blue stained glass, which looks like a modernist Mayan temple as it catches the afternoon sunlight. It is commonly said to be bt Niemeyer, but is in fact by another Brazilian Le Corbusier disciple, Edgar de Oliveira da Fonseca. The best time to visit is late afternoon, when the sunlight streams through the immense monotone stained-glass windows.

There is a small **Sacred Art Museum** in the crypt, which has a handful of relics, including the fonts used for the dunking of imperial Brazilian babies, and Dom Pedro II's throne.

● *The tram to Santa Teresa leaves from behind the cathedral, the entrance is on Rua Senador Dantas. Soon after leaving the station the tram traverses the Arcos da Lapa offering wonderful views. See page 62, for further information.*

★ Lapa

Only a decade ago Lapa, which lies just south of the cathedral between the centre and Glória, was a no-go area; tawdry and terrifying – walked only by the prostitutes and thugs, and with drug addicts chasing the dragon in the crumbling porticoes of the colonial and art nouveau buildings. The area can still feel a little edgy, especially on weekdays after dark, but it has undergone an unimagined renaissance. This was once the Montmartre of Rio; the painter Di Cavalcanti wrote poetically of wandering its streets at night on his way home to Flamengo, past the little cafés and ballrooms, and the rows of handsome townhouses. Now the cafés are alive again, spilling out onto the streets, and the ballrooms and townhouses throb with samba and electronica. Opera is once more performed in the concert halls of the ***Escola da Música****, and the area's once notorious thoroughfare, Rua do Lavradio, is now lined with smart clubs and restaurants, playing host to one of the city's most interesting bric-a- brac and antiques markets (see page 194). The area is best just for a wander, although be very careful here after dark on weekdays.*

Sights

The Arcos da Lapa and around

Map 2, G8, p248

These much-photographed, white arches were built in 1744 as an aqueduct to carry water between Morro do Castelo and Santa

Teresa. They now carry the tram – one of the city's most delightful journeys (see page 62). Bars huddle under their southern extremity on **Avenida Mem de Sá**, one of Rio's most popular nightlife streets. Street performers (and vagrants) often gather in the cobblestone square between the Arcos and the cathedral. There are a number of moderately interesting buildings off this square. The eclectic baroque/neoclassical **Escola da Musica da Universidade Federal do Rio de Janeiro** (*R do Passeio 98*), open officially just for performances, has one of the city's best concert halls. A stroll away is the bizarre baroque facade of another prestigious classical concert hall, the **Sala Cecília Mereilles** (*Largo da Lapa 47*). More picturesque are the **Ladeira do Santa Teresa stairs** which wind their way steeply from the square by the cathedral, and from the back of Rua Teotônio, to Santa Teresa. They are much beloved of music video directors and fashion photographers. The steps are tiled in red, gold and green and lined by little houses, many of which are dishevelled and disreputable, but wonderfully picturesque. Be vigilant here.

Rua do Lavradio

Map 2, F/G7, p248

This was one of urban Rio's first residential streets and is lined by handsome 18th-, 19th- and early-20th-century townhouses. These are now filled by samba clubs, cafés, bars and antiques shops. Any day is good for a browse and a wander, and Saturdays here are wonderful when the area is pedestrianized to hold a market and live street tango, attracting throngs of people from all sections of Carioca society. Some of the houses here were once grand. Number 84 once belonged to the marquis who gave the street its name. Further along is what was once Brazil's foremost Masonic lodge, the imposing **Palácio Maçônico Grande Oriente do Brasil**, which, tellingly, has had as its grand masters King Dom Pedro I and one of the country's most important republican politicians, José Bonífacio Andrada e Silva.

Central station and Praça da República

Centro do Brasil, or Dom Pedro II railway station as it is also known, once served much of the country, but now serves only Rio. This brutal 1930's art-deco temple to progress was one of the city's first modernist buildings, and was recently made famous by the Walter Salles film Central Station. *The film's thronging crowd scenes were set here, and are recreated every morning or evening with hundreds of thousands of people bustling in and out of trains leaving for the northern and western parts of Rio, and the buzz of touts including professional letter writers like those featured in the film.*

Praça da República or Campo de Santana is an extensive and picturesque public garden close to the railway station, designed in the late 19th century by the French landscape gardener Auguste Glaziou. It is a haven during the heat of the day; agoutis and the occasional marmoset can be seen here at dusk. A plaque at Praça da República 197 marks the house of Marechal Deodoro da Fonseca, who proclaimed Brazil a republic in 1889. *Map 2, C3/D4, p248*

Casa da Moeda
Praça da República e R Azeredo Coutinho 173, **T** 021-25090796.
Mon-Fri 0900-1700, US$1.50. *Map 2, D5, p248*

The Casa da Moeda, which holds the Brazilian national archive, is a temple to bureacracy and a national treasure. Nowhere celebrates the document as an end in itself with quite the same enthusiasm as Brazil. Here, visitors have the privilege of seeing, at first hand, millions of priceless bits of paper with elaborate seals and ribbons and other such emblems of the Brazilian state. The building itself is also of interest – a fine piece of Carioca neoclassicism, which once housed the Mint.

Palácio Duque de Caxias

Praça Duque de Caxias 25, the opposite side of Av Presidente Vargas from Praça da República. *Map 2, C4, p248*

The Palácio is not open to the public. However, in front of it stands the **Panteão Duque de Caxias**, a statue of Duke Luís Alves de Lima e Silva; though long dead, he remains patron of the Brazilian army. He was a skilful soldier and is the nearest thing the country, which has never been threatened militarily by anyone, has had to a military hero. He was responsible for crushing Paraguay in the lop-sided 19th-century war waged against the little republic by Brazil, Argentina and Uruguay. The art-deco Palácio, which is wonderfully over the top and grandiose, is an apotheosis to the general in stone, stucco and glass, and is now an army administrative headquarters.

Palácio do Itamaraty

Av Marechal Floriano 196, **T** 021-22532828. *Free guided tours on Mon, Wed and Fri, hrly between 1315-1615. Map 2, B4, p248*

Built in neoclassical style in the 1850s for the coffee baron Francisco José da Rocha, the Palácio do Itamaraty became the president's residence between 1889 and 1897. Now it houses the **Museu Histórico e Diplomático** which comprises numerous treasures from porcelain and tapestries to sculpture, painting and jewellery. The map and book collections are among the best in Latin America. Be sure to visit the beautiful garden.

Centro Cultural Light

Av Marechal Floriano 168, **T** 021-22112921 *Mon-Fri 1000-1900, Sat-Sun 1400-1800. Map 2, C5, p248*

The imitation US neoclassical Light Cultural Centre is named after the former state electricity company. Di Cavalcanti paintings are preserved here, and there is also a children's theatre.

Cidade Nova and the Sambódromo

Map 2, E1-F1, p248

The Cidade Nova is the centre of Carnival Rio, for here lies the **Sambódromo**, (*R Marquês de Sapucaí, **T** 021-25026996, Tue-Sun 1100-1700*) – Oscar Niemeyer's 650-m-long stadium street, purpose- built for the annual Carnival parades (see page 179). The area has long been important for black Carioca culture. **Praça Onze** near the Sambódromo is today the terminus of the city's main thoroughfare, Avenida Presidente Vargas. But it was once a square and an established meeting place for *capoeristas* whose acrobatic martial art to the rhythm of the *berimbau* and hand clap inspired much Carnival choreography. A replica of the head of a Nigerian prince from the British Museum, erected in honour of **Zumbi dos Palmares,** sits on Avenida Presidente Vargas itself. Zumbi was a Bantu prince who became the most successful black slave emancipator in the history of the Americas, founding a kingdom within Brazil in the 19th century.

Candelária

From its little island in a river of trafic, the Italianate domes of the Church of Candelária, Rio's best-loved and most ostentatious church, sits looking down the busy thoroughfare of Avenida Presidente Vargas. Nearby are a handful of cultural centres, which host some of Brazil's most interesting temporary exhibitions.

Sights

Igreja de Nossa Senhora da Candelária

Praça Pio X, **T** 021-22332324. *Mon-Fri 0730-1200, 1300-1630, Sat 0800-1200, Sun 0900-1300, free.* *Map 6, A1, p256*

Candelária has long been the church of high-society Rio. Celebrities still gather here in the Italianate marble interior for the city's most prestigious weddings; herding together for the photographers from *Caras* magazine beneath the cavernous dome and sumptuous painted ceiling. The church itself is European in style and material. It is modelled on the Basilica da Estrela in Lisbon. The tiles in the dome are from that city, the marble inside is Veronan and the heavy bronze doors were commissioned from France. All were shipped across at vast expense in the late 18th century, during an era when, even though such materials were readily available in Brazil at similar quality and far lower prices, snobbery demanded that they be imported. The church was built on the site of a chapel founded in 1610 by the Spaniard Antônio Martins Palma who arrived in Rio after surviving a terrible storm at sea. He erected the chapel in homage to Nuestra Señora de Candelária, the patron saint of his home, La Palma, in the Canaries.

Espaço Cultural dos Correios

R Visconde de Itaboraí 20, **T** 021-25038770. *Tue-Sun 1200-2000.* *Map 6, B4, p256*

A number of cultural centres have opened in this area in recent years. The Espaço Cultural dos Correios is in a smart Edwardian building with a little private park and is a great stop over for an air-conditioned juice or coffee. It holds temporary exhibitions and cultural events, and a postage stamp fair on Saturdays.

Centro Cultural Banco do Brasil

R Primeriro de Março 66, with another entrance on Av Presidente Vargas, **T** 021-38082089. *Tue-Sun 1230-1900.* *Map 6, A3, p256*

The Centro Cultural Banco do Brasil (CCBB) is housed in a fine turn-of-the-19th-century, neoclassical building with a beautiful glass-domed roof. The centre hosts some of the city's more distinguished art shows, including some excellent photographic exhibitions. It also has an arts cinema, library, multimedia facilities and lunchtime concerts (around US$5). There is also an air-conditioned restaurant.

Fundaçao Casa França-Brasil

R Visconde de Itaboraí 78, corner of Av Presidente Vargas
T 021-22535366. *Tue-Sun 1200-2000.* Map 6, A4, p256

The Fundaçao Casa França-Brasil is a Franco-Brazilian cultural centre which holds temporary exhibitions exploring the long relationship between the two countries. The building itself dates from the first French Artistic Mission to Brazil and was the first neoclassical building in Rio. It was designed by the French architect Granjean de Montigny and commissioned by King João VI. A year after its inauguration, it was stormed by troops loyal to the king's son, Dom Pedro I, who suppressed crowds who had gathered here to demand that the Portuguese court remained in Brazil. Several protestors were killed and the house was given the nickname 'the Butcher's of Bragança' after the surname of the Portuguese royal family. The interior of the building is entirely neoclassical, although the pillars and mouldings are made of wood. The roof is a hybrid between the colonial Brazilian style and the newly introduced European fashion. It was built as a customs house and the strongroom can still be seen.

Espaço Cultural da Marinha

Av Alfredo Agache, on the waterfront, **T** 021-21046025. *Tue-Sun 1200-1700, US$2.* Map 6, north of A5, p256

The newest of the cultural centres near Candelária is the Naval Cultural Centre. This former naval establishment, built on a jetty over the bay, now contains museums of underwater archaeology and navigation. *Galeota*, the boat used by the Portuguese royal family for sailing around Guanabara Bay is kept here, and a World War II submarine and warship, the *Bauru* is moored outside. The museum is very popular with children and is crowded at weekends.

Praça Mauá and the port area

*The **Praça Mauá**, which lies north of Avenida Presidente Vargas, marks the end of the city centre and the beginning of the port zone. Many of the empty warehouses here are used as workshops by the samba schools for the construction of their beautiful Carnival floats. The area would be unremarkable were it not for the Benedictine **Mosteiro de São Bento**, whose sober Brazilian baroque facade sits on a promontory looking out over the bay.*

Sights

★ Mosteiro de São Bento

R Dom Gerardo 68, **T** 021-22917122. *Mon-Sun 0800-1000, 1430-1800, free, modest dress, no shorts. Access via R Dom Gerardo 68, turning left off Av Rio Branco; by a lift from R Dom Gerardo 40, behind the RBI building; or by taxi from centre, US$5.* *Map 2, just north of A9, p248*

The monastery of São Bento is widely publicized as a World Heritage site, which it is not; but of all the city's colonial buildings this is the most worth visiting, and it is a building of global importance. It began life in 1586 with a group of monks, who arrived in Rio from Salvador, and gradually grew to become the most powerful monastery in the city, with the finest building and art work being produced in the 17th century. The jewel in the mitre is the monastery's church, dedicated to Nossa Senhora de Monserrat (usually referred to as the **Igreja do Mosteiro de São Bento**). This may appear austere from the outside, but hidden within is some of the most lavish baroque art in Brazil. The three doors giving access to the nave were sculpted by Father

! Arriving at the monastery by lift is a magical experience, as you are whisked from the heat and bustle of the dock area to an oasis of calm, which beautifully sets the mood for a wander around the monastery buildings.

Domingos da Conceição; the sculptures of St Benedict, St Escolastica and Our Lady of Monserrat are particularly remarkable. The latter, also by Domingos de Conceição, has painted birds' eggs for eyes. The painting is as wonderful as the carving; particularly the panels in the Blessed Sacrament chapel by Ínacio Ferreira Pinto. '*O Salvador*', the masterpiece of Brazil's first painter, Frei Ricardo do Pilar, hangs in the sacristy.

The enormous candelabras, which are attributed to Mestre Valentim, Rio's most celebrated church artisan, are moulded from solid silver specially imported from Peru and the mines of Potosí in Bolivia at a price higher than Brazil's own gold. The monastery's **library** (open to men only), preserves a number of priceless religious manuscripts alongside 200,000 other books.

● *Every Sunday at 1000 there is a Latin Mass with plainsong. Arrive an hour early to get a seat. On other days, Mass is at 0715 and the monks often sing at vespers.*

Morro da Conceição

Map 2, north of A8, p248

Close to the Praça Mauá, via a moderate climb, is the **Morro da Conceição**, a hill which the first Portuguese settlers used to survey the bay. The first constructions on the hill were religious, and a bishop's palace, the **Palácio da Conceição**, was built in 1702. This and the subsequent **Fortaleza da Conceição** are owned by the army and, aside from a small museum in the Palácio, are closed to the public. However, the area around the buildings is perfectly safe to visit. Look out for another of Rio's few remaining public oratories above the door of the Fortaleza; it is illuminated at night.

! A strange but popular sight on Rio's beaches, during the winter months, are the penguins that occasionally find themselves off course during their migration from the Straits of Magellan to the milder climates up the coast.

Ilha Fiscal

T 021-38706879. *Ferries leave Fri-Sun 1300, 1430 and 1600 (30 mins later from Oct-Mar).* *Map 1, D12, p246*

Just offshore, but connected to the mainland by a causeway to Ilha das Cobras, is the Ilha Fiscal. It was built as a customs house at the Emperor's request, but he deemed it too beautiful, and said that it should be used only for official parties; only one was ever held, five days before the Republic began. It is now a museum, linked with the Naval Cultural Centre (see page 53). The island is passed by the ferry to Niterói (see page 91).

Ilha de Paquetá

Ferries leave every 2 hrs from Praça 15, US$1, 1 hr, ***T*** *021-25337524; hydrofoils leave between 1000-1600 hrly, US$4.20, 20 mins,* ***T*** *021-33970656. Buses from Praça 15: 119 from Glória, Flamengo and Botafogo; 154/413/455/ 474 from Copacabana, or 415 passing Leblon via Ipanema. For organized trips, see Tour operators, page 26.* *Off the map*

Paquetá Island, the second largest in Guanabara Bay, is noted for its gigantic pebble-shaped rocks, butterflies and orchids. The only real reason to come here is for the wonderful views, but there are a few historical buildings on the island, including the **house of José Bonifácio**, a Carioca anti-slavery campaigner, and the newly refurbished **Solar d'el Rei** which houses a library. At the southwest tip is the interesting **Parque Darke de Mattos**, with beautiful trees, lots of birds and a lookout on the Morro da Cruz. The island has several beaches, but the water is none too clean. The only means of transport are bicycles and horse-drawn carriages.

The southern suburbs

Cariocas, as the citizens of Rio are known, have been defined by Priscilla Ann Gosling as 'people who go to the beach before, after or instead of work'. And it is in the city's southern suburbs, or Zona Sul, where their obsessions with the *praia* (beach) most truly comes to the fore. The Zona Sul proper begins in Copacabana, a sweeping crescent of sand, broken by *postos* of lifeguard stations. These are numbered and continue through the Arpoador and Ipanema to Barra Da Tijuca. Each attracts a different crowd – from gay men with tiny waists and inflated chests, to the famously toned and tanned Carioca women. 'Where do you go on the beach?' is the defining question for Cariocas seeking to establish social status. Between Copacabana and the city centre are a series of giant boulders, like the Sugar Loaf, and white-sand bays, backed by what were at various stages of the city's existence, the most fashionable seaside suburbs. As Guanabara Bay has become steadily more polluted, these have moved further and further out, and the most desirable spot is now Ipanema. The safest places for a lounge or swim are in front of the major hotels which have their own security, such as the Meridien on Copacabana beach or the Caesar Park on Ipanema.

Glória, Catete and Flamengo

The first bay after the city centre is the Enseada da Glória, fronting the suburb of the same name and sitting next to the Santos Dumont Airport. Avenida Infante Dom Henrique, a broad avenue lined with an eclectic mix of grand houses and squat office blocks, leads from here to what was once the city's finest beach, Flamengo, a long stretch of sand separated from the rest of southern Rio by the Morro da Viúva or Widow's Peak. The suburb of Catete sits just behind Flamengo. These three areas were once the heart of recreational Rio; the public posing spots of choice for the belle époque middle and upper classes, with beaches which were perhaps the most coveted urban swimming spots in the world. Now the water is polluted and swimming ill advised. These suburbs are pleasant for a stroll and preserve a few sights of interest.

▸▸ *See Sleeping p112, Eating and drinking p138*

Sights

Parque do Flamengo

Av Infante Dom Henrique. *Metrô Glória, Catete, Largo de Machado or Flamengo. Closed to traffic on Sun. Be careful after dark.*

Map 3, A-L8, p250

Before the pollution became too much, Burle Marx, Brazil's 20th-century Capability Brown, designed this handsome stretch of waterfront public gardens, watched over by the stands of stately royal palms. The gardens separate Infante Dom Henrique from the sea, and stretch from Glória through to Widow's Peak at the far end of Flamengo. They were built on reclaimed land and opened in 1965 to mark the 400th anniversary of the city's founding. They are dotted with bandstands, children's play areas, temporary stages for night and daytime shows, and a handful of monuments and museums. These include the striking post-modern **Monumento aos Mortos da Segunda Guerra Mundial** (National War Memorial to Brazil's dead in the Second World War), a gently curved slab supported by two slender columns, representing two palms uplifted to heaven. It looks particularly striking at sunset. In the crypt are the remains of the Brazilian soldiers killed in Italy in 1944-45. (*Tue-Sun1000-1700, for crypt and museum*). Beach clothes and rubber-thonged sandals are not permitted. The **Praça Paris** (*Av Infante Dom Henrique 75*), with illuminated fountains and gardens built in homage to French style, sits opposite the monument and is a very pleasant public space.

Museu de Arte Moderna

Av Infante Dom Henrique 85, **T** 021-22404944, www.mamrio.com.br. *Tue-Sun 1200-1700 (last entry 1630), US$2.* *Map 2, H11, p248*

Just beyond the War Memorial at the far northern end of the Parque do Flamengo is the Museum of Modern Art, another striking modernist building with a small collection of international and domestic modern and contemporary art, including drawings by the distinguished Carioca artist Cândido Portanari and etchings of everyday work scenes by Gregório Gruber.

Nossa Senhora da Glória do Outeiro

Ladeira da Glória, **T** 021-22252869. *Tue-Fri 1300-1700, Sat-Sun 0800-1200, closed Mon, US$1. Metrô Glória.* *Map 3, C6, p250*

This beautiful little early-18th-century church built on a hill overlooking the Parque do Flamengo was a favourite of the imperial family. Dom Pedro II was baptized here. The building is polygonal, with a single tower, and contains some of the finest *azulejos* in the city and a fine carved altar by Mestre Valentim. A and **Museum of Religious Art** stands behind the church.

Museu da República

R do Catete 153, Catete, **T** 021-25573150. *Tue-Sun 1200-1700, US$2.50. Bus 571 from Copacabana, Metrô Catete.* *Map 3, E5, p250*

The former residence of a coffee baron, the Barão de Nova Friburgo, the palace was built in 1858-1866 and was converted in 1887 into the presidential seat, until the move to Brasília. The ground floor comprises the sumptuous rooms of the coffee baron's former mansion. The first floor is devoted to the history of the Brazilian Republic. You can also see the room where former President Getúlio Vargas shot himself. Behind the museum is the **Parque do Catete** with many birds and marmosets.

Museu do Folclore Edison Carneiro

R do Catete 181, Catete, **T** 021-2850441. *Tue-Fri 1100-1800, Sat-Sun 1500-1800, free. Bus 571 from Copacabana, Metrô Catete.* *Map 3, E5, p250*

An eclectic selection of items and objects related to folklore and popular culture, including a selection of ceramic figures, Candomblé and Umbanda costumes, religious objects, ex-*votos* and displays on many of Brazil's festivals. It has a small, but excellent library, with friendly staff and a range of books on Brazilian culture, history and anthropology.

Museu Carmen Miranda

Opposite Rui Barbosa 560, Parque do Flamengo (in front of the Morro da Viúva) **T** 021-55125970. *Mon-Fri 1100-1700, US$0.30.* *Map 3, just off L6, p250*

Over 3,000 items related to the famous Portuguese singer who emigrated to Brazil and then Hollywood, and is forever associated with Rio. These include her famous gowns, fruit-covered hats, jewellery and reviews, recordings and occasional showings of her films.

Santa Teresa

This hilly inner suburb southwest of the centre is one of Rio's most picturesque – colourful trams wind up the hilly streets lined with pretty colonial houses and lavish mansions towards the forested slopes of Tijuca National Park, leaving in their wake sweeping views of Guanabara Bay and the Sugar Loaf. If it weren't for its proximity to favelas, *the suburb would be one of the city's most idyllic. As it is, a number of Rio's glitterati live behind the high walls of many of the colonial and 19th-century buildings. Mick Jagger met Luciana Morad at a party in one of the mansions, and Ronnie Biggs lived here before his deportation to the UK. A tram ride from the cathedral to Santa*

Teresa over the Arcos de Lapa viaduct is an unmissable Rio experience. The suburb is a popular spot for lunch. Rio's equivalent of the Buena Vista Social Club play at the Aprazível restaurant every Sunday competing for attention with the wonderful views of the bay. There are a wealth of excellent, small restaurants around the Largo do Guimarães and the Largo das Neves – a little community in its own right, sitting at the end of the tram line.

▸▸ *See Sleeping p114, Eating and drinking p139, Bars and clubs p161*

Sights

Convento da Santa Teresa

R Joaquim Murtinho e Ladeira de Santa Teresa.
Map 3, north of A4, p250

Santa Teresa's sense of separation is reflected not only in the suburb's geography, but also its history. In 1624, Antônio Gomes do Desterro chose the area for its combination of proximity to Rio and isolation, and erected a hermitage dedicated to Nossa Senhora do Desterro. The name was changed from Morro do Desterro to Santa Teresa after the construction in 1750 of a convent of that name dedicated to the patroness of the order. The convent exists to this day, but it can only be seen from the outside; the Carmelite nuns do not admit visitors.

Santa Teresa's colonial houses with a view

Map 3, B1, p250

Santa Teresa is best seen by tram or on foot. It is a good place to wander around or stop at a streetside café to admire the view. Always be vigilant with your camera and money; robberies are not unknown here. The better colonial houses, most of which are private residences, include the castle-like **Casa de Valentim** in Vista Alegre, the tiled **Chácara dos Viegas** in Rua Monte Alegre and the **Chalé Murtinho**. This was the house in which Dona Laurinda Santos Lobo

Safety in Santa Teresa

In recent years, visitors have been put off going to Santa Teresa because of a reputation for crime which has spilled over from neighbouring *favelas*. However, It would be a great shame to miss this unique 'town within a city'. The crime rate has been reduced, and normally a policeman rides each tram but you are advised not to take valuables or look 'wealthy'. A T-shirt, shorts and enough money for a meal should be sufficient. Avoid long walks on streets that are far from the main centres of Largo das Neves and Largo do Guimarães.

held her famous artistic, political and intellectual salons at the turn of the 20th century. The house was in ruins until it was partially restored and turned into a cultural centre, **Parque das Ruínas** (*R Murtinho Nobre 41, daily 1000-1700*). It has superb views of the city, an exhibition space and an open-air stage with live music Thursdays. A bridge connects it to the Chácara do Céu (see below).

★ Santa Teresa tram

US$0.40 single. Buses 206/214 from Av Rio Branco in the city centre to Santa Teresa and vice versa. At night, take a taxi (US$7 to the centre or Ipanema). *Map 2, F8, p248*

Santa Teresa is best visited on the traditional open-sided tram; the *bondinho*. This can be caught from the terminus next to the cathedral or from Cinelândia; take the Metrô to Cinelândia station, go to Rua Senador Dantas then walk along to Rua Profesor Lélio Gama (look for Banco do Brasil on the corner). The station is up this street. Enjoy the trip as it passes over the **Arcos da Lapa** aqueduct, winding its way up to the district's historic streets. The journey ends at the Largo das Neves *praça* where the tram turns round for the journey back to Rua Profesor Lélio Gama. As the

Arcos da Lapa

From the 17th to the mid-18th century, work was done in various stages to bring water from the Rio Carioca to the city centre through Santa Teresa, thus lessening the suburb's isolation. This culminated in the construction of the Aqueduto dos Arcos (Arcos da Lapa, see also page 47), which carried water from Santa Teresa to the Chafariz da Carioca, with its 16 fountains, in the centre of the city. The aqueduct's use was changed at the end of the 19th century with the introduction of electric trams in Rio. The inaugural run along the tracks laid on top of the arches was on 1 September 1896.

trams are open-sided, the views wonderful; but be careful with your camera and valuables.

Museu Chácara do Céu

R Murtinho Nobre 93, **T** 021-22850891. *Daily except Tue 1200-1700, US$2. Santa Teresa tram to Curvelo station, walk along R Dias de Barros following signposts to Parque das Ruínas. Map 3, A2, p250*

The Chácara do Céu, or Fundação Raymundo Ottoni de Castro Maia, sells and displays a wide range of art objects and works by modern painters, including Brazilian; exhibitions change through the year. Castro Maia's former residence, now the **Museu Açude**, a small handicrafts museum, is also interesting (see page 83).

Pão de Açúcar, Botafogo and Urca

Pão de Açúcar or the Sugar Loaf, looms over Botafogo, the next of the Guanabara Bay coves after Flamengo. It stretches from the Widow's Peak to the tiny suburb of Urca which huddles around the Sugar Loaf's flanks. A remnant of forest, still home to marmosets and rare birds, shrouds the boulder's sides and a cable car straddles the distance between its summit, the Morro da Urca hill and the suburbs below, making one of the continent's most breathtaking views easily accessible to everyone. Food, drink and shade are abundant at the top. Urca and Botafogo have a few sights of interest, make convenient bases for the centre and have reasonable accommodation and restaurant options, particularly in the lower price ranges.

▸▸ *See Sleeping p114, Eating and drinking p140, Bars and clubs p161*

Sights

★ Pão de Açúcar (the Sugar Loaf)

Av Pasteur 520, Praia Vermelha, Urca. *Daily 0800-2200. Cable car US$15, every 30 mins. Buses 107 (from the centre, Catete or Flamengo) and 511 from Copacabana (512 to return) take you to the cable car station. Or walk 10 mins northeast from behind the Rio Sul shopping centre.* *Map 4, C12, p252*

The western hemisphere's most famous monolith rises almost sheer from the dark sea to just under 400 m; towering over Botafogo beach and separating Guanabara Bay from the open Atlantic Ocean. The views from the top, out over Copacabana, Ipanema and the mountains and forests of Corcovado and Tijuca are as unforgettable as the view from New Yorks's Empire State building or Victoria Peak in Hong Kong. They are a definite must-see and are easily accessible by cable car, extensive paths, plentiful shade and various snack bars. Come early for the clearest air, best views and smallest crowds.

The cable car station is in Praça General Tiburcio in the heart of Urca's military district and next to the Rio de Janeiro Federal University. Rides go up in two stages, the first to the summit of **Morro da Urca**, the smaller rock which sits in front of the Sugar Loaf, and the second to the top of the Sugar Loaf itself. Allow at least two hours for your visit.

Big brother

Paul Landowski's 'Christ the Redeemer' looms over the city, keeping a watchful eye on Rio's pleasure-loving inhabitants.

A
OSORIO

1 Capoeira, the only sport to have originated in the Americas, is played out with impossible speed in Rio's streets and parks. ▸▸ *See page 198.*

2 The historic buildings on and around Praça 15 de Novembro are the focal point of Rio's colonial heritage. ▸▸ *See page 32.*

3 Perhaps the most famous party in the world – for five days each year life goes on hold for the swirling, reverberating, joyous Carnival.
▸▸ *See page 179.*

4 'The whole world tries, but only Brazil has won the world cup five times'. The huge Macaraña football stadium is a tribute to the passion and pride the game inspires.
▸▸ *See page 85.*

5 Clinging to the hills above some of Rio's most affluent suburbs, Rochina favela is a world apart and where much of the city's poor live.
▸▸ *See page 78.*

6 Founded in 1808, the botanic gardens remain a haven of peace within the city and protect a number of rare birds and plants.
▸▸ *See page 73.*

Pão de Açúcar

Climb or take the cable car to the top of the Sugar Loaf for a bird's eye view of the city and beaches.

Flying saucer museum

The dramatic Museu de Arte Contemporanea in Niterói is an architectural marvel designed by Oscar Niemeyer.

Colonial charm

Ride Rio's last remaining tram from the cathedral through the winding, cobbled streets of Santa Teresa.

Where do you go on the beach?

The defining question for Cariocas seeking to establish social status. The beach at Ipanema is currently one of the most fashionable.

Moonlighting

As the sun sets the city comes alive with the sensual sounds of samba. Sip caipirinhas and soak up the carnival vibe of Brazil's former capital.

Pirate retreat

Escape the hustle and bustle in Vila do Abraão, Ilha Grande's main village. Legend has it that the island's beauty is secured by a swashbuckling curse.

Around Pão de Açúcar

Map 4, C12, p252 and around

There is more to the Sugar Loaf than the views from the top. Few visitors bother with the boulder's environs, yet their secluded little beaches, remnants of forest and little colonial suburbs are well worth seeing. The best place to begin is at **Praia Vermelha**, the beach to the south of the rock, where there is a simple restaurant with wonderful views. The **Pista Cláudio Coutinho** (*daily 0700-1800*) walking track runs from here along the waterfront around the foot of the rock. You'll see plenty of wildlife here at dawn, especially marmosets and brilliantly-coloured birds, like the endangered seven-coloured or green-headed tanager (*tangara fastuosa*), along with various intrepid climbers scaling the hulking granite. About 350 m from the beginning of the Pista Coutinho is a turn off to the left for a path which winds its way up through the forest to the top of **Morro da Urca**, from where the cable car can be taken for US$10. You can save even more money, but use more energy, by climbing the Caminho da Costa, a path to the summit of the **Pão de Açúcar**. Only one stretch, of 10 m, requires climbing gear, but if you wait at the bottom of the path for a group going up, they will usually let you tag along. This way you can descend to Morro da Urca by cable car for free and walk down from there.

● *There are 35 rock-climbing routes up the boulder, with various degrees of difficulty. The best months for climbing are April to August. See page 204 for climbing clubs.*

Museu do Índio

R das Palmeiras 55, **T** 021-22868899. *Mon-Fri 1000-1730, Sat-Sun 1300-1700 (shop closes for lunch 1200-1400). US$1.75. 10-min walk from Metrô Botafogo, bus 571 from Catete passes close by. Map 4, C3, p252*

A Funai-run musem set up by Marechal Rondon with some 12,000 objects from over 180 Brazilian Indian groups, including basketry, ceramics, masks and weapons as well as 500,000 documents, 50,000 photographs and various documentary films and videos. The garden includes an Indian *maloca* (house) built by Guaraní people. There is also a small, well-displayed handicraft shop and a library of ethnology at the same location, which has friendly and helpful staff. The museum is popular with children.

Museu Villa-Lobos

R Sorocaba 200, **T** 021-22663845, www.museuvillalobos.org.br. *Mon-Fri 1000-1700, free.* *Map 4, C3, p252*

Such was the fame and respect afforded to Latin America's most celebrated composer that this museum was founded only a year after his death in 1960. Inside the fine 19th-century building is a collection of his personal objects, including instruments, scores, books and recordings. The museum has occassional temporary shows and concerts, and supports a number of classical music projects throughout Brazil. For more information on Villa-Lobos see the box on page 171.

Museu Internacional de Arte Naif do Brasil (MIAN)

R Cosme Velho 561, 30 m uphill from the Corcovado station, **T** 021-22058612. *Tue-Fri 1000-1800, Sat-Sun and holidays 1200-1800, closed Mon, US$3.20, discounts available.* *Map 4, north of A1, p252*

One of the most comprehensive museums of naive and folk paintings in the world with a permanent collection of some 8,000 works by naive artists from about 130 countries. The museum also hosts several thematic and temporary exhibitions throughout the year. Parts of its collection are often on loan to other museums and exhibitions around the world. There is a coffee shop and a souvenir shop where you can buy small paintings by some of the artists on display, books, postcards and T-shirts. Courses and workshops on painting and related subjects are also available.

Largo do Boticário

R Cosme Velho 822. *Map 4, north of A1, p252*

This pretty, shady little square, close to the terminus for the Corcovado cog railway and surrounded by 19th-century buildings, offers a glimpse of what the city looked like before the various 20th-century municipal authorities succumbed to dreams of positivism and functionalism. That the square exists at all is thanks to concerned residents, who sought to preserve it, and were instrumental in rebuilding and refurbishing the buildings using rubble from colonial buildings demolished in the city centre. Many of the doors once belonged to churches. The four houses that front the square are painted different colours (white, pale blue, caramel and pink), with different features picked out in decorative tiles, woodwork and stone.

Copacabana and Leme

Copacabana, which is called Leme at its northern end, epitomizes Rio both for better and for worse. At first sight it looks magnificent; a splendid sweeping crescent of broad fine sand stretching for almost 8 km, washed by a bottle-green Atlantic and watched over by the Morro do Leme – another of Rio's beautiful forest-covered hills. Behind it is a wide, neon-lit avenue lined with high rises, the odd grand hotel and various bars, clubs and restaurants. The tanned and toned flock here in little bikinis, sungas *and bright beach wraps, playing beach volleyball on the sand, jogging along the wavy black-and-white dragon's tooth pavements, busking, playing capoeira and selling wares. But like much of Brazil, the devil is in the detail, and up close Copacabana looks a lot uglier than it does from afar. The sand may be clean enough but those bottle-green waves are far from it. Many of the bars and hotels are tatty and tawdry. Some are peopled with a* pattaya *crowd of young, thin Cariocas and fat older foreigners looking to buy more than drink. And at night Copacabana can be dangerous. Soliciting is rife and muggings are not uncommon.*

▸▸ *See Sleeping p115, Eating and drinking p141, Bars and clubs p161*

Buses 119, 154, 413, 415, 455 and 474, between Av Nossa Senhora de Copacabana and the city centre, are plentiful and cost US$0.40. If you are going to the centre from Copacabana, look for 'Castelo', 'Praça 15', 'E Ferro' or 'Praça Mauá' on the sign by the front door. 'Aterro' means the expressway between Botafogo and the centre (not open on Sunday). From the centre to Copacabana is easier as all buses in that direction are clearly marked. The 'Aterro' bus takes 15 minutes. Numerous buses run between Copacabana and Ipanema, and the 2 beaches are connected by R Francisco Otaviano and R Joaquim Nabuco, immediately west of the Forte de Copacabana.

Sights

Copacabana beach and Avenida Atlântica

Map 4, H5-G10, p252

Copacabana exploded in population after the construction of the *túnel velho* (old tunnel), in 1891. The new tunnel was built in the 20th century and has been growing – mostly upward– ever since, from its original seafront thoroughfare, Avenida Atlântica. Now this, like the suburb's other streets, is packed with high-rise flats and hotels which crowd around the neoclassical facade of the belle époque **Copacabana Palace Hotel**.

Apart from on New Year's Eve, when the whole suburb becomes a huge party venue and bands play along the entire length of the beach, Copacabana is a place for little more than landscape and people watching. There are few other sights and the sea is good for swimming only when the current is heading out from the shore. The best way to enjoy the area is to wander along the promenade between Avenida Atlântica and the beach, stopping for the odd coconut in one of the numerous beachfront snack bars, and gazing at the diverse crowd which gathers at each one. Everyone looks at everyone in Rio so don't be afraid to surreptitiously stare.

Copacabana - What's in a name?

Copacabana is most famously a beach in Brazil; but it is also a beach in New South Wales, a nightclub in New York, a small town in Bolivia and a song by Barry Manilow. All of these, one might think, owe their name to Brazil's Copacabana. But it is not so. Copacabana is an Inca word meaning 'beholder of the blue horizon' or 'beholder of the precious stone'. The original Copacabana was a port for the islands of the Sun and the Moon on the shores of Lake Titicaca, endowed with spiritual significance for the Inca people. These islands were the mythical navel of the world, and the birthplace of the incarnation and the sun deities with which they are associated. As far as we know, the Incas never made it to Rio, and certainly were not directly responsible for naming Rio's Copacabana. For this we must thank the Virgin Mary. In 1576, after surviving a storm on the lake, some fisherman commissioned Francisco Yupanque, a direct descendant of the Inca nobility, to carve a statue in homage to Our Lady, whom they credited with having rescued them. The statue, which had strong Inca features, was placed inside a purpose-built church in the town of Copacabana, which was renamed Nuestra Señora de Copacabana. It quickly became a pilgrimage centre, especially for sailors, and copies of the Inca Virgin were often carried on voyages between Spain and the New World. In the 17th century, a boat sailing from Spain to South America came into difficulties during a storm in the Atlantic. The sailors prayed to an image of Nuestra Señora de Copacabana and, like those Inca fishermen, they were saved. Their captain promised to build a chapel to the Virgin when he reached land, and he did so in Rio de Janeiro. The chapel, Nossa Senhora de Copacabana, and the original image left there by the ship's captain, stood until 1914, when it was razed to the ground to make way for the Forte de Copacabana.

Ipanema, Arpoador and Leblon

Like Copacabana and Leme, Ipanema and Leblon are essentially one long curving beach integrated by the monolithic **Dois Irmãos** *rocks at the western end and the* **Arpoador** *rocks at the eastern. Also like Copacabana, there are few sights beyond the sand, the landscape and the beautiful people who inhabit them. However, comparisons end there. Ipanema and Leblon are as fashionable and cool as Copacabana is grungy and frenetic. If Copacabana is samba, then Ipanema is bossa nova: wealthy, sealed off from the realities of Rio in a neat little fairy-tale strip of streets and watched over by twinkling lights high up on the flanks of the Morro Dois Irmãos rocks. They look so romantic that it is easy to forget that they come from the world's largest* favela.

Closeted and cosseted though it may be, this is the suburb in which to base yourself while in Rio. Almost all of the city's best restaurants and bars lie here (and in the suburbs of Gávea and Lagoa which lie behind). The streets are fairly clean and usually walked by nothing more dangerous than a small white poodle, there is plenty of reasonable accommodation which doesn't rent by the hour at the lower end of the market, and the sea is good for swimming and surfing (see page 205).

▸▸ *See Sleeping p120, Eating and drinking p143, Bars and clubs p162*

Sights

★ The beaches

Map 5, H1-H9, p254

Like Copacabana, Ipanema and Leblon are places for people-watching. A half-day wandering around Ipanema/Leblon followed by a half-day wandering around Copacabana/Leme can be most interesting. The crowds are quite different. While Copacabana attracts a real cross section of Rio society, from the poor to the wealthy, Ipanema/Leblon are predominantly haunts of the fashionable peacocks, who emerge early to strut in small

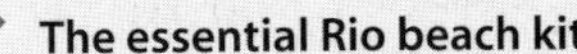

The essential Rio beach kit

To get the best out of Rio, dress as the locals do – become a Carioca. Leave your board shorts, sense of shame and awareness of time in the hotel, and go out in search of the essential Carioca uniform. If you you are a man, the first thing you will need is a *sunga*, a tiny piece of square lycra; if you are a woman you'll need a tiny bikini or *tanga*, see page 189 for the most fashionable places to buy. The next essential is a *canga* – a sarong of the kind ubiquitous in Asia – which is used as a wrap, towel and beach mat. You will then need a *frescobol* kit – a wooden racket and a rubber ball to hit back and forth across the sand – and a pair of *Havaianas* – Brazilian flip flops. Both are available for next to nothing in the supermarket. A small white poodle (for women) and pair of cheap sunglasses (for men) complete the outfit.

swimming gear and fan out their pectorals along the beachfront promenade, especially around *posto nove*. This is a Vanity Fair which should not be missed, especially if you like photography. Beyond the people and the breathtaking landscape, there is little to see here. But there is plenty to do, especially for avid consumers. Shopping is best on and around Garcia D'Avila and the Hippy Fair (see page 194), where you will find everything from high quality Brazilian designer swimwear to seed bracelets and T-shirts with pictures of Bob Marley.

Casa de Cultura Laura Alvim

Av Vieira Souto 176, **T** 021-2671647. *Map 5, H9, p254*

Those seeking culture but reluctant to leave the beach should head for the Casa de Cultura Laura Alvim, a complex comprising an art cinema, art galleries (with temporary exhibitions), workshop spaces and a bookshop.

Gávea, Lagoa and Jardim Botânico

Just inland from Ipanema and Leblon, nestled under the forested slopes of Corcovado and the Tijuca National Park, and spread around the picturesque saltwater lagoon, ***Lagoa Rodrigo de Freitas****, are these three mainly residential suburbs. All have lively top-end nightlife. Gávea tends to attract the young and wealthy, while the 30-somethings dine in the restaurants in Lagoa, overlooking the lagoon and go out to clubs in Leblon.*

▸▸ *See Eating and drinking p147, Bars and clubs p164*

Sights

Lagoa Rodrigo de Freitas and around

Map 5, centre, p254

The Lagoa is yet another of Rio de Janeiro's unbelievably beautiful natural sights and has long been admired. Darwin and German naturalists Spix and Martius, all wrote of its natural beauty in their accounts. It is best seen in the early evening, when golden sunlight bathes the rainforest-clad slopes of the Serra da Carioca which rise high above to reach their spectacular pinnacle with the distant statue of the xenon-white Christ.

Like Copacabana and Guanabara Bay, it could be even more beautiful if only it were looked after a little better. The canal which links the lake to the sea is far too narrow to allow for sufficient exchange of water; pollution makes it unsafe for swimming, and occasional summer algal blooms have led to mass fish deaths.

The lake is surrounded by a series of parks. The nearest is the **Parque Tom Jobim** and contiguous are **Brigadeiro Faria Lima**, **Parque do Cantagalo** and **Parque das Taboas**. All have extensive leisure areas popular with roller skaters and volleyball players. There are live shows and *forró* dancing in the **Parque dos Patins**. Nearby is the **Parque Carlos Lacerda** and the **Parque**

da Catacumba (*Av Epitacio Pessoa, daily 0800-1900*), an open-air art gallery with sculptures by local artists in a landscaped park.

Jardim Botânico

R Jardim Botânico 1008, **T** 021-2947494, www.jbrj.gov.br. *Daily 0800-1700, US$2. Bus 170 from the centre, or any bus to Leblon, Gávea or São Conrado marked 'via Jóquei'; from Glória, Flamengo or Botafogo take 571; from Copacabana, Ipanema or Leblon take 572 (584 back to Copacabana). Information in English is available from Beatriz Heloisa Guimaraes, of the Society of Friends of the Garden.*
Map 5, B2, p254

These extensive 137-ha gardens protect some 70,000 rare vascular plants, and are home to some 140 species of birds and butterflies, including the brilliant blue morphos. There are stately stands of 40-m-high royal palms, large tropical ficus and ceiba trees and pau de Brasil, from whom Brazil gets its name.

The gardens were founded in 1808 by the king, Dom João VI, as a nursery for European plants and new specimens from around the world. When the electric tramline arrived in this part of the city housing and industries soon followed, but the gardens remained a haven of peace. There is a **herbarium**, an **aquarium** and a library as well as the **Museu Botânico**, housing exhibitions on the conservation of Brazilian flora, and the **Casa dos Pilões**, the first gunpowder factory in Brazil. A new pavilion contains sculptures by Mestre Valentim transferred from the centre. Many improvements were carried out before the 1992 Earth Summit, including a new **orquidario**, an enlarged book shop and a smart café.

Birdwatchers can expect to see rarities including social flycatchers, great and boat-billed kiskadees, cattle tyrants, sayacas, palm and seven-coloured (green-headed) tanagers as well as over 20 different kinds of hummingbirds, roadside hawks, laughing falcons and various toucans and parakeets. There are marmosets in the trees.

Best

Views

- From the **Sugar Loaf** first thing in the morning, p64.
- From **Corcovado** at sunset, p76.
- From the **Museu de Arte Contemporânea** in Niterói, p91.
- From **Três Picos** mountain in Itatiaia National Park, p97.
- From the **Pico do Papagaio** on Ilha Grande, p104.

Parque Lage

R Jardim Botânico 414. *Daily, 0900-1700, free.* *Map 5, north of A5, p254*

This park is more jungle-like than the Botanical Gardens and has a series of small grottos, an old tower and lakes. The **Escola de Artes Visuais** (Visual Arts School) is in a large colonial house in the park.

The Planetário

R Padre Leonel Franco 240, Gávea. **T** 021-22740096, www.rio.rj.gov.br/planetario. *US$5. Buses 176/178 from the city centre and Flamengo; 591/592 from Copacabana.* *Map 1, G10, p246*

This small planetarium was inaugurated in 1979, with a sculpture of the Earth and Moon by Mario Agostinelli. On Wednesday evenings at dusk, in clear weather, astronomers give guided observations of the stars. On Saturday and Sunday there are shows for children at 1630 and for adults and children over 12 at 1800 and 1930.

Instituto Moreira Salles

R Marques de São Vicente 476, **T** 021-5126448. *Tue-Fri 1300-2000, Sat-Sun 1300-1800.* *Map 1, G10, p246*

This cultural centre is housed in a 19th-century mansion with gardens landscaped by Burle Marx. There are a number of exhibition halls, library and a small auditorium for concerts and films.

Corcovado and the Christ statue

There are only a few famous sights in the world that exceed even the high expectations over-exposure has placed on them. The view from Rio's Corcovado Christ is one of them. Come, if you can, for dusk. Almost a kilometre above the city and at the apex of one of the highest pinnacles in Tijuca forest stands Christ; lit in brilliant xenon and with arms open to embrace the urban world's most breathtaking view. At his feet to the west is a panoply of bays, fringed with white, and backed by twinkling skyscrapers and the neon and argon of street lights. To the east, as far as the eye can see, lie long stretches of sand washed by green and white. And in front and to the south, next to tens of kilometres of ocean beaches, is the sparkle of Niterói, watched over by low grey mountains and connected to Rio by a long sinuous bridge, which threads its way across the 10-km expanse of Guanabara Bay. As the light fades from rich yellow and red through to violet, lilac and peacock blue, the tropical forest at Christ's back comes to life in a chorus of cicadas and evening birdsong loud enough to drown even the chatter of a thousand tourists.

---

*If going by **car**, drive through Túnel Rebouças from the Lagoa and then look out for the Corcovado signs to your right before the 2nd tunnel. Touts on the Corcovado road may try to convince you the road is closed in order to take you an alternative route and charge a hefty fee. Entrance is US$2.20 for the vehicle, plus US$2.20 per passenger. If coming down after dark try to go in company or at weekends when more people are about. If going by **foot**, catch bus 206 from Praça Tiradentes (or 407 from Largo do Machado) to Silvestre (the railway has no stop here now). It is a steep 9-km walk to the top. Take the narrow street to the right of the station, go through the gate and continue to the park entrance. Walkers are not usually charged. Allow a minimum of 2 hrs for the climb and consider taking a taxi back down if after dusk. **Taxis** wait in front of the station and offer tours for around US$25.* *For further details of tours, see page 26.*

Sights

★ Statue of Cristo Redentor (Christ the Redeemer)

T/F 021-5581329, www.corcovado.com.br. *Daily 0830-1900.* *Map 1, F11, p246*

The idea for a grand monument on Corcovado had long been a dream of Emperor Dom Pedro II, who used to come here on horseback to admire the sweeping views of the city. In the 1880s, he approved the construction of a cog railway up the mountain (see below), pulled by a specially designed steam train, '*Maria Fumaça*'.

It wasn't until the 1920s, when Brazil had become a republic, that plans for a grand monument were finally realized. A group of determined Catholics decided that the hill should be crowned with a statue of Christ, and in 1921 launched a competition under the auspices of a designated 'monument week'. The first sketches, by Carlos Oswaldo, depicted Christ carrying a cross, holding a globe in his hands and standing on a pedestal symbolizing the world. These were rejected in favour of Heitor da Silva Costa's 30-m-tall Christ the Redeemer with arms outstretched to embrace the city, based on Leonardo da Vinci's famous study of the human body. The detail of the figure itself was designed by the French sculptor Paul Landowski, who was responsible for the equally monumental art-deco statue of Sainte-Geneviève in Paris. Landowski created an enormous prototype bust of Christ in terracotta, and subsequently carved the body out of soapstone. This was cut into blocks, shipped to Rio and carried up the mountain on the cog railway for re-assembly. The statue was finally opened to the public in 1931, and illuminated from a switch in Rome using a signal sent by Marconi, the inventor of the radio.

! To see the city by day and night go up at 1500 or 1600 and descend on the last train, approximately 1815.

Corcovado Cog Railway

Cosme Velho 513, on the northern side of Rebouças tunnel from the Lagoa, **T/F** 021-5581329, www.corcovado.com.br. *Daily 0830-1900, every 30 mins, US$8 return, single tickets available. Bus 180 from centre or Glória/Flamengo, 583 from Copacabana, Micrônibus from Santa Teresa.* *Map 4, north of A1, p252*

The 3.8-km railway was opened on 9 October 1884 by Emperor Dom Pedro II and offers fine views. Steam trains were used initially, but electric trains replaced them in 1910. The current rolling stock is Swiss and dates from 1979. Average speed is 15 kph on the way up and 12 kph on the way down; the journey takes about 10 minutes. Mass is held on Sunday in a small chapel in the statue pedestal. From the upper terminus there is a climb of 220 steps to the top or you can take the newly installed escalator, near which there is a café.

Corcovado Cog Railway Cultural Centre

Cosme Velho 513, **T** 021-25581329. *Daily 0830-1830.*
Map 4, north of A1, p252

The station at Cosme Velho also houses a small museum, which displays aspects of the entire history of Corcovado and the statue, comprising photos and newspaper reports and the 4-m-high prototype head, sculpted in Paris. Also on display are a 19th-century Swiss carriage and the engine of Brazil's first electric train, used in 1910, which replaced the original steam engine.

South of Leblon and Tijuca National Park

Rio de Janeiro spreads into suburbs beyond Ipanema and Leblon. The roads which connect them to the inner southern beaches cling to the coast, cutting through dramatic monolithic granite mountains and winding at times in two tiers above the green of the Atlantic. The first suburb after Leblon is São Conrado, once the wealthiest in Rio and a microcosm for the country as a whole. A stone's throw from the windows of the fortified high-rise beachfront penthouses and the ultra-exclusive shops of the fashion mall are the shanty town breeze block shacks of the world's largest favela, *Rocinha. Stray bullets from the* favela *are occasionally embedded into the concrete of the tower blocks and what were among the most desirable residences in the country are now almost impossible to sell. While the* favela *continues to grow, the municipal government and police seem to continue to pursue an aggressive policy towards those who live there.*

▸▸ *See Sleeping p122, Bars and clubs p166*

Sights

Rocinha favela

Map 1, G10, p246

Many Brazilians like to think of themselves as beyond prejudice and social divide, and Cariocas are forever talking about the democracy of the beach, where people from all walks of life meet. But the reality is very different. Most upper- and middle-class Brazilians are no more likely to meet or socialize with someone from a *favela* than are most tourists. The two worlds simply do not come into contact, nor have the opportunity to do so despite their close proximity. Two nations of 'have' and 'have not' exist side by side with all the contact that a Londoner has with a Sudanese villager. Foreigners who choose to visit the *favelas* and then return to their hotels in Ipanema or elsewhere are in the rare position of being able to catch a glimpse of both. Some consider such tours voyeuristic, but they do offer insights into the reality of day-to-day life for most of Brazil, both poor and rich. Rocinha has a tourist

! Poverty and crime levels are extremely high in *favelas*, in no circumstances should you attempt to venture into a slum unless accompanied by a recommended tour guide.

The Favelas

Brazil's reputation as a violent country comes almost exclusively from the gun fights against the police and the inter-gang wars that take place in the slums of Rio de Janeiro, São Paulo, and other big cities. Such slums are known as *favelas* and many are highly dangerous, closed communities where strangers enter in peril of their lives; like the *favela* so shockingly portrayed in the multi-award winning film, *Cidade de Deus* (City of God). The film was no exaggeration: a study undertaken in 2002 found that in the 14 years to that date almost 4,000 under-18 year olds were killed by firearms in Rio, compared to just under 500 children killed in the fighting between Palestinians and Israelis in the same period. The study also estimated that there were between 5,000-6,000 armed children in the city.

For some years now there has been a stand-off between the drug gangs and their child soldiers and the police, while Rio's streets have remained relatively safe for tourists. But in mid-2004, after three police officers were shot, the city police announced a knee-jerk offensive, called Operation Maximum Pressure, targeting the drug gangs with a 'shoot first, ask questions later' policy. When Deputy State Governor, Luiz Paulo Conde, announced plans to build 10-ft-high concrete walls around Rocinha and Vidigal *favelas*, gang members took their fight to the streets of Copacabana, exchanging gunfire with the police on Avenida Atlântica.

But all is not bad news. While the authorities use little more than intimidation and brute force against the urban poor, more enlightened individuals, like the wife of the culture minister, Flora Gil, and musicians like Grupo Afro Reggae in Rio are making a real difference by bringing education and the hope of work to the young, urban poor. Crime statistics have shown a marked decrease. But yet government bodies have shown little interest in following their example.

information post with guides from the community who will take visitors on an hour-long tour, minimum of four people, US$6 per person, but it is best to visit on an organized tour. See Tour operators page 26.

Pedra da Gávea and Pedra Bonita

Map 1, H8, p246

The large, flat-topped monolith of Pedra da Gávea can be climbed or scrambled up for magnificent views, but beware of snakes. The trek to the top and back takes about five hours for the reasonably fit. People sometimes camp on top especially during full moons. If you choose to do so be sure to go in a group of at least six. Banditry is not unknown. Behind the Pedra da Gávea is the Pedra Bonita, which can be reached in about 30 minutes at an easy pace from the parking place for the hang-gliders. There are good views of Barra da Tijuca, Rio and the Ilhas Cagarras from the top. A road, the Estrada das Canoas, climbs up past these two rocks on its way to the Tijuca National Park. There is a spot on this road which gives access to the *rampa de asa delta*, which is one of the chief hang-glider launch sites in the area (see Sport, page 201).

Barra da Tijuca

Buses 175/176 from the city centre ; 179 from Botafogo, Glória or Flamengo; 591/592 from Leme; 523 from Copacabana via Leblon. A taxi to Zona Sul costs US$15 (US$22.50 after midnight). A comfortable bus, Pegasus, goes along the coast from the Castelo bus terminal to Barra da Tijuca and continues to Campo Grande or Santa Cruz, or take the free Barra Shopping Centre bus. Bus 700 from Praça São Conrado goes the full length of the beach to Recreio dos Bandeirantes. *Map 1, H8, p246*

This predominantly residential suburb of beachside apartment blocks, ugly shopping malls and long, broad car-friendly avenues was modelled on South Beach Miami and many of the residents look like they'd love to live there. This is a cultural wasteland, with such vulgar delights as a giant fibreglass Statue of Liberty standing outside the Liberty Shopping Mall. However, the beaches are fabulous, especially for surfers. Beyond is the slightly scruffier suburb of Recreio dos Bandeirantes, with even more magnificent surf beaches and more shopping centres and apartment blocks. There are plenty of restaurants and snack bars along the seafront in both suburbs, and air-conditioned eating options on the ground floor of any of the shopping malls.

Bosque da Barra/Parque Arruda Camara
Av das Americas at Av Ayrton Senna, Barra da Tijuca,
T 021-33256519. *Daily 0700-1800.* *Map 1, H8, p246*

A small nature reserve set up to preserve the sandbank vegetation that existed all along this part of the coast, before the city reached here. Many shore and land birds and small animals can be seen around the natural lagoons in the very early morning, even from the cycle and jogging paths.

Museu Casa do Pontal
Estrada do Pontal 3295, Recreio dos Bandeirantes, **T** 021-4903278.
Tue-Sun 0900-1730, US$2.75. *Map 1, H3, p246*

Set in a pleasant site near the Grumari mountains, this museum houses a collection of Brazilian folk art, put together by French designer Jacques van de Beuque. Expressive figurines made from painted wood or clay represent diverse aspects of the country's culture and history from banditry in the northeastern backlands to Carnival in Bahia and urban and rural life and eroticism. Some of the displays are animated with sound. The museum is best visited on a tour of Barra or western Rio as the museum is difficult to reach by public transport.

Parque Ecologico Municipal Chico Mendes

Av Jarbas de Carvalho 679, Recreio dos Bandeirantes, **T** 021-4376400. *Daily 0900-1730, free.* *Map 1, H3, p246*

A 400,000-sq-m park with ecological trails focused on a small lake, the Lagoinha das Tachas, and its surrounding *restinga* marsh ecosystem. The lake and marsh provide a home for broad-nosed caymans and many birds.

★ Tijuca National Park

Daily 0600-2100. Bus 221 from Praça 15 de Novembro, 233 (which continues to Barra da Tijuca) or 234 from the rodoviária *or from Praça Saens Pena, Tijuca (the city suburb, not Barra - reached by Metrô), or bus 454 from Copacabana to Alto da Boa Vista, for the park entrance.* *Map 1, F7, p246*

Tijuca National Park is the largest area of urban rainforest in the world; it is a haven for city-weary Cariocas, some 200 species of birds, numerous small mammals including primates and hundreds of species of endangered Atlantic coast rainforest plants. The forest drips with natural springs, many of which have been diverted through bamboo channels to form natural showers – be sure to bring your swimming gear. There is plenty of shade and the views from the various vantage points are almost as impressive as those from Corcovado.

The vegetation in the Parque Nacional da Tijuca is not primary. Most is natural regrowth and planned reforestation. It is a testament to what humans can do to regenerate lost forest. The first Europeans in the area cut down trees for use in construction and as firewood. The lower areas were cleared to make way for sugar plantations. When coffee was introduced to Rio de Janeiro in 1760, further

! Corcovado sits in Tijuca National Park and it is possible to walk or drive up the road immediately behind the Christ. Views are wonderful.

A walk in the park

One of the best walks in the park is to the Pico da Tijuca (1,022 m). Views from the top are wonderful and the walk offers the chance to see plenty of animals. Allow two to three hours. To get to the trailhead, enter the park at Alto da Boa Vista and follow the signposts (maps are displayed) to Bom Retiro, a good picnic place (1½ hours' walk). At Bom Retiro the road ends and there is another hour's walk up a decent footpath to the summit (take the path from the right of the Bom Retiro drinking fountain; not the more obvious steps from the left). The last part consists of steps carved out of the solid rock. There are several sheer drops at the summit which are masked by bushes - be wary, especially if you take children. The route is shady for almost its entire length. The main path to Bom Retiro passes the Cascatinha Taunay (a 30-m waterfall) and the Mayrink Chapel (built 1860). Panels painted in the chapel by Candido Portinari have been replaced by copies, and the originals will probably be installed in the Museu de Arte Moderna. Beyond the chapel are the restaurant A Floresta and Major Archer's house, now in ruins. Allow at least five to six hours for the excursion. Maps of the park are available.

Other viewpoints not passed on the walk to the peak are the Paulo e Virginia Grotto, the Vista do Almirante, the Mesa do Imperador and the Vista Chinesa (420 m), where from a Chinese-style pavilion one can see the Lagoa Rodrigo de Freitas, Ipanema and Leblon. The **Museu Açude** (*Estrada do Açude 764, Alto da Boa Vista, Floresta da Tijuca, Thu-Sun 1100-1700*), preserves Castro Maia's former residence and has a brunch with live music between 1230 and 1700 every Sunday (*T 021-4922119, www.visualnet.com.br/cmaya*).

If hiking in the national park other than on the main paths, a guide may be useful, contact the Sindicato de Guías, **T** 021-2674582. See also Tours, page 26.

swathes were cut down for *fazendas*. But the deforestation destroyed Rio's watershed and in 1861, in one of the world's first conservation projects, the Imperial government decided that Tijuca should become a rainforest reserve. The enormous task of reforesting the entire area was given to an army major, Manuel Gomes Archer, who took saplings from other areas of Atlantic forest and replanted Tijuca with native trees and a selection of exotics in fewer than 13 years. The names of the six slaves who did the actual manual work is not known. Reforestation was continued by Tomas de Gama. In 1961 Tijuca was joined to several other patches of remnant forest to form a national park of 3,300 ha.

Northern Rio

The area north of the city centre, known as the Zona Norte, gradually becomes as ugly as the Zona Sul is beautiful. There are no spectacular granite mountains here; instead, the city becomes a plain of shallow hills covered first in modest, lower-middle-class houses, and then in a seemingly endless *favela* of breeze blocks, broken only by giant concrete roads and open sewers which pour their filth into Guanabara Bay. This is where most of Rio lives. Close to the city centre, in the suburbs of São Cristovão and Maracanã, which remain relatively affluent, there are a few sights of interest.

Sights

Cemitério dos Ingleses

R da Gamboa 181, Morro da Providência, Gamboa. *Map 2, A1, p248*

This is the oldest cemetery in Rio and was granted to the British community by Dom João, Regent of Portugal, in 1810. Catholics who could afford a burial were laid to rest inside their churches (the numbers on the church floors mark the graves), but the British in Rio, being non-Catholic, were not allowed to be buried in the religious establishments. However, Brazil was under the control of Britain and the English were a powerful force in Rio. The empire was forced to grant land to them for a church and a burial ground for their dead.

Maracanã Football Stadium

Maracanã, **T** 021-25689962. *Daily, 0900-1700 (0800-1100 on match days), US$0.50. Guided tour of the stadium (in Portuguese) from Gate 16, US$2, recommended. Metrô: (linha 2) Maracanã station. Buses 238/239 from centre; 434/464 from Glória, Flamengo and Botafogo; 455 from Copacabana; 433/464 from Ipanema and Leblon.* Map 1, D8, p246

Before Homebush was built in Sydney, this was the world's largest sports stadium, and it remains the venue for many of Brazil's most important football matches: the derby against Argentina, the *Copa das Americas* and many games in the national and state football championships. It has a seating capacity of 200,000. This is where Pelé scored his 1,000th goal in 1969 and coming here for a match is a real experience. The crowds are noisy and colourful, bringing horns, trumpets, rattles and, of course, dozens of samba drums which are played throughout the game. They can be notoriously unforgiving of errors. In the international against Argentina in 2003, they became so disgusted with their national team's performance that they cheered for Argentina instead. There are three types of ticket: *cadeiras* (individual chairs), the most expensive; *arquibancadas* (terraces), good for watching the game, but don't sit between two rival groups of fans; and *geral* (standing), the cheapest, which are not recommended, are uncomfortable and not safe. Prices vary according to the game, but it's much more

! Don't be tempted to buy a club shirt or favour on match day; if you find yourself in the wrong place, you could be in trouble. See also Sport, page 199, for further information.

expensive to buy tickets from agencies than it is at the gate. Hotels can arrange visits to football matches; a good idea on Sunday when the Metrô is closed and buses are very full. Don't take valuables or wear a watch; take special care when entering and leaving the stadium. The rivalry between the local clubs (Flamengo and Vasco da Gama) is intense, often leading to violence, so it is advisable to avoid their encounters.

Quinta da Boa Vista

São Cristovão, 3 km west of Praça da República, **T** 021-25033072.
Daily 0700-1800, free. Metrô São Cristovão; safest to take a taxi.
Map 1, D8-9, p246

This large palace and extensive park, beyond the Sambódromo, was the seat of the imperial family, and their private leisure area between 1809 and 1889. Their former palace now houses the Museu Nacional (see below). The park itself is the best example of a grand, European-style landscaped park in Brazil, with mock-Greek temples, grottos and a large, artificial lake. The park fills with people at the weekend, playing football, preaching about the imminent apocalypse from appallingly loud megaphones, hawking and touting, and the air is thick with the smell of hot dogs and corn on the cob. The park's gates are a replica of Robert Adam's gates on Sion House in England and were donated to the Kind by the then Duke of Northumberland.

In recent years the Quinta da Boa Vista has had the problem of thieves operating by the park entrance and in the park itself. If you are comfortable in crowds, perhaps the best time to visit is Saturday, or better still, Sunday afternoon. There are more people and therefore more police, because it is full of Cariocas looking for fun and relaxation. It is a good time for people watching (but don't take an expensive camera).

● *The **Jardim Zoologico**, also in the Quinta da Boa Vista, is one of the best and most modern zoos in South America (see Kids, page 213)*

Museu Nacional

Quinta da Boa Vista, **T** 021-25628262. *Tue-Sun 1000-1600, US$2. Some collections open to qualified research students only. Metrô: São Cristovão (cross the railway line, a short walk to the park); taking a taxi to the main door is safer than the bus.* *Map 1, D8, p246*

This former Imperial Palace in the Quinta da Boa Vista is a fairly modest three-storey Palladian mansion with a grand, though crumbling, facade looking out over a formal Italian courtyard garden. There are two inner courtyards and two unfurnished rooms: the Throne Room, and the Ambassadorial Reception Room on the second floor, which has a modicum of original fittings. The museum's collections are a real miscellany. In the Entrance Hall is the famous Bendegó meteorite from Bahia; the largest found in South America. Its original weight, before some of it was chipped off, was 5,360 kg. Besides several foreign collections of note (for example, of Peruvian and Mexican archaeology, Graeco-Roman ceramics and Egyptian mummies), the museum contains collections of Brazilian Indian weapons, dresses, utensils, as well as minerals and historical documents. There are also collections of stuffed birds and animals, fish and butterflies. Collections are poorly displayed and the museum is in need of renovation.

Igreja de Nossa Senhora da Penha de França

Largo da Penha 19, **T** 021-38875155. *Wed-Mon 0700-1800. Free bus 497 from Copacabana, 340/346 from centre.* *Map 2, B1, p248*

This little neo-gothic church on the summit of one of the city's great boulders is an important pilgrimage centre (see Festivals and events page 185). The views from the balustrade are marvellous. The church itself can be reached by a 365-step stairway or a funicular. The church in its present form dates from the early 20th century but is based on an early-18th-century chapel. The first religious building, a hermitage, was built in 1632.

Listings

Museums and galleries

- **Museu da Imagem e do Som** images of cinema and Carioca musicians, and recordings of popular music, p38.
- **Museu Histórico Nacional** collection of historical treasures, p38.
- **Museu Naval e Oceanográfico** collection of paintings, weapons and figureheads, p39.
- **Museu Nacional de Belas-Artes** 20,000 pieces of decorative, popular and fine art, p41.
- **Espaço Cultural da Marinha** underwater archaeology and navigation, linked to the museum on Ilha Fiscal, p53.
- **Museu de Arte Moderna** collection of international and domestic modern and contemporary art, p59.
- **Museu da República** former coffee baron's mansion, now houses exhibitions of the Brazilian Republic, p59.
- **Museu do Folclore Edison Carneiro** items and objects related to folklore and popular culture, p60.
- **Museu Carmen Miranda** items related to the famous Portuguese singer, p60.
- **Museu do Índio** objects from over 180 Brazilian indigenous groups, p65.
- **Museu Villa-Lobos** personal items belonging to the composer, including instruments, scores and books, p66.
- **Museu Internacional de Arte Naif do Brasil** extensive collection of naive and folk paintings, p66.
- **Museu Casa do Pontal** Brazilian folk art, p81.
- **Museu Nacional** collection of objects from meteorites to historical documents, set in the former Imperial Palace, p87.
- **Museu de Arte Contemporânea** Niterói's space-age modern art museum, with a fantastic view of Rio, p91.
- **Museu do Carnaval** photographs and information about Rio's infamous Carnival, p180.

Around Rio de Janeiro

Niterói

Cariocas are rude about everywhere, but they are especially rude about their neighbour across Guanabara Bay. The only good thing about Niterói, they say, is the view it has of Rio de Janeiro. As a result few visitors make it here. But Niterói is well worth a visit. Its ocean beaches are less polluted and far less crowded than Rio's, and Oscar Niemeyer's architectural homage to the incumbent jet age, the ***Museu de Arte Contemporânea****, is one of his very best buildings. There is no reason to stay overnight in Niterói, but the city is worth a day-trip or a visit on the way to Búzios. Tourist information is available from* ***Neltur****, Estrada Leopoldo Fróes 773, São Francisco,* ***T*** *021-27102727.* *Map 7, inside back cover*

Ferries from the 'Barcas' boat terminal at Praça 15 de Novembro every 10 mins, journey time is 15-20 mins and costs US$0.50. Catamarans (aerobarcas) *also leave every 10 mins but take only 3 mins and cost US$2.50. Fares are half-price between 0700-1000. The slower ferry gives the best views. Ferries and catamarans leave Niterói for Rio de Janeiro from the terminal at Praça Araribóia. Bus 996 Gávea-Jurujuba, 998 Galeão-Charitas, 740-D /741 Copacabana-Charitas, 730-D Castelo-Jurujuba, US$0.60-0.75 all go from Rio-Niterói. If you are driving, the bridge across Guanabara Bay is well signposted. There is a toll of US$2.*

Sights

★ Museu de Arte Contemporânea

Mirante da Praia da Boa Viagem **T** 021-26202400. *Tue-Sun 1100-1800, US$1.50.*

This concentric space-age building, surrounded by long, curved walkways, is rapidly becoming the most famous work by Brazil's celebrated disciple of Le Corbusier, Oscar Niemeyer. It is in a fabulous location – perched on a promontory next to a pearl-white beach and lush, granite mountains, and with a sweeping view across Guanabara Bay to Rio. The building itself looks like a Gerry Anderson vision of the future; one can almost imagine Thunderbird 1 taking off through its centre. The main gallery is a white circle of polished concrete perched on a low monopod and sitting in a reflection pool. It is reached by a serpentine ramp which meets the building on its second storey. The exhibitions comprise seasonal shows and a permanent collection of Brazilian contemporary art of all disciplines. Niemeyer overcomes the problem of the unsuitability of a curved space for the exhibiting of art by using an inner hexagonal core enclosed by flat-screen walls. But he fails to overcome another – the glimpses of the stunning panorama of Rio through the gaps in the hexagon are far more captivating than most of the art. The building is also worth seeing at dusk when it is lit, and the sky above the streetlights of Rio is infused with lilac, and the distant figure of the Corcovado Christ shines brilliant xenon-white over the dark mass of mountains.

Fortaleza da Santa Cruz

Estrada General Eurico Gaspar Dutra, **T** 021- 27107840. *Daily 0900-1600, US$1.50. Guides are compulsory.*

This 16th-century fort, still used by the Brazilian military and perched on a rocky promontory at the mouth of Guanabara Bay, is the most important historical monument in Niterói. In addition to the usual gamut of cannon, dungeons and bulwarks, the tour includes a visit to gruesome execution sites and a little chapel dedicated to Saint Barbara. The statue of the saint inside was originally destined for Santa Cruz dos Militares in Rio but any attempts to move her image from here have allegedly been accompanied by violent storms.

Praça da República

Many buildings associated with the city's period as state capital are grouped around the Praça da República. However, none are open to the public. The city's main thoroughfare, Avenida Ernâni do Amaral Peixoto, which runs from this *praça*, is lined with buildings similar to Avenida Presidente Vargas in Rio. At the end of the avenue is the dock for Rio and a statue of the Indian chief Araribóia.

The beaches

Buses 38/52 from Praça General Gomes Carneiro or from the street directly ahead of the ferry entrance, at right angles to the coast street.

Although many of the beaches close to the centre of Niterói have lively nightlife (especially Icaraí which sits in the most upmarket neighbourhood), most are as unsuitable for bathing as those in urban Rio. For swimming, head for the ocean beaches. The coastal road continues around the bay, past Preventório and Samanguaiá, to Jurujuba, a fishing village at the end of the bus line (sit on the right of the bus, it's a beautiful drive). About 2 km from here, along a narrow road, are the attractive twin beaches of **Adão** and **Eva** beneath the Fortaleza da Santa Cruz. These are relatively clean and have wonderful views of Rio across the bay. The surf beaches of **Piratininga**, **Camboinhas**, **Itaipu** and **Itacoatiara** are 40 minutes' further, through picturesque countryside. They are cleaner and even more beautiful, although the undertow at Itacoatiara can be dangerous.

Búzios

Búzios is the principal resort of choice for Carioca and Mineira upper-middle classes searching for their idea of St Tropez sophistication. When it was discovered by Brigitte Bardot in 1964, it was little more than a collection of colonial fishermen's huts, and a series of pristine beaches hidden beneath steep hills covered in maquis-like vegetation. Now there are strings of hotels behind all of those beaches, and the huts have become lost within a designated tourist village of bars, bikini boutiques and restaurants; most of which are strung along the pretty little main street – Rua das Pedras. Bardot sits here, too , cheesily immortalized in brass and subsequently in tens of thousands of pictures taken by the troops of cruise-line passengers who fill Búzios's streets in high season. St Tropez this is not, but it can be fun for 20-somethings who are single and looking not to stay that way; the beaches are beautiful and there are a few romantic hotels with wonderful views.

Tourist information is available from ***Manguinos***, ***T*** *0800-249999, the main office (24-hour), on the western edge of the peninsula, and Praça Santos Dumont,* ***T*** *024-26232099, in the centre of town. Also see www.buziosonline.com.br.* *Map 7, inside back cover*

▸▸ *See Sleeping p123, Eating and drinking p150, Bars and clubs p166*

Buses from Rio's rodoviária, *4 daily (US$8, 2½ hrs). Buses to Cabo Frio leave more frequently, from where it's 30 mins to Búzios. Buy the ticket in advance during major holidays. The Búzios* rodoviária *is a few blocks' walk from the centre. By car the journey along the BR106 takes about 2½ hrs from Rio. Traffic can be appalling on Sunday nights and holidays.*

Sights

The beaches

During the daytime, the best option is to head for the beaches, of which there are 25. The most visited are **Geribá** (many bars and restaurants; popular with surfers), **Ferradura** (deep blue sea and calm waters), **Ossos** (the most famous and close to the centre), **Tartaruga** and **João Fernandes**. The better surf beaches like **Praia de Manguinhos** and **Praia de Tucuns** are further out of town.

● *To help you decide which beach suits you best, take one of the* *schooner trips, which pass many of the beaches, or hire a beach buggy. Schooner trips cost around US$10-15 for 2-3 hrs and can be arranged through Escuna Queen Lory, **T** 024-26231179.*

Itatiaia National Park

*Deep valleys shrouded in pristine rainforest, hiding rocky, clear-water rivers and icy waterfalls; walks of anything from an hour to two days along little winding mountain trails, watched over by some of the world's rarest birds and mammals; picturesque little hotels and guesthouses to suit all budgets ... and all within easy reach of Rio. This 30,000-ha national park, set in the Serra de Mantiqueira mountains, is a must for those who wish to see virgin rainforest and its animals, and are unable to visit the Amazon or Pantanal. This is good hiking country with walks through subtropical and temperate forests, grasslands and paramos to a couple of peaks just under 3,000 m. The best trails head for **Pedra de Taruga** and **Pedra de Maçã** and the Poranga and Véu da Noiva waterfalls. The **Pico das Agulhas Negras** and the **Serra das Prateleiras** (up to 2,540 m) offer decent rock climbing.* Map 7, inside back cover

▸▸ See Sleeping p, Eating and drinking p151

The park is a 2-hr drive from Rio along the motorway to São Paulo, known as the 'Dutra'. There are 2 entrances; one is via Itatiaia, from where a road leads to the park Visitors' Centre and the hotels; the 2nd provides access to the Abrigo Rebouças lodge – the starting point for the higher peaks in the park. This is reached via BR354 which leaves north from the town of Engenheiro Passos, the next town west of Itatiaia town on the Dutra. The Dutra is well-signposted from Rio, and can be reached from Lagoa via the Rebouças tunnel. There are direct buses from Rio de Janeiro to Resende and from there to Itatiaia town. A bus from Itatiaia town, marked Hotel Simon or 504 Circular, goes to the park 4 times a day; coming from Resende this may be caught at the crossroads before Itatiaia.

Sights

The Visitors' Centre and Museu de História Natural

Park Entrance, Tue-Sun 1000-1600, US$1.50

The Visitors' Centre is helpful and can provide maps and directions to all the trail heads, although not much English is spoken. The adjacent museum has a depressing display of stuffed animals from the 1940s; all of which exist in fully animated form in the park itself.

The trails

*Information and maps can be obtained at the park office (above) or from Ibama, **T** 024-33521461, www.ibama.gov.br.*

There are some excellent trails within the park leading to magnificent views of the Atlantic coastal forest and the Rio de Janeiro coastline, and to some beautiful waterfalls. The trails cut through the forest, bushland and up into the alpine paramo which is dotted with giant granite boulders within seemingly endless folds of misty mountains. Walking the trails can be one of the best ways of seeing a good cross section of the habitats and their flora and fauna. Be sure to take plenty of water, insect repellent and a fleece for the higher areas. Many of the trails begin just behind the Hotel Simon (see page 125) or a little beyond the Visitors' Centre.

A Maçico das Prateleiras This is a full day's walk to one of the highest peaks in the park (2,548 m) and, when there is no mist, the views are magnificent. Take the trail from the Abrigo Rebouças mountain lodge, reached from the BR354 road which heads north out of Engenheiro Passos – the next town beyond Itatiaia on BR116 (the Dutra). From here it is a 1½ hour walk.

Pico das Agulhas Negras The highest point in the park (2,787 m) is reached via the same route as Maçico das Prateleiras

The flora and fauna of Itatiaia

Wildlife has been protected here since the 1930s and the park is an important haven for myriad rare species listed as critically endangered or endangered by CITES. Brown capuchins and southern masked titi monkeys are common, the latter recognizable by its loud hee-haw like call. There are also agoutis, sloths, peccaries and other rare mammals like jaguar, ocelot and puma. Sources vary on the number of bird species in the park from 270 to 400, but many species are endemic making it a top birdwatching destination. There are scores of spectacular tanagers, humming birds (including the ultra-rare Brazilian ruby, with emerald wings and a dazzling red chest), and cotingas (including the swallow-tailed, shrike-like and black-and-gold; which as far as we are aware has never been photographed). Guans literally squawk and flap next to the park roads. Other specialities include white-bearded ant shrike and black-capped manakins.

The vegetation is stratified by altitude so that the plateau at 800-1,100 m is covered by forest, ferns and flowering plants (such as orchids, bromeliads and begonias), giving way on the higher escarpments to pines and bushes. Higher still, over 1,900 m, the distinctive rocky landscape has low bushes and grasses, isolated trees and many unique plants adapted to the high winds and strong sun. There is also a wide variety of lichens.

(above), but with a turn to the east at the Abrigo Rebouças instead of west. The upper reaches are only accessible with a rope and moderate climbing experience. Another full day's walk.

Tres Picos This six-hour walk, leaving from a trail signposted off to the right about 3 km beyond the Visitors' Centre, is one of the best for a glimpse of the park's various habitats. The first half of the trail is gentle, but after about an hour the path gets progressively steeper. An hour or so beyond the steep trail is the Rio Bonito – a great place for a break with a beautiful waterfall for swimming. There are wonderful views from the top – another 45 minutes further on.

The Piscina do Maromba One of the best and most refreshing places to swim in the park – in a natural pool formed by the Rio Campo Belo and situated at 1,100 m. Trails leave from behind Hotel Simon.

Waterfalls There are a number of waterfalls in the park, most of which have pools where you can swim. The most accessible is Cachoeira Poranga – left off the park road about 3½ km beyond the Visitors' Centre. Itaporani and Véu da Noiva are reached by a trail just beyond the Poranga trail, which leaves from next to the road bridge and divides after about 1 km; take the left trail for Véu da Noiva, the right trail for Itaporani.

Petrópolis and around

Emperor Pedro I, who tired of the sticky summer heat in Rio, longed for a summer palace in the cool of the Atlantic coast mountains, but abdicated before he could realise his dream. When the new Emperor, Pedro II, took the throne, he quickly approved the plans of German architect Koeler, for a palace to be built, together with a new city, to be settled by immigrants. The result was Petrópolis. The city was founded in 1843 and in little over a decade had become a bustling Germanic town and an important imperial summer retreat. The Emperor and his family would spend as much as six months of each year here, and a number of grand houses and administrative buildings were constructed. Many of these still stand – bizarre Rhineland anomalies in a neotropical landscape. Nearby is another relic of the short-lived imperial ages: Teresópolis, named after Empress Teresa Cristina, who used it as her summer residence and the access point for the Serra dos Órgãos which is famous throughout the Americas for its beautiful rainforest scenery and birdwatching.

Tourist information is available from ***Petrotur****, Praça da Confluência ,* ***T*** *024-22433561, Mon-Fri 0900-1830. It has a list of tourist sites, hotels and a free city map. There is also a tourist kiosk on Praça Dom Pedro II , Mon-Sat 0900-1800, Sun 0900-1700.* *Map 7, inside back cover*
▸▸ *See Sleeping p126, Eating and drinking p151*

Única Fácil buses leave Rio for Petrópolis every 15 mins (US$3), every hr on Sun. The journey takes abour 1½ hrs. Sit on the left of the bus for the best views, and bring travel sickness pills if you are prone to nausea on bendy roads. Return tickets are not available, so buy tickets for the return on arrival in Petrópolis. The ordinary buses leave the rodoviária *in Rio; a/c buses leave hourly from 1100, from Av Nilo Peçanha. There are 8 buses daily from Petrópolis to Teresópolis, US$3.*

Sights

Centro histórico and Casa de Petrópolis

Instituto de Cultura, R Ipiranga 716, Petrópolis, **T** 024-22372133. *Tue-Sun 1100-1900, Sat 1100-1300, US$2.*

Three rivers dominate the layout of Petrópolis: the Piabanha, Quitandinha and Palatino. In the historic centre (*centro histórico*), where most of the sites of tourist interest are to be found, the rivers have been channelled to run down the middle of the main avenues. Their banks are planted with fine trees and flowers, and the overall aspect is completely different from elsewhere in Brazil. You quickly get a sense that this was a city built with a specific purpose and at a specific time in Brazil's history. The facades of many of the mansions (not open to the public) built by the imperial and republican aristocracy can be seen on Avenida Koeler and Avenida Ipiranga.

! The Orquidário Binot (R Fernandes Vieira 390, Petrópolis, T 024-22420833) has one of the best collections of orchids in the state and is well worth seeing even if you don't intend to buy.

Among them are the neoclassical **Palácio Rio Negro** (Av Koeler *255*), the summer palace of the current President; the **Palácio da Princesa Isabel** (Av Koeler 42); and the **Casa de Rui Barbosa**, in the eclectic style (Av Ipiranga 405). Another palace is the mid-19th-century **Casa do Barão do Rio Branco** (Av Barão do Rio Branco 279). It was here that the Treaty of Petrópolis was signed, settling with Bolivia the issue of the annexation of Acre in 1903.

The **Casa de Petrópolis** (Av Ipiranga 716, **T** 024-22420653) is one of the few Koeler buildings open to the public. Its lavish, wonderfully over-the-top interior has been lovingly restored and serves as an exhibition and concert space.

The Museu Imperial

R da Imperatriz 220, Petrópolis, **T** 024-22378000. *Tue-Sun, 1100-1700, US$2. Expect long queues in high season.*

Brazil's most visited museum, the imperial palace, is so well kept you might think the imperial family had left the day before, rather than in 1889. The modest but elegant building, neoclassical in style, is fully furnished, but it's worth a visit just to see the crown jewels of both Pedro I and Pedro II. In the palace gardens is a pretty French-style tearoom, the Petit Palais. Descendants of the original family live in a house behind the palace.

Catedral de São Pedro de Alcântara

R São Pedro de Alcântara 60, Petrópolis. Tue-Sat 0800-1200.

This Gothic-revival church, completed in 1925 contains the tombs of the Emperor Dom Pedro II, Empress Doña Teresa and Princess Isabel. Dom Pedro II died in France in 1891, where he was given a Head of State funeral through the streets of Paris, before being transferred to Lisbon until President Vargas arranged to have his body brought back to Brazil. The imperial chapel is to the right of the entrance.

Teresópolis

Information from Secretaria de Turismo, Praça Olímpica, **T** 021-27423352, ext 2082; Terminal Turístico Tancredo Neves, Av Rotariana at the entrance to town from Rio, **T** 021-27423352.

Near the Serra dos Órgãos, 91 km north of Rio, at an altitude of 910 m, this is the highest city in the state of Rio de Janeiro. Because of its height above sea level and the relatively low temperatures, the area was not exploited by the early colonists since they could not grow the tropical crops which were in demand in Europe.

Building in recent years has destroyed some of the city's character, but most visitors do not go only to see the town. Its location, at the foothills of the Serra dos Órgãos, with the associated outdoor activities, is an essential part of the charm.

The Serra dos Órgãos

Ranger station headquarters, **T/F** 021-26421070. *Park entrance US$1, extra charge for Pedra do Sino. Tourist information available from Ibama, **T** 021-22311772, www.ibama.gov.br.*

These mountains near Teresópolis, named after their strange rock formations, which are said to look like Organ pipes, preserve some of the most diverse stretches of Atlantic coast forest in the state of Rio de Janeiro. The wildlife, plants and birdwatching here are excellent, as are the walks and rock climbs. The best way to see the park is on foot; there are many trails. Hikes that cut through the forest and head up into the alpine slopes include the ascent of the **Dedo de Deus** ('God's finger'), a precipitous peak which requires some climbing skills to ascend. Others head to the highest points in the park, such as the **Pedra do Sino** ('Bell Rock' – 2,263 m), a three-

! If you have a car, a good way to see the park is to do the Rio-Teresópolis-Petrópolis-Rio road circuit, stopping off for walks in the forest. This can be done in a day.

The flora and fauna of Serra dos Órgãos

The park belongs to the threatened Mata Atlântica coastal rainforest; a Conservation International designated global biodiversity hotspot and the preserve of what are probably the richest habitats in South America outside the Amazonian cloud forests. There are 20-30-m-high trees, such as paineiras (floss-silk tree), ipês and cedros, rising above palms, bamboos and other smaller trees. Flowers include begonias, bromeliads, orchids and quaresmeiras (glorybushes).

The park is home to numerous rare and endemic birds including numerous cotingas, the rarest of which is the grey-winged cotinga, guans, tanagers, berryeaters and trogons. Mammals include titi and capuchin monkeys, all of the Amazonian cats including jaguar and oceleot, tapir and white-collared peccary. Reptiles include the sapo-pulga, the flea-toad, which at 10 mm long vies with the Cuban pygmy frog as the smallest amphibian in the world.

to-four-hour climb up a 14 km-path; the west face of this mountain is one of the hardest climbing pitches in Brazil. Other popular walks include the **Pedra do Açu** trail and walks to a variety of anatomically named peaks and outcrops: **O Escalavrado** ('The Scarred One'), **O Dedo de Nossa Senhora** ('Our Lady's Finger'), **A Cabeça de Peixe** ('Fish Head'), **A Agulha do Diabo** ('The Devil's Needle') and **A Verruga do Frade** ('The Friar's Wart').

The park has two ranger stations, both accessible from the BR116: the Sede is closer to Teresópolis (from town take Av Rotariana), while the Sub-Sede is just outside the park proper, off the BR116. By the Sede entrance is the **Mirante do Soberbo**, with views to the Baía de Guanabara. Anyone can enter the park and hike the trails from the Teresópolis gate, but if you intend to climb the Pedra do Sino, you must sign a register (those under 18 must be accompanied by an adult and have authorization from the park authorities).

Ilha Grande

Ilha Grande is a mountain ridge, covered in tropical forest, sticking out of an emerald sea and fringed by some of the world's most beautiful beaches. As there are no cars or roads – just trails through the forest – the island is still relatively undeveloped, and with luck it will remain so. Much of Ilha Grande forms part of a state park and biological reserve, and cannot even be visited. The island was a notorious pirate lair in the 16th and 17th centuries, and then a landing port for slaves. By the 20th century it had become the site of an infamous prison for the country's most notorious criminals, including the writer Graciliano Ramos, whose Memórias do cárcere *relate his experiences. The prison was closed in 1994 and is now overgrown rubble. Since then Ilha Grande has been a well-kept Brazilian treasure, which is now beginning to be discovered by the international backpacker circuit.* *Map 7, inside back cover*

▸▸ *See Sleeping p128, Eating and drinking p152*

Ferries and fishing boats take 2 hrs to reach Vila do Abraão from Angra dos Reis or Mangaratiba. Both are connected to Rio by regular buses. Bicycles can be hired and tours arranged, ask at pousadas. *Boat trips cost US$10, see tours page 26. Recommended boats are Victória Régia (owned by Carlos, contact at Pousada Tropicana), Papyk or André Maru (owned by André).*

 Sights

The beaches

The beach at Abraão may look beautiful on first arrival, but beaches further afield are even more spectacular. The two most famous are **Lopes Mendes** – a long stretch of sand on the eastern, ocean side, backed by flatlands and patchy forest, and **Aventureiro**, fringed by coconut palms and tropical forest, and whose powder- fine sand is pocked with boulders, and washed by transparent aquamarine. Lopes Mendes is a two-hour walk from Abraão. Aventureiro is over six hours, but it can be reached via the *Maria Isabel* or *Mestre Ernani* boats (**T** 021-33619895 or **T** 021-92695877), which leave from the quay in front of the BR petrol station in Angra dos Reis. A few fishermen's huts and *barracas* provide food here and allow camping. Good beaches closer to Abraão include the half-moon bay at **Abraãoozinho** (15-minute walk) and **Grande das Palmas**, which has a delightful tiny whitewashed chapel (1½ hour walk). Both lie east of the town, past the Hotel Sagu. Boat trips can be organized to **Lagoa Azul**, which has crystal-clear water and reasonable snorkelling, **Freguesia de Santana** and **Saco do Céu**.

The trails

There are a couple of good treks over the mountains to **Dois Rios**, where the old jail was situated. There is still a settlement of former prison guards here, who have nowhere to go. The walk is about 13 km one way, takes about three hours and affords beautiful scenery and superb views. You can also hike to **Pico do Papagaio** (980 m) a stiff, three-hour climb through forest, for which a guide is essential; the view from the top is breathtaking. **Pico da Pedra d'Água** (1,031 m) can also be climbed.

★ Paraty and around

Paraty is one of Brazil's prettiest colonial towns and one of Rio de Janeiro state's most popular tourist destinations. It is at its most captivating at dawn, when all but the dogs and chickens are sleeping. As the sun peeps over the horizon, the little rectilinear streets are infused with a rich, golden light which warms the whitewash and brilliant blue-and- yellow window frames of the colonial townhouses and the facade of the Manueline churches. Brightly-coloured fishing boats bob up and down in the water in the foreground, and behind the town the deep green of the rainforest-covered mountains of the Serra da Bocaina sit shrouded in their own self-generated wispy cloud. The town was founded in the 17th century as a gold port and most of its historical buildings date from this period.

The town's environs are as beautiful as Paraty itself. Just a few kilometres away lie the forests of the ***Ponta do Juatinga*** *peninsula, fringed by wonderful beaches, washed by little waterfalls and still home to communities of* Caicara *fishermen, who live much as they have done for centuries. Islands pepper the bay, some of them home to ultra-rare animals, like the tiny golden-lion tamarin monkey which is found nowhere else. The best way to visit these destinations is on a boat trip, operated by the town's fishermen. The rustic, hippy resort of* ***Trindade****, a short bus ride away, has a fabulous beach and is popular with backpackers.* *Map 7, inside back cover*

▸▸ *See Sleeping p129, Eating and drinking p152, Bars and clubs p166*

The rodoviária *in Paraty is at the corner of R Jango Padua and R da Floresta, 9 buses daily to Rio , 4 hrs, US$8.10. Taxis US$4 from the bus station to the historic centre. Tourist information is available from Centro de Informaçôes Turísticas, Av Roberto Silveira, near the centre,* ***T*** *024-33711266. The best map is in the* Welcome to Paraty *brochure, www.eco-paraty.com. More information is available at www.paraty.com.br.*

Sights

Centro histórico

Paraty is not a town with any individually outstanding buildings; it is pretty as a whole and the best way to see it is leisurely to wander around the town centre, which covers only 2 km. The centre comprises a cluster of cobbled streets lined with whitewashed houses, whose window frames are painted in rich yellows and deep blues. **Rua do**

Comércio has the best buildings. Today the houses are occupied by restaurants, *pousadas* and shops. The **Casa da Cadeia**, close to Santa Rita Church (*Wed-Sun, 0900-1800, US$1*), is the former jail, complete with iron grilles in the windows and doors. It is now a public library and art gallery. Paraty's four churches were built to accord with social status and race; of the four, one is for the 'freed coloured men', one for the blacks and two are for the whites. **Santa Rita** (1722), built by the 'freed coloured men' in elegant Brazilian baroque, faces the bay and the port. It is probably the most famous 'picture postcard' image of Paraty and houses the interesting **Museum of Sacred Art**. **Nossa Senhora do Rosário e São Benedito** (*R do Comércio, Tue 0900-1200*) was built by black slaves and is small and simple. **Nossa Senhora dos Remédios** (*Mon, Wed, Fri, Sat 0900-1200, Sun 0900-1500*) is the town's parish church, the biggest in Paraty. The church was started in 1787, but never finished as it was built on unstable ground, so the architects decided not to add weight to the structure by putting up the towers. The facade is leaning to the left, which is clear from the three doors: only the one on the right has a step. **Capela de Nossa Senhora das Dores** (*Thu 0900-1200*) built in 1800, is a small chapel facing the sea. It was used mainly by the wealthy whites in the 19th century.

Forte do Defensor Perpétuo

On the headland north of town, about 15 mins' walk from the centre via the Rio Perequê Açu bridge. *Tue-Sun 0900-1800, US$1.*

This small fort, built in 1822, and with extant cannon affords good views of the bay and the red-tile and whitewash of the town. There is a **Museum of Arts and Popular Tradition** on the site, with carved wooden canoes, musical instruments, fishing gear and other handmade items from local communities. Also on the headland is the **gunpowder store** and, set in the grass, enormous hemispherical iron pans, which were used for extracting whale oil to use in lamps and to mix with sand and cement for building.

The bay

Paraty sits in a bay of tiny islands, many of them fringed with little beaches, dotted with fishing communities, and still covered in patches of Atlantic-coast rainforest. Brightly-coloured fishing boats leave from the jetty in Paraty for tours around the bay (see Tours, page 26). Smaller boats can be rented for around US$10 for an hour.

The beaches

Praia do Pontal, the town beach, is five minutes' walk from the historic centre across the river, but is a little unprepossessing. There are far better beaches a little further afield. The long, broad and clean stretches of **Praia da Conçeicao**, **Praia Vermelha** and **Praia da Lula**, all of which have simple restaurants, are backed by forest and washed by gentle waves. The **Saco da Velha**, further south still, is small and intimate, protected by an island and surrounded by rainforested slopes. The small town of **Paraty Mirím**, 17 km away has a vast sweeping beach with a fine old Manueline church sitting on its white sand alongside a handful of ruined colonial buldings. It can be reached by boat or bus, and has simple restaurants and spots to camp. Fishing boats leave from here for other islands and beaches, including the **Praia do Pouso da Cajaíba**, which has lodgings of the same name, the spectacular sweep at **Martim do Sá** and the **Saco do Mamanguá** – a long sleeve of water that separates the Ponta da Juatinga and Paraty Mirím and has good snorkelling.

The gold trail

Tours leave from Teatro Espaço, R Dona Geralda 327, **T** 021-3371157, at 1000.

This partly-cobbled trail through the mountains was built by slaves in the 18th century to bring gold down from Ouro Preto before transporting it to Portugal. Recently restored, it can be visited, along with the ruins of a toll house, on foot or horse on a day trip.

Trindade

Located 30 km south of Paraty via a steep, winding 7-km road off the BR101 (Rio-Santos road). Paraty-Ubatuba bound buses will drop off at the turning to Trindade. In high season there are vans from here to Trindade (US$2). In low season frequent cars pass and hitching here is quite normal.

Ramshackle little Trindade may not be as beautiful in its own right as Paraty, but its setting – sandwiched between rainforested slopes and bottle-green sea – is equally spectacular; and unlike Paraty it has a long, broad beach. The town has long been a favourite hangout for young, middle-class surf hippies from São Paulo and Rio, who still come here in droves over Christmas and New Year. These days it is gradually finding its place on the international backpacker circuit and it's easy to see why. The beach is spectacular, the *pousadas* and restaurants cheap and cheerful, and there are a number of campsites. Sadly there is no sewage treatment, and when the town is full, foul black water flows from the town onto the sand. There are plenty of fairly unprepossessing restaurants along the town's main drag, Avenida Principal. All serve the usual 'and beans, rice and chips' combinations. There are even more beautiful beaches outside of town – beyond the upmarket *condo* at Laranjeiras. The most famous is **Praia do Sono** – one of the most impressive stretches of sand in the country. To get there take a bus to Laranjeiras and walk east along the trail for one to two hours. There are restaurants and a campsite.

Sleeping

There are plenty of places to stay in Rio but, with a few notable exceptions, the city's hotels are a disappointment. Aside from the Copacabana Palace and the Glória, those in the higher and medium price range are a mix of anonymous business-chain towers and fading leftovers from the 1970s, complete with peeling period decor. With luck, the opening of Philippe Starck's Rio Universe in 2005/6 may well shock Rio into realizing international standards. Those at the lowest end are almost invariably dubious hot-pillow establishments in equally dubious areas. Those on a budget should head for the hostels, which are almost all new, safe and in decent areas. The best and safest places to stay in Rio are Ipanema and southern Copacabana. Central Rio is attractive by day but can be unsafe by night, and is not recommended as a base. If you need to be close to the centre, stay in Glória, Flamengo, Catete or Botafogo; the former has a beautiful, grand hotel, and the latter has a lively hostel scene.

Sleeping codes

Price

LL	US$200 and over	**C**	US$35-49
L	US$150-199	**D**	US$20-34
AL	US$100-149	**E**	US$15-19
A	US$66-99	**F**	US$10-14
B	US$50-65	**G**	under US$10

Prices are for a double room in high season.

All accommodation in Rio is considerably more expensive over New Year and Carnival; reserve well in advance. All of the hotels listed (aside from the hostels) have air conditioning. A useful website is: www.hostelriodejaneiro.com.

Self-catering apartments are a popular form of accommodation in Rio, available at all price levels. Furnished apartments for short-term let, accommodating up to six, cost around US$300 per month in Cinelândia and Flamengo; US$25 a day or US$500-600 a month for a simple studio in Copacabana, Ipanema and Leblon; and up to $2000 a month for a luxurious residence sleeping four to six. Heading south, past Barra da Tijuca, virtually all the accommodation available is self-catering. Renting or sharing a flat can be much better value than a hotel room. Blocks consisting entirely of short-let apartments can attract thieves, so check the (usually excellent) security arrangements; residential buildings are called *prédio familial*. Higher floors (*alto andar*) are considered quieter.

Self-catering apartments are listed in the *Guia 4 Rodas* and Riotur's booklet, *RIO*. Agents and private owners advertise under '*Apartamentos – Temporada*' in publications like *Balcão* (twice weekly), *O Globo* or *Jornal do Brasil* (daily). Advertisements are classified by district and size of apartment: '*vagas e quartos*' means shared accommodation; '*conjugado*' (or '*conj*') is a studio with limited cooking facilities; '*3 quartos*' is a three-bedroom flat. There should always be a written agreement when renting.

Central Rio

Hotels

LL-A **Aeroporto Othon**, Av Beira Mar 280, Centro, **T** 021-25441231, www.othon.com.br. *Map 2, F11, p248* Modest little block five minutes from both the airport and the Museu de Arte Moderna. Rooms are simple, tiled and painted in white with sparse furniture and heavy hardwood beds. The best have balconies overlooking Guanabara Bay. The hotel has an unillustrious restaurant and bar. 'Corporate' rates booked through the website are almost a quarter of the rack rate.

A **Guanabara Palace**, Av Presidente Vargas, 392, Centro, close to the Uruguaiana Metrô station, **T** 021-22161313, www.windsorhoteis.com. *Map 2, B8, p248* Reasonably well-maintained 1950s business hotel with kitschy rooms, a pool, sauna, bar, parking and a very average restaurant. Orientated towards the business traveller, services include internet access and a small conference centre. Local calls are included in the daily rate.

Glória, Catete and Flamengo

Hotels

AL-A **Flórida**, Ferreira Viana 71/81, Catete, **T** 021-25565242, www.windsorhoteis.com. *Map 3, F6, p250* Business-orientated hotel with respectable facilities and one of the city's largest convention centres, bars (for private hire), a restaurant, gym and modestly decorated, no-nonsense, modern rooms.

AL-A **Glória**, R do Russel 632, Glória, **T** 021-25557572, www.hotelgloriario.com.br. *Map 3, D7, p250* Stylish and elegant

1920s hotel, which, although not as grand as the Copacabana Palace (see page 115), has far more charm than any of the others in this price range in Copacabana or Ipanema. Rooms have mock-Edwardian decoration with ornate mirrors, ottomans and fussy, heavy curtains. The hotel has two pools, a spa, an in-house theatre and excellent business facilities.

AL-A **Novo Mundo**, Praia do Flamengo 20, Catete, **T** 021-25574355, www.hotelnovomundo-rio.com.br. *Map 3, E7, p250* Standard four-star rooms in a big 1950s block near the beach. The suites have balcony views of the Sugar Loaf. Services include a currency exchange, tour reservations, and a newly renovated conference and business centre.

D **Imperial**, R do Catete 186, Catete, **T** 021-25565212, www.imperialhotel.com.br. *Map 3, F5, p250* One of the city's very first grand hotels, built in the late 19th century. Rooms are divided between the grander, older main building with its large but rather frayed rooms, and the annex whose modern US-style motel rooms are better equipped but overlook the parking lot.

D **Inglês**, R Silveira Martins 20, Glória, **T** 021-25583052, www.hotelingles.com.br. *Map 3, E6, p250* Popular cheapie next to the Metrô and in front of the Museu da República. The better rooms have been refurbished and have a/c.

D **Paysandu**, R Paissandu 23, Flamengo, **T** 021-25587270, www.paysandu.com. *Map 3, D1, p250* Wonderful old, art-deco tower in a good location next to the Palácio de Republica and Flamengo gardens, with spartan rooms but helpful staff. Organized tours available.

D **Único**, Ferreira Viana 54, Catete, **T** 021-22059932, **F** 22058149. *Map 3, F5, p250* Plain rooms with TV, a/c and fridge.

Hostels

G **King Hostel**, R Barão de Guaratiba 20, Catete, **T** 021- 22450286, www.kingalbergue.hpg.ig.com.br. *Map 3, D6, p250* Cheap and cheerful hostel with dorms and doubles. A stroll from Catete Metrô.

Santa Teresa

Numerous bed and breakfast options in Santa Teresa can be found on www.camaecafe.com.br.

Pão de Açúcar, Botafogo and Urca

Hostels

F **Ace Backpackers**, R São Clemente 23, 1st Floor, Botafogo, **T** 021-25277452, www.copacabanahostel.com.br. *Map 4, C5, p252* Very popular, lively hostel with helpful friendly staff and tiny but scrupulously clean dorms and doubles. Services include communal kitchen, tours, internet, laundry, communal TV with DVDs, and phone/fax. 20m from the Botafogo Metrô station.

F **Carioca Easy**, R Marechal Cantuaria 168, Urca, **T** 021-22957805, www.cariocahostel.com.br. *Map 4, C10, p252* Bright little hostel in a colonial house in one of the safest and most spectacular neighbourhoods in Rio – at the base of Sugar Loaf. Facilities include a small pool, kitchen, bike rental and boat trips. Dorms and one basic double room (**D**) with en suite bathroom.

F **The IYHA Chave do Rio de Janeiro hostel**, R General Dionísio 63, Botafogo, **T** 021-22860303, www.riohostel.com.br. *Map 4, E1, p252* Large four-storey hostel with 70 beds. Small, tiled dormitory rooms for between four and eight people with aluminium bunks, separate women's bathrooms, cybercafé, laundry, TV lounges with cable TV and a kitchen (available only to IYHA members). Can be noisy.

G **El Misti Hostel**, Praia de Botafogo 462/9, Botafogo, **T** 021-22260991, www.elmistihostel.com. *Map 4, C5, p252* A small hostel in a converted colonial house with six dorms and two doubles – all simply decked out with plain white walls and polished wooden floors. Bathrooms are shared and other services include a kitchen, internet, capoeira classes and a tour service. The Metrô is one block away and buses stop nearby. Breakfast and linen included.

Copacabana and Leme

Hotels

LL **Copacabana Palace**, Av Atlântica 1702, **T** 021- 25487070, **F** 22357330, www.copacabanapalace.com.br. *Map 4, H6, p252* The best hotel in Rio for leisure or business and one of the best in the world; dripping in 1920's elegance, adorned with the photographs of the numerous kings, presidents, stars and statesmen who have stayed there. *Flying Down to Rio*, in which Fred Astaire and Ginger Rogers first danced together, was filmed here. The plushest rooms are the sixth-floor suites, which have their own designated lifts and pool. The Cipriani restaurant has the best cooking in Rio – come for cocktails and dinner if you can't afford to stay (see Eating, page 141).

LL **Marriott**, Av Atlântica 2600, **T** 021-25456500, www.marriott.com. *Map 5, D13, p254* Rio's newest and plushest Business hotel with 245 rooms, an executive floor,12 meeting rooms and a gamut of other business services. As personality-free as most of the hotels in the chain.

LL-L **Pestana Rio Atlântica**, Av Atlântica 2964, **T** 021-25486332, www.pestana.com. *Map 4, E12, p252* The best option in Copacabana after the Copacabana Palace, with spacious, bright rooms and a rooftop pool and terrace with sweeping views. Part of the well-managed Portuguese Pestana group. While the modern building is unprepossessing, rooms have large, ocean-facing French windows and discreet, contemporary decoration. Service is of a very high standard.

LL-AL **Le Meridien**, Av Atlântica 1020, **T** 0800-111554, www.meridien-br.com. *Map 4, G8, p252* A dull, modern tower at the city end of Copacabana with small, business-like, scrupulously maintained rooms remarkable only for their wonderful views. Breakfast, too, comes with a wonderful view. Cordon bleu chef, Paul Bocuse's newly renovated Le Saint-Honoré French restaurant is one of the best in the city (see page 142).

LL-AL **Sofitel Rio Palace**, Av Atlântica 4240, **T** 021- 25251232, www.accorhotels.com.br. *Map 5, H12, p254* Enormous, characterless beachfront hotel with 356 rooms, 32 suites, a pool and five restaurants. Rooms are less anonymous than the hotel itself and the suites even show a slight touch of design savvy. The best have ocean views. Excellent business facilities outside the norm include mobile phone rental facility.

L-A **South American Copacabana**, R Francisco de Sá 90, **T** 021-25220040, **F** 22670748, southamerican@uol.com.br. *Map 5, G11, p254* Two blocks from the beach but in Arpoador, which is safer than Copacabana. The front rooms are noisy; others are garishly decorated but well-maintained. Helpful staff.

Best

Rooms for a splurge in Rio

- The sixth floor suites at the **Copacabana Palace**, p115
- Room 21 in **Casas Brancas**, Búzios, p123
- The luxury chalets in the **Hotel Donati**, Itatiaia, p125
- The suites at **Sítio do Lobo**, Ilha Grande, p128
- The suites in the **Hotel Coxixo**, Paraty, p130

AL **GranDarrell Ouro Verde**, Av Atlântica 1456, **T** 021-25421887, www.grandarrell.com.br. *Map 4, H7, p252* One of the better small hotels in Copacabana in a 1950's beachfront tower. Spacious, classically decorated rooms come complete with grand mirrors and mock Edwardian furniture. Good for families – the hotel has a kid's club. Rooftop sundeck with views but no pool.

A-B **Benidorm Palace**, R Barata Ribeiro 547, **T** 021-25488880, www.benidorm.com.br. *Map 5, D12, p254* A hotel which is as tacky as its name might suggest, with old-fashioned, though well-maintained rooms, some of which look rather *Saturday Night Fever*. Sauna, pool, bar and restaurant.

A-B **Debret**, Av Atlântica 3564, **T** 021-25220132, www.debret.com. *Map 5, F11, p254* Bright, spacious, modern seafront rooms (others are a little dark) in a tower next to the Arpoador. Convenient for both Copacabana and Ipanema. Designated business rooms available to corporate travellers.

A-B **Savoy Othon Travel**, Av Nossa Senhora 552, **T** 021-25250282, www.othon.com.br. *Map 4, H5, p252* Yet another anonymous Copacabana tower, two blocks from the beach, with equally anonymous, though spacious, early 1990s rooms. Absurd rack rates; good corporate rates.

B Copacabana Sol, R Santa Clara 141, **T** 021-25494577, www.copacabanasolhotel.com.br. *Map 5, C12, p254* Old-fashioned and rather tawdry rooms in a small tower four blocks from the beach. Helpful staff, quiet location and a decent breakfast.

B-C Rio Copa, Av Princesa Isabel 370, **T** 021-22756644, www.riocopa.com.br. *Map 4, G7, p252* Simple, plain, though rather faded, rooms two blocks back from beach. English-speaking staff, sauna, small gym and a rooftop pool.

Hostels

F Che Lagarto, R Anita Garibaldi 87, **T** 021-22562776, www.chelagarto.com. *Map 4, H3, p252* A self-proclaimed party hostel three blocks from the beach run by, and catering to, 20-something travellers. Well-equipped kitchen, internet, large breakfasts, cable TV, airport or bus station transfer and advice on the current best night spots. Four-to six-bed dorms and double rooms (D), all en suite, some with a/c.

F Shenkin Hostel, R Santa Clara 304, **T** 021-22573133, www.shenkinhostel.com. *Map 4, H3, p252* IYHA party hostel with its own bar, seven blocks from the beach. Bright and airy dorms, some with a/c, singles and doubles, services include decent breakfast, internet and airport and bus station transfers.

F-G Copacabana Praia, R Tenente Marones de Gusmão 85, Bairro Peixoto, **T** 021-22353817, **F** 22375422, www.center.com.br/copapraia. *Map 4, H3, p252* Dorms and doubles with private bathrooms (some with a/c and TV, E-D) in a quiet residential area, four blocks from the beach. Services include a kitchen, telephones, private lockers in the dormitories. Private rooms also available.

F-G **Mario's Hostel**, R Leopoldo Miguez 10, **T** 021-31856604, www.marioshostel.com. *Map 5, E12, p254* Dorms, singles and doubles, a large kitchen, dining room in a scruffy building, four blocks from the beach. Services include airport pick-up and internet. Can be noisy.

G **Copa Chalet**, R Henrique Oswald 103, **T** 021-22360047, www.copachalet.com. *Map 4, G3, p252* Pleasant hostel, three blocks from the beach, with mock-Moorish touches and a little garden area. A range of rooms and dorms including a suite. Very friendly and reasonably tranquil. Price includes breakfast.

G **Rio Backpackers**, Travessa Santa Leocádia 38, **T** 021- 22363803, www.riobackpackers.com.br. *Map 4, D11, p252* Another new party hostel, popular with Brazilians. Tiny but bright and clean dorms, singles and doubles. The large living area includes a bar, pool table, stereo, cable TV, internet access and hammock- draped veranda.

Self-catering apartments

Copacabana Holiday Hotel, R Barata Ribeiro 90A, **T** 021-25421525, www.copacabanaholiday.com.br. *Map 4, G7, p252* Well-equipped, small apartments from US$500 per month, minimum 30-days let.

Fantastic Rio, Av Atlântica 974, Suite 501, **T/F** 021-25432667, hpcorr@hotmail.com. *Map 4, G8, p252* All types of furnished accommodation from US$20 per day. Owned by Peter Corr.

Paulo de Tarso, Av Princesa Isabel 236, Apto 102, **T** 021-25425635, pauldetarso@ig.com.br. *Map 4, G8, p252* Apartments near Copacabana beach from US$25 per person. Several languages spoken, very helpful.

Rio Residences, Av Prado Júnior 44, Apto 508, **T** 021- 25414568, **F** 25416462. *Map 4, G7, p252* Swiss-run, includes airport transfer.

Yvonne Reimann, Av Atlântica 4066, Apto 605, **T** 021-22270281 *Map 5, H12, p254* All apartments with phone, near beach, a/c, maid service, English, French, German spoken. Apartments owned by the agency, prices from US$50 per flat.

Ipanema, Arpoador and Leblon

Hotels

LL-L **Caesar Park**, Av Vieira Souto 460, **T** 021-25252525, www.caesar-park.com. *Map 5, H6, p254* Anonymous chain hotel with mock 19th-century flourishes in a beachfront tower. Some rooms have beach views. Decent service includes beach patrol and childminding. Pool, sauna, restaurant and business facilities.

LL-L **Marina Palace** and **Marina All Suites**, Av Delfim Moreira 630 and 696, **T** 021-22941794, and **T** 021-25404990, www.hotelmarina.com. *Map 5, H2, p254* Two 1980's towers almost next door to each other. The former has smart, modern but standard four-star rooms and a rooftop pool, the latter is a luxury boutique with 'designer' suites and is favoured by the likes of Giselle Bundchen. By international standards it is shabby. But it has an excellent sea-view restaurant and a fashionable restaurant bar.

L **Best Western Sol Ipanema**, Av Vieira Souto 320, **T** 021-26252020, www.bestwestern.com. *Map 5, H8, p254* Part of the world's largest hotel chain, with the usual catalogue furniture rooms and technically courteous, efficient service. Popular with agencies and business travellers.

A **Mar Ipanema**, R Visconde de Pirajá 539, **T** 021-38759190, www.maripanema.com. *Map 5, H4, p254* Simple, smart, modern rooms in a tower one block from the beach. The front rooms on the lower floors are noisy. Bar, restaurant and beach umbrellas.

A-B **Arpoador Inn**, R Francisco Otaviano 177, **T** 021-25230060, **F** 25115094. *Map 5, H10, p254* Well-maintained, undistinguished rooms; some overlooking the beach, with off-season special offers and a seafront restaurant, which is a good spot for watching the world go by – though the service is so slow that the coffee arrives cold.

A-B **Ipanema Inn**, R Maria Quitéria 27, behind Caesar Park, **T** 021-25233092, **F** 25115094. *Map 5, H6, p254* Plain and modest rooms, some in need of renovation, half a block from the beach.

B **San Marco**, R Visconde de Pirajá 524, **T** 021-25405032, www.sanmarcohotel.net. *Map 5, G5, p254* Newly renovated two-star hotel with modestly decorated, simple rooms and a free *caipirinha* for every internet booking. Price includes breakfast. Two blocks from beach.

B-C **Atlantis Copacabana**, Av Bulhões de Carvalho 61, **T** 021-25211142, atlantishotel@uol.com.br. *Map 5, H11, p254* Fading Arpoador hotel in a quiet, safe street very close to the beach. The best rooms are on the upper floors. Small rooftop pool, sauna and excellent special rates.

Hostels

F **Che Lagarto**, R Barão de Jaguaripe 208, **T** 021-22474582, www.chelagarto.com. *Map 5, F6, p254* Bright red, party hostel with young staff and a terrace with views of Corcovado. Sister hostel to the Che Lagarto in Copacabana (see page 118) with similar services, dorms and doubles.

F **Ipanema Beach House**, R Barão da Torre 485, **T** 021- 32022693, ipanemahouse@hotmail.com. *Map 5, G6, p254* Party hostel with a pool and a lively bar. Services include car parking, internet, money exchange, laundry service, airport pick-up and bike rental. Breakfast is included. Rooms are small but well looked after.

F **Harmonia**, R Barão da Torre 175, Casa 18, **T** 021-25234905, www.hostelharmonia.com. *Map 5, G8, p254* Small hostel in a residential building, three blocks from beach. Doubles or dorms, kitchen facilities, broadband internet, very welcoming and helpful.

G **Albergue Hostel Ipanema**, R Barão da Torre 175, Casa 14, **T** 021-22477269, www.geocities.com/hostelipanema. *Map 5, G8, p254* Modest little hostel with small rooms housed in a converted residential house with dorms, singles and doubles. English spoken, children welcome, internet, bike rental, breakfast and shared kitchen.

G **Casa 6**, R Barão da Torre 175, Casa 6, **T** 021-22471384, www.casa6ipanema.com. *Map 5, G8, p254* Charming, colourful but simple, French-owned B&B in a townhouse three blocks from the beach. Good long-stay rates.

G **Crab Hostel**, R Prudente de Moraes 903, **T** 021-22677353, www.crabhostel.com. *Map 5, H7, p254* Brand new hostel, one block from the beach with a pool, sauna, cable TV and all rooms with en suites. Excellent value.

South of Leblon and Tijuca National Park

Hotels

LL **Sheraton**, Av Niemeyer 121, Vidigal, São Conrado, **T** 021-22741122, www.sheraton-rio.com. *Map 1, H9, p246* One of the

Sheraton group's poorest hotels – a 1970's slab of concrete in painful need of restyling and refurbishing. Wonderful beach views, though, and a decent pool area.

Búzios

The best rooms on the peninsula are not on the beaches but are those on the Morro da Humaitá hill, 10 minutes' walk from the town centre, which have a superb view. Prior reservations are needed in summer, during holidays such as Carnival and New Year's Eve, and at weekends. Several private houses rent rooms, especially in summer and holidays. Look for the signs: *'alugo quartos'*.

Hotels

LL **Boca do Ceu**, Mirante de João Fernandes, R Hum, **T** 022-26234713, www.bocadoceu.com. Super-luxurious private home/mini-*pousada* (owned by a famous Uruguayan interior designer) with the best views on the peninsula out across a carefully designed swimming pool and garden. All the fittings are by famous designers. Nonetheless somewhat overpriced.

LL-L **Casas Brancas**, Alto do Humaitá 8, **T** 022-26231458, www.casasbrancas.com.br. Far and away the best hotel in Búzios; a series of rooms perched on the hill in mock-Mykonos buildings with separate terraces for the pool and spa areas. Sweeping views over the bay. Wonderfully romantic at night when it is candlelit. If you can't afford to stay, come for dinner.

LL-L **El Cazar**, Alto do Humaitá 6, **T** 022-26231620. Next door to Casas Brancas (above) and almost as luxurious; though a little darker inside. Beautiful artwork on the walls and Central Asian *kelims* on the wooden floors. Tasteful and relaxing.

AL Pousada Pedra da Laguna, R6, Lote 6, Praia da Ferradura, **T/F** 022-26231965, www.pedradalaguna.com.br. Spacious rooms, the best have a view, 150 m from the beach. Part of the Roteiros de Charme.

A-AL Pousada Byblos, Alto do Humaitá 14, **T** 022-26231162, www.byblos.com.br. Wonderful views out over the bay and bright, light rooms with tiled floors and balconies.

A Pousada Hibiscus Beach, R 1, no 22, Quadra C, Praia de João Fernandes, **T** 022-26236221, www.hibiscusbeach.com. A peaceful spot, run by its British owners, 15 pleasant bungalows, garden, pool, light meals available, help with car/buggy rentals and local excursions. One of the best beach hotels.

A-B Brigitta's Guest House, R das Pedras 131, **T/F** 022-26236157, www.buziosonline.com.br/brigitta. Beautifully decorated little *pousada* where Bardot once stayed, with just four rooms on the main street of Rua das Pedras. The delightful restaurant, bar and tea house overlooking the water are worth a visit.

Hostels

C-E Praia dos Amores, Av José Bento Ribeiro Dantas 92, **T** 022-26232422, www.buziosturismo.com/auberge. IYHA, not far from the bus station, next to Praia da Tartaruga and just under 1 km from the centre. The best value in Búzios. Recommended.

Itatiaia National Park

Basic accommodation in cabins and dormitories is available in the park; you will need to book 30 days in advance in high season. Bookings can be made by writing to Administração do Parque Nacional de Itatiaia, Caixa Postal 83657, Itatiaia 27580-000, RJ.

Hotels

A **Hotel Donati**, Estrada Parque, **T** 024-33521110, www.hoteldonati.com.br. One of the most delightful hotels in the country; mock-Swiss chalets and rooms, set in tropical gardens visited by animals every night and early morning. A series of trails lead off from the main building and the hotel can organize professional birdwatching guides. Decent restaurant and two pools. Highly recommended. Map on website.

A **Simon**, Km 13 on the road in the park, **T** 024-33521122, www.hotelsimon.com.br. A 1970's concrete block at the top of the park, which marks the trailhead for the higher walks to Agulhas Negras and Três Picos. Wonderful views from fading rooms.

B **Pousada do Elefante**, R Maricá 255, **T** 024-33521699. 15 minutes' walk back down hill from Hotel Simon (above). Good food, swimming pool, lovely views, cheap lodging. Possibility of pitching a tent on the premises, located close to the national park.

B-C **Hotel Cabanas de Itatiaia, T** 024-33521252 Magical views from these comfortable but ridiculously Swiss chalets on a hillside. Pool and good restaurant.

C-D **Cabanas da Itatiaia**, **T** 024-33521152/33521252, www.hotelcabanasitatiaia.com.br. Price per person. Simple chalets in secondary forest overlooking a stream in the lower reaches of the park. The sister hotel (A **Ideia dos Passaros**) opposite has a pool. Both share facilities and are very friendly and helpful. Great breakfasts, good off-season rates and a riverside sauna.

D **Hotel Alsene**, at 2,100 m, 2 km from the side entrance to the park. *Take a bus to São Lourenço and Caxambu, get off at Registro,* walk or hitch from there (12 km). Very popular with climbing and trekking clubs, dorms or camping, chalets available, hot showers, fireplace, evening meal after everyone returns, drinks but no snacks.

Hostels

F **Ipê Amarelo**, R João Maurício Macedo Costa 352, Campo Alegre, **T/F** 024-33521232. IYHA. Nine small apartments, 15 fixed tents, sauna, swimming pool and large lawn for camping. A little inconvenient for the park.

Petrópolis and around

There are many cheap hotels in Rua Delfim Moreira, near the *praça* in Teresópolis. Ibama has some hostels (www.ibama.com.br), US$5 full board, or US$3 for the first night, US$2 thereafter, most of which are a bit rough.

Hotels

L **Fazenda Rosa dos Ventos**, Km 22 on the road to Nova Friburgo, Teresópolis, **T** 021-27428833. In the Roteiros de Charme group. One of the best hotels in inland Rio with a range of chalets set in one million square metres of private forest and with wonderful views.

L **Pousada da Alcobaça**, R Agostinho Goulão 298, Correas, Petrópolis, **T** 024-22211240, www.pousadadaalcobaca.com.br. In the Roteiros de Charme group. Delightful, family-run, large country house set in flower-filled gardens leading down to a river, with pool and sauna. Worth stopping by for tea on the terrace, or for dinner at the restaurant. Recommended.

A **Campo de Aventuras**, Paraíso Açu, Estrada do Bonfim 3511, Serra dos Órgãos, in the Petrópolis side of the park, **T** 024-21426275, or

T 021-29733618. Various types of accommodation, from rooms to chalets. Specializes in adventure sports (credit cards not accepted).

A **Cabanas Açu**, Estrada do Bonfim, Km 3.5, Serra dos Órgãos, **T** 021-29835041. Inside the park, cabins, restaurant, sports include riding, canoeing and fishing. Credit cards accepted.

A **Fazenda Montebello**, at Km 17 on R Petrópolis, Teresópolis, **T/F** 021-26446313. Modern hotel with pool, price includes three meals. Recommended.

A **Margaridas**, R Bispo Dom José Pereira Alves 235, Trono de Fátima, Petrópolis, **T** 024-22424686. A chalet-type hotel set in lovely gardens with a swimming pool, charming proprietors.

A **Riverside Parque**, R Hermogéneo Silva 522, Retiro, Petrópolis, **T** 024-22310730, **F** 22432312. Five minutes from the centre, with a helpful owner who can arrange tours in surrounding countryside.

B **Casablanca Centre**, R General Osório 28, Petrópolis, **T** 024-22422612. Old 1960's block with a range of reasonable rooms and a restaurant. Somewhat faded.

B **York**, R do Imperador 78, Petrópolis, a short walk from the *rodoviária*, **T** 024-22432662, **F** 22428220. Convenient, helpful, fruit and milk from the owners' own farm for breakfast. Recommended.

C **Comércio**, R Dr Porciúncula 55, opposite the *rodoviária*, Petrópolis, **T** 024-22423500. One of the cheapest options. Very basic with shared bath.

C **Várzea Palace**, R Sebastião Teixeira 41, Teresópolis, **T** 021-27420878. Simple hotel with very friendly staff. Highly recommended.

Hostels

F **Retiro da Inglesa**, Km 20 on road to Nova Friburgo, Fazenda Boa Esperança, Teresópolis, **T** 021-27423109. In the beautiful Vale dos Frades. Book in advance for January and February, dormitory accommodation and family rooms, camping beside the hostel.

Ilha Grande

There are many *pousadas* in Abraão and reservations are only necessary in peak season or on holiday weekends.

LL-L **Sítio do Lobo**, Enseada das Estrelas, outside Abraão, **T** 024-22274138, www.sitiodolobo.com.br. An architect-commissioned house converted into a small boutique hotel, sitting on an isolated peninsula with its own little dock. The views are marvellous; sea, rainforest, mountains and sunsets. The best room are the suites; the others, which overlook the pool, are a little boxy. Access to the rest of the island is only by boat. The best food on the island.

AL-B **Sankay**, Enseada do Bananal, 1 hr by boat from Angra or Abraão, **T** 024-33651090, www.pousadasankay.com.br. Another beautiful little *pousada* perched on a peninsula with wonderful views. Rooms are simple with brick or stone walls. The best is the *cavalo marinho* (sea horse) suite. Sauna and bar, dinner included.

B **Ancoradouro**, R do Praia 121, **T** 024-33615153, www.ancoradouro.ilhagrande.com. *10 mins walk east of the jetty.* Clean, simple rooms with en suites in a beachfront building.

B-C **Farol dos Borbas**, Praia do Abraão, **T** 024-33615260, www.ilhagrandetour.com.br. *1 min from the jetty.* Simple, well-maintained, fan-cooled rooms with tiled floors and breakfast tables and chairs. The best have balconies; the worst have no windows. Boat trips organized.

C **Porto Girasol**, R do Praia 65, **T** 024-3361527, portogirasol@ilhagrande.com. Simple rooms in a mock-colonial beach house five minutes east of the jetty.

C-E **Pousada Cachoeira**, Angra dos Reis, **T** 024-33615083, www.cachoeira.com. Price per person. Great little *pousada* full of character; with little rooms in chalets in a forest garden. English spoken. Good breakfasts. Map on website.

D **Estalagem Costa Verde**, R Amâncio Felicio de Souza 239A, **T** 024-31047490, www.estalagemcostaverde.com.br. *In town, half a block behind the church.* Bright hostel with light, well-maintained rooms decorated with a little thought. Great value. Map on website.

D **Colibri**, R da Assembléia 70, Abraão **T** 024-33615033, www.colibriresort.com. Smart little hostel, rooms decorated with a personal touch and an outdoor breakfast area. Tours around the island. Map and directions on the confusing website.

F **Albergue Holdandes**, R Assembléia de Deus, **T** 024-33615034. Price per person. Four little chalets and rooms lost in the forest. Great atmosphere. Be sure to reserve.

Paraty and around

There are many options in Paraty and two beautiful places in the hills nearby. Browse through: www.paraty.com.br/frame.htm for still more options. Expect no frills in Trindade.

AL Pousada do Ouro, R Dr Pereira (or da Praia) 145, Paraty, **T/F** 024-3712221, www.pousadaouro.com.br. Near Paraty's eastern waterfront and built as a private home from a fortune made on the gold route. Plain rooms in an annex and suites in the main building. The grounds house an open-air poolside pavilion, in a tropical garden. The icons of previous guests, like Mick Jagger, Tom Cruise and Linda Evangelista, adorn the lobby.

AL Pousada do Sandi, Largo do Rosário 1, Paraty, **T** 024-33712100, www.pousadadosandi.com.br. An 18th-century building with a grand lobby, comfortable, mock-colonial rooms and an adjoining restaurant and pool area.

AL Pousada Pardieiro, R do Comércio 74, Paraty, **T** 024-33711370, www.pousadapardieiro.com.br. Tucked away in a quiet corner, with a calm, sophisticated atmosphere. Attractive colonial building with lovely gardens, delightful rooms facing internal patios and a little swimming pool. Always full at weekends, does not take children under 15.

AL-A Bromelias Pousada & Spa, Rodovia Rio Santos, Km 562, Graúna, Paraty, **T/F** 024-33712791, www.pousadabromelias.com.br. An Asian-inspired spa *pousada* with its own aromatherapy products and a range of massage treatments. Accommodation is in tastefully decorated chalets perched on a hillside overlooking the sea and islands. Pool, sauna and restaurant.

A-B Hotel Coxixo, R do Comércio 362, Paraty, **T** 024- 33711460, www.hotelcoxixo.com.br. A converted colonial building in the heart of the 17th-century town, which has been turned into a temple to its Brazilian movie-star owner, Maria Della Costa. Black and white pictures of her from the 1950s adorn every corner. Rooms are decked out in Catholic kitsch. The best rooms in the hotel, and in Paraty, are the plush colonial suites.

A-B Le Gite d'Indaiatiba, Rodovia Rio-Santos, Km 562, Graúna, Paraty, **T** 024-33717174, www.legitedindaiatiba.com.br. French-owned *pousada* with carefully designed, stylish chalets set in gardens on a hillside. Sweeping views of the sea and bay of islands. French food to match the location.

A-B Morro do Forte, R Orlando Carpinelli, Paraty, out of the centre, **T/F** 024-3711211, www.pousadamorrodoforte.com.br. Lovely garden, good breakfast, pool, German owner, Peter Kallert, offers trips on his yacht. Recommended.

B Pousada Capitão, R Luiz do Rosário 18, Paraty, **T** 024-33711815, www.paraty.com.br/capitao. Converted, colonial building, close to the historical centre, swimming pool, English and Japanese spoken.

B Pousada do Corsário, Beco do Lapeiro 26, Paraty, **T** 024-33711866, www.pousadadocorsario.com.br. New building with a pool and its own gardens; next to the river and two blocks from the centre. Simple but stylish rooms, most with hammocks outside. Highly recommended.

B Pousada Mercado de Pouso, Largo de Santa Rita 43, Paraty, **T/F** 024-33711114, www.paraty.com.br/mercadodepouso. Historic building close to waterfront decked out in lush wood, with good sea views. Family atmosphere, no pool.

B-C Pousada Arte Colonial, R da Matriz 292, Paraty, **T** 024-33717231, www.paraty.com.br/artecolonial. One of the best deals in Paraty, colonial building in the centre decorated with style and a genuine personal touch, artefacts and antiques collected from all over the world by its French owner. Friendly, helpful, beautiful and with breakfast. Highly recommended.

C-D **Solar dos Gerânios**, Praça da Matriz, Paraty, **T/F** 024-33711550, www.paraty.com.br/geranio. Beautiful colonial family house on main square in traditional rustic style that is a welcome antidote to the more polished *pousadas*. Rooms have lovely wooden-lattice balconies – ask for the corner one which has two. Very reasonably priced, English spoken. Warmly recommended.

D **Chalé e Pousada Magia do Mar**, Praia de Fora, Trindade, **T** 024-33715130. Thatched-roof hut with space for four. Views out over the beach.

D **Marendaz**, R Patitiba 9, Paraty, **T** 024-33711369. Family-run, simple, charming, a block from the historical centre.

D **Pousada Marimbá**, R Principal, Trindade, **T** 024-33715147. Simple, colourful rooms and a little breakfast area.

D-E **Pousada do Careca**, Praça Macedo Soares, Paraty, **T** 024-33711291. Very simple rooms in the historic centre. Those without street windows are musty.

D-F **Ponta da Trindade Pousada & Camping**, Trindade, **T** 024-33715113. Simple, fan-cooled rooms and a sand-floored campsite with cold-water showers and no power.

Hostel

F **Casa do Rio**, R Antônio Vidal 120, Paraty, **T** 024-33712223, www.paraty.com.br/casadorio. Little house with riverside courtyard and hammocks. Kitchen, price includes breakfast. Offers jeep and horse riding trips to waterfalls, mountains and beaches. Dorms a little crowded.

Eating and drinking

Cariocas have never been gourmets. The beach, they might say, is too inviting for anyone to spend time indoors slaving over a hot stove. Eating out for leisure has long meant dressing up in a pair of tiny trunks or a bikini, grabbing a juice and a pastry at a stand up street stall and wolfing it down as quickly as possible before heading for the sea. Dinner would be similarly streetside - *bacalhau* fish balls and frothy cold beer at a little *botequim* bar, accompanied by busy chit chat and an absolute minimum of formality.

Thankfully for tourists seeking good food, Rio de Janeiro is home to more than just Cariocas. French, Italians, Japanese and *Paulistas* (from São Paulo) have, over the last few decades, gradually been introducing the idea of proper food to the city. And although they are still relatively hard to find there are now some excellent restaurants in all of Rio's *bairros*.

Bookings are recommended for the better restaurants. Most of Rio's bars serve light food, and some are bar-restaurants - see also Bars and clubs pages 155-166.

Eating codes

Price

¥¥¥¥	US$20 and over
¥¥¥	US$10-19
¥¥	US$5-9
¥	under US$5

Price per head for a two-course meal excluding drinks

Central Rio

¥¥¥ **Albamar**, Praça Marechal Âncora 184, Centro, **T** 021-22408378. *Map 2, C11, p248* A long-established Rio seafood restaurant as popular today with politicians and businessmen as it has been since its opening 70 years ago in the old Mercado Municipal. Getulio Vargas, Juscelino Kubitschek, Fernando Henrique Cardoso and almost all of the other Brazilian presidents have dined here on dishes like *bacalhau* and oysters, and whiting fillet à la Albamar, which have been on the menu for as long as anyone can remember. Great views out across Guanabara Bay.

¥¥¥ **Cais do Oriente**, R Visconde de Itaboraí 8, Centro, **T** 021-22332531, www.caisdooriente.com.br. *Map 2, B10, p248* Wonderful restaurant with a range of different spaces, each with a different atmosphere; from a formal Portuguese-style belle époque dining-room to an informal palm-shaded, open-air patio and a terrace with live music. The menu by French chef Alex Giraud is similarly varied, with a broad selection of fusions and Mediterranean, Brazilian and oriental dishes.

¥¥¥ **Republique**, Praça da República 63 (2nd floor), Centro, **T** 021-25329000. *Map 2, E4, p248* A long-established Rio favourite, now newly refurbished by the architect, Chico Gouveia (whose

Best

Fine dining

- **French** - Carême Bistrô in Botafogo, p140
- **Italian** - Cipriani in Copacabana, p141
- **Seafood** - Satyricon in Ipanema, p144
- **Intimate dining** - Carlota in Leblon, p145
- **Fusion cooking** - Merlin O Mago in Paraty, p153

decoration is based on the colours of the French flag), and serving daring and ambitious South American fusion cooking from distinguished Rio chef Paulo Carvalho who worked for some 16 years at Le Saint-Honoré.

Adega Flor de Coimbra, R Teotônio Regadas 34, Lapa, **T** 021-22244582. *Map 2, H8, p248* *Chope* and reliable Portuguese food, including excellent *bacalhau* and sardines in olive oil served in a little restaurant bar founded in 1938 and which was the home of the Carioca painter, Cândido Portinari. This was once a haunt of Rio's left-wing intelligentsia, who would gather here to discuss political theory over a glass of chilled French wine. Now the eclectic crowd is decidedly capitalist, mostly young after-workers, and is particularly lively on Fridays.

Cantina Hombu, Espaço Cultural Hombu, R Mem de Sá 33, Centro, **T** 021-25078073. *Map 2, G8, p248* Informal but superior Bahian restaurant in a beautifully restored colonial house in the liveliest part of Lapa. The *moquecas* are large enough for two.

Café da Moda, R Gonçalves Dias 49, 3rd floor, Centro, **T** 021-22220610. *Map 2, D8, p248* A café devoted to the narrow waistline and located within the Folic shop. Salads are named after famous models - Gisele Bündchen, Kate Moss, Claudia Schiffer and so on with more macho options for men - Zulu comprises buffalo, mozzarella, maize, tomato, croûtons, lettuce and a garnish of marjoram. Light meals are also available.

Al Kuwait, Av Treze de Maio, Centro, **T** 021-22401114. *Closed at the weekend.* *Map 6, E6, p256* Charming Middle Eastern fan-cooled restaurant with wood panelling in unprepossessing alley off Treze de Maio. No English menu but helpful staff. Try a traditional kofta or the daily special.

Bar das Artes, Paço Imperial, Praça 15 de Novembro 48, Centro, **T** 021-22155795. *Map 2, C10, p248* Neat, clean and peaceful café on the ground floor of the Paço Imperial (formerly the Royal Palace) in the busy centre of Rio. Salads, sandwiches, light meals and desserts like strawberry strudel.

Confeitaria Colombo, R Gonçalves Dias 32 (near Carioca Metrô station), Centro, **T** 021-22322300, www.confeitariacolombo.com.br. *Afternoons only during the week.* *Map 2, D9, p248* The only remaining belle époque Portuguese coffee house in Rio serving a range of café food, cakes, pastries and light lunches. The *Feijoada Colonial* on Saturdays is accompanied by live *choro*.

Mala e Cuia, Av Presidente Wilson 123, Centro, **T** 021-25245143. *Map 2, G10, p248* Good value Minas food with as much as you can eat for a set price.

Sabor Saúde, R da Quitanda 21, Centro, **T** 021-22526041. *Breakfast and lunch only.* *Map 2, C10, p248* Vegetarian and wholefood including sandwiches (whose content you can compile yourself), quiches, pastries, salads and light dishes like grilled salmon with rosti.

¥ **Verde Vício and Balanceado**, R Buenos Aires 22 and 27, Centro, **T** 021-22339602 and **T** 021-25181661. *Map 2, B9, p248* Soups, salads, pastas and quiches in two per-kilo wholefood restaurants.

Glória, Catete and Flamengo

¥¥¥ **Colonial**, Hotel Glória, R do Russel 632, **T** 021-25557572. *Map 3, D7, p250* A formal open-plan dining room decorated with old prints and staffed by black-tie waiters. The broad international menu created by named Swiss chef Fredy Rothen is strong on seafood and pasta.

¥¥ **Alcaparra**, Praia do Flamengo 144, Flamengo, **T** 021-25577236. *Map 3, G6, p250* Elegant traditional Italian/ Portuguese restaurant overlooking the sea. A long-established favourite of senior politicians and business people, who often ask for the *bacalhau*.

¥¥ **Alho e Óleo**, R Buarque de Macedo 13, Flamengo, **T** 021-25578541. *Map 3, G6, p250* Fashionable Italian with a strong emphasis on home-made pasta like the *Picatina Al Capone* - tagliatelle with beef medallions in a cream sauce.

¥¥ **Lamas**, Marquês de Abrantes 18A, Flamengo, **T** 021-25560799. *Map 3, I5, p250* This famous café brasserie with its conservative décor of white tablecloths and dark wood has been serving steaks, *bacalhau* and draught *chope* beer to the Rio intelligentsia since 1874. It is still a wonderful place to see the city's movers and shakers and gives a real sense of how European the city once was.

¥ **Amazônia**, R do Catete 234B, Catete. *Map 3, F5, p250* Downstairs for one-price counter service, upstairs for good, reasonably priced evening meals.

Ɏ **Estação República**, R do Catete 104, Catete, **T** 021-22252650. *Map 3, E5, p250* Over 40 different dishes from soups and sushi to salads and stews in this per-kilo restaurant housed in the Palácio do Catete.

Ɏ **Galícia Grill**, R do Catete 265 at Largo do Machado, Catete. *Map 3, H5, p250* Popular pizza served quickly and efficiently.

Santa Teresa

ɎɎɎ **Aprazível**, R Aprazível 62, Santa Teresa, **T** 021-38524935. *Map 3, D1, p250* One of Rio's best tables with a view - with a range of Brazilian dishes, the best of which are seafood, served in an intimate garden setting on a hillside overlooking Guanabara Bay. At lunchtime on Sundays live *choro* and samba are performed by Rio's equivalent of the Buena Vista Social Club.

ɎɎ **Adega do Pimenta**, R Almirante Alexandrino 296, Santa Teresa, **T** 021-22247554. *Closed Tue and Sat. Map 3, C2, p250* A very small, German restaurant in the Largo do Guimarães with excellent sausages (and numerous mustards to eat them with), sauerkraut, apple strudel, Black Forest gateau and cold beer.

Ɏ **Bar do Arnaudo**, Largo do Guimarães, R Almirante Alexandrino 316, Santa Teresa, **T** 021-22527246. *Map 3, C2, p250* A modest-looking restaurant decorated with handicrafts, but serving generous portions of wonderful northeastern Brazilian cooking. Try the *carne do sol* (sun-dried beef, or jerky) with *feijão de corda* (brown beans and herbs), or the *queijo coalho* (a country cheese, grilled).

Ɏ **Sobrenatural**, R Almirante Alexandrino 432, Santa Teresa, **T** 021-22241003. *Lunch only, closed Mon. Map 3, C2, p250* A charming rustic restaurant serving fish caught daily from owner's boat. For a light lunch, order a mix of the various delicious appetisers. On the same square as the Adega do Pimenta.

Pão de Açúcar, Botafogo and Urca

Those on a tight budget will find a number of enticing bars and restaurants on Rua Visconde de Caravelas in Catete, like **Aurora** (corner of Rua Capitão Salomão 43) and **Botequim** (no 184), both with varied menus, and good value, simple fare. **Cobal Humaitá**, is a daytime fruit market with many popular restaurants. **Chez Michou** and the ubiquitous chain restaurant **Habib's**, both in Shopping Rio Sul serve, respectively, very cheap crêpes and Arabic fastfood.

ΨΨΨΨ **Carême Bistrô**, R Visconde de Caravelas 113, Botafogo, **T** 021-25375431. *Map 4, E2, p252* An elegant and intimate little restaurant serving some of the best French bistro food in Rio. The original chef, Christophe Faivre, who created much of the menu, worked at Guy Savoy in Paris. He has since been replaced by his once junior chef, Flavia Quaresma, who continues to produce house favourites like coq au vin, and Argentinian executive chef, Guillermo Martin Lusardi, who has created a delicious new degustation menu.

ΨΨ **Rajmahal**, R General Polidoro 29, Baixo, Botafogo, **T** 021-25426242, www.raajmahal.com.br. *Map 4, D5, p252* One of the few restaurants in Brazil offering authentic Indian food with a huge menu including a range of vegetarian dishes like mater paneer.

ΨΨ **Yorubá**, R Arnaldo Quintela 94, Botafogo, **T** 021-25419387. *Evenings only, except at the weekend; closed Mon-Tue.* *Map 4, E5, p252* Rio's favourite Bahian restaurant, and voted the best Brazilian restaurant in the city by *Veja* magazine in 2002. The menu comprises the usual run of Bahian food from *acarajé* (beans fried in *dendê* palm oil) to *vatapá* alongside more unusual dishes like chicken in ginger sauce with cashew nut rice.

Brazilian food

Traditional southern Brazilian cooking is dominated by Portuguese staples like *bacalhau*, thick, fleshy camp-fire stews like *feijoada*, barbecued meats served on a spit and pasties stuffed with chicken, sticky cheese, ham or palm hearts. All these are served alongside beans, rice, *manioc* flour, perfunctory salads and vegetable side dishes like mashed squash. Other than salt and weak chilli sauce, condiments are non-existent. Northern Brazilian cooking, or at least that of Bahia is more sophisticated largely thanks to the influence of West African techniques and ingredients. Herbs and spices make an appearance; dishes require various stages of preparation, and meat and fish are seasoned or marinated and served in carefully prepared sauces based on coconut milk or the oil of the African *dendê* palm. Readily available Bahian dishes include *moqueca* (fried fish served in a sauce of chilli pepper, coriander, lemon, tomato and onion) and *vatapá* (chicken stewed in coconut milk and seasoned with sliced shrimps, onion, chilli pepper and olive oil).

Copacabana and Leme

ΨΨΨΨ **Cipriani**, Copacabana Palace, Av Atlântica 1702, **T** 021-25487070. *Map 4, H6, p252* Rio's best Italian food served in a conservative dining room decked out with chandeliers, thick white tablecloths and staffed by waiters in black tie. This is a sister restaurant to the Cipriani restaurants in Venice (chef Francesco Carli made his name there) and New York. The pasta and seafood dishes are faultless, particularly the *taglierni verdi del Cipriani gratinati al prosciutto*. Dress smart casual. Best for dinner.

Best

Tables with a view

- **Casas Brancas** in Búzios, p123
- **Aprazível** in Santa Teresa, p139
- **Le Saint-Honoré** in Copacabana, p142
- **Bar d'Hotel** in Leblon, p145
- **Sushinaka** in Lagoa, p148

ΨΨΨ **Le Pré-Catelan**, Hotel Sofitel, Av Atlântica 4240, Copacabana, **T** 021-25251160. *Map 5, H12, p254* Intimate dining with piano tinkling and low lights and a superlative menu of French dishes from Roland Villard, whose signature dishes include rosemary steamed whiting fillet in a langoustine and coconut sauce.

ΨΨΨ **Le Saint-Honoré**, Hotel Le Méridien, Av Atlântica 1020, Copacabana, **T** 021-38738880. *Map 4, G8, p252* French food from Dominique Oudin, the disciple of the restaurant's illustrious founder Paul Bocuse, whose signature dishes include *terrine de foie gras com gelado de maracujá e gengibre* (foie gras terrine with ginger and passion fruit jelly) and *pintado da Amazônia com purê de batata-doce* (Amazon *pintado* catfish with sweet potato purée). Wonderful views out over the beach.

ΨΨ **Azumi**, R Ministro Viveiros de Castro 127, Copacabana, **T** 021-25414294. *Map 4, G7, p252* The most popular Japanese restaurant in Brazil for visiting Japanese, who claim that the Ohara family produce authentic traditional Japanese home cooking in traditional Japanese restaurant surrounds.

Ψ **A Marisquera**, R Barata Ribeiro 232, Copacabana, **T** 021-25473920. *Map 4, H5, p252* Reasonable seafood dishes and Brazilian standards – usually a choice of meat or fish accompanied by rice, beans, chips and salad.

Ɏ **Cervantes**, R Barata Ribeiro 07-B and Av Prado Júnior 335B, Copacabana, **T** 021-22576147. *Open all night, queues after 2200.* *Map 4, G7, p252* Stand-up bar or sit-down, a/c restaurant. Said to serve the best sandwiches in town, a local institution. Attracts a colourful, bizarre crowd.

Ɏ **Chon Kou**, Av Atlântica 3880, Copacabana, **T** 021-22873956. *Map 5, G12, p254* A traditional Chinese restaurant which also offers an extensive sushi menu. Sit upstairs for good a/c views over Copacabana beach accompanied by piped music. A welcome change from most of the other options in this area.

Ɏ **Churrascaria Palace**, R Rodolfo Dantas 16B, Copacabana, **T** 021-22870592. *Map 4, H6, p252* Twenty different kinds of barbecued meat served on a spit at your table with buffet salads to accompany. Good value.

Ɏ **Estação Minas**, R Figueiredo Magalhães 131A, Copacabana, **T** 021-22558995. *Map 4, below H4, p252* A wealth of different meats, stews and salad combinations made from ingredients from the owners' farm in Minas Gerais.

Ɏ **Taberna do Leme**, corner of Princesa Isabel and Av NS Copacabana. *Map 4, G8, p252* A simple, friendly bar/restaurant with helpful waiters and tables on pavement. Comprehensive menu in English includes delicious crab pancakes. Warmly recommended for eating as well as drinking.

Ipanema, Arpoador and Leblon

ɎɎɎɎ **Antiquarius**, R Aristides Espínola 19, Leblon, **T** 021-22941049. *Map 5, H1, p254* One of Rio's most vaunted restaurants by hotel concierges is a place to be seen rather than to eat well.

Jewel-encrusted fifty-somethings gather here in the mock-European home surrounds to dine on heavy, overly-salted and overly-expensive Portuguese cooking.

ΨΨΨΨ **Esplanada Grill**, R Barão da Torre 600, Ipanema, **T** 021-25122970. *Map 5, G5, p254* By far the best *churrascaria* in Rio - with as much you can eat of the very best cuts of meat from central Brazil and Argentina served on spits at your table, accompanied by a vast buffet spread of side dishes and salads.

ΨΨΨΨ **Gero**, R Aníbal de Mendonça 157, Ipanema, **T** 021-22398158. *Map 5, G5, p254* Rio's most fashionable restaurant is owned and carefully overseen by São Paulo restaurant entrepreneur, Rogerio Fasano. The light Italian menu is strong on fish, but at times light on flavour, and is accompanied by a respectable wine list. Come here for a window on Rio's Vanity Fair – TV Globo Becky Sharps and Beau Brummels mingle with smug old money and nouveaux riches, and the modernist brick space and long, cool bar serve as a tasteful backdrop to their picturesque ostentation.

ΨΨΨΨ **Satyricon**, R Barão da Torre 192, Ipanema, **T** 021-25210627. *Map 5, G8, p254* Ronaldo's and Rio's favourite seafood restaurant draws a lively crowd to a large dining room which precludes intimacy, and is particularly crowded on Saturdays when there is a seafood buffet. The squid, in particular, is excellent and the sushi bar the best in the city.

ΨΨΨΨ **Zuka**, R Dias Ferreira 233, Leblon, **T** 021-32057154. *Map 5, G1, p254* One of wealthy Rio's most popular restaurants and posing spots, with an exciting and eclectic fusion of world cuisines - French and Japanese, American fast food and Italian are thrown together by ex-Nobu chef Felipe Bronze and presented on huge rectangular plates. Delights include teriyaki-glazed foie gras.

ɎɎɎ **Bar d'Hotel**, Hotel Marina All Suites, Av Delfim Moreira 696, Leblon, **T** 021-21721100. *Map 5, H2, p254* Light but very well-flavoured fish dishes (and excellent cocktails) – served to people with tiny waists in a casual, cool, bright and spacious dining room/bar overlooking the water. Come for breakfast, lunch or dinner.

ɎɎɎ **Bistrô ZaZá Tropical**, R Joana Angélica 40, Ipanema, **T** 021-22479101. *Map 5, H7, p254* Hippy, chic, pseudo- Moroccan/ French restaurant that attracts a mix of tourists and bohemian Zona Sul Cariocas. Good fish dishes and cocktails and good fun. Evenings are best for intimate dining when the tables are lit by candles.

ɎɎɎ **Capricciosa**, R Vinícius de Moraes 134, Ipanema, **T** 021-25233394. *Map 5, G8, p254* The best pizzas in Rio - which are very ordinary by international standards (think Pizza Express with more cheese) and a crowd of posers and shakers including many TV Globo faces. Queues can be long.

ɎɎɎ **Carlota**, R Dias Ferreira 64, Leblon, **T** 021-25406821 *Map 5, G1, p254* The sister restaurant to Carla Pernambuco's Carlota in São Paulo is the best of many on a street lined with restaurants and bars. The décor is simple - all white with candles, offsetting a sophisticated crowd of creative industry types and social circuit intellectuals. The Italian food is the best in Ipanema/Leblon and the crowd one of Rio's more sophisticated. The crispy prawns with parma ham risotto is excellent.

ɎɎɎ **Garcia and Rodrigues**, Av Ataulfo de Paiva 1251, Leblon, **T** 021-25128188. *Map 5, G1, p254* This French-owned delicatessen restaurant tucked away on a busy main street would be more attractive were it closer to the beach, but it's air-conditioned interior and light Frenchified café food and exclusive reputation lures many *mauricinio* Cariocas for lunch and breakfast. They also serve sumptuous ice cream and decent coffee.

ŸŸŸ **Siri Mole and Compania**, R Francisco Otaviano 50, Arpoador, **T** 021-22670894. *Map 5, H11, p254* Quality Bahian seafood in elegant a/c surrounds, including *moquecas* for one which serve for two, and thick, dark, properly prepared coffee. The restaurant also has a popular bar next door.

ŸŸ **Alessandro & Frederico**, R Garcia d'Ávila, 134D, Ipanema, **T** 021-25210828. *Map 5, G5, p254* Upmarket café on the busiest upmarket shopping street in Ipanema/Leblon, serving decent latte, breakfasts and brunches to people with Louis Vuitton handbags. Great juice bar next door.

ŸŸ **Casa da Feijoada**, R Prudente de Moraes 10, Ipanema, **T** 021-25234994. *Map 5, H9, p254* Brazilians flock here for the national dish which gives this restaurant its name - a thick meaty stew made from a large variety of farmyard animals and served with black beans, rice and strong, sweet *cachaça*. Come for lunch or dinner with a very empty stomach.

ŸŸ **Pizzaria Guanabara**, Av Ataulfo de Paiva, Leblon, **T** 021-22940797. *Map 5, G1, p254* The pizzas here are dreadful. And they're overpriced. And the restaurant itself looks very down at heel: aluminium tables and chairs spill out onto the pavement and a TV blares inside. But for some reason, known only to Cariocas, this is a lynchpin on the Zona Sul nightlife scene - on Fridays and Saturdays, in the small hours, there are always Brazilian celebrities here chewing the fat and the rubbery mozzarella, which makes it great for lively people-watching. If you can get a table.

ŸŸ **Yemanjá**, R Visconde de Pirajá 128, Ipanema, **T** 021-22477004. *Map 5, G9, p254* Decent Bahian cooking including *moqueca*, *vatapá* and various other dishes cooked in *dendê* palm or coconut oil.

Ψ **Aipo e Aipim**, R Visconde de Pirajá 145, Ipanema, **T** 021-22678313. *Map 5, G9, p254* Plentiful, tasty food sold by weight at this popular chain (with another branch in Copacabana).

Ψ **Amarelinho**, R Farme de Amoedo 62, Ipanema. *Until 0300* *Map 5, H8, p254* Corner *lanchonete* with tables outside. Fresh food, friendly service and doors open.

Ψ **Celeiro**, R Dias Ferreira 199, Leblon, **T** 021-22747843; also at R Vinícius de Moraes 71B, Ipanema. *Map 5, G1, p254* Some of the best salads and per-kilo food in the city, with various Bahian dishes from *moqueca* to *vatapá*.

Ψ **Empório Saúde**, R Visconde de Pirajá, 414, Ipanema, **T** 021-25221494. *Closed Sun and evenings.* *Map 5, G6, p254* A large variety of vegetarian comfort-cooking from quiches to stews in a cramped indoor setting, some tables outside.

Ψ **Gergelim**, R Vinícius de Moraes 121, Ipanema, **T** 021-25237026. *Map 5, G8, p254* Vegetarian whole food in an impersonal, clinical but a/c modern café. Good desserts.

Ψ **New Natural**, R Barão da Torre 173, Ipanema, **T** 021-36834608. *Map 5, G8, p254* Popular per-kilo lunchtime vegetarian restaurant and wholefood shop. Excellent value and plenty of choice.

Gávea, Lagoa and Jardim Botânico

ΨΨΨΨ **Olympe**, R Custódio Serrão 62, Lagoa, **T** 021-25394542, www.claudetroisgros.com.br. *Map 5, A7, p254* An elegant, understated restaurant in a quiet back street which vies with Le Saint-Honoré and Carême Bistrô for the mantle of best French restaurant in Rio. It takes its name from its French chef, who cooks a mixture of traditional cuisine and Franco-Brazilian fusions.

ỲỲỲ **Guimas**, R José Roberto Macedo Soares, Gávea, **T** 021-22597996. *From 2200.* *Map 5, D1, p254* Towards the end of the week this is one of the places where trendy Rio under 30s gather to be seen before moving down the street to the two tatty bars on the corner of Praça Santos Dumont. The restaurant itself is modest, with only a handful of tables, a modest front. The food is traditionally Portuguese and uncomplicated, with excellent *bacalhau*.

ỲỲỲ **Rhapsody**, Av Epitácio Pessoa 1104, Lagoa, **T** 021-22472104. *Map 5, F5, p254* Dinner and dancing with a lake view for a wealthy30- and 40-something crowd. The restaurant is divided into three spaces: a piano bar, where live bands play until the small hours; a main dining room; and a veranda. Most come here for the evening rather than solely for the Italian and French food, which, while perfectly respectable, is not up to the standard of others in this price bracket.

ỲỲỲ-ỲỲ **Sushinaka**, Av Epitácio Pessoa 1484, Lagoa, **T** 021-25220998. *Map 5, F7, p254* Sushi and sashimi with a wonderful view out over the lagoon and to the Corcovado Christ. The dining room is large and elegant, and the diners some of the Zona Sul's most fashionable. Of the various dishes, the most celebrated is the vast Sushinaka spread with some 80 pieces of sushi, sashimi and others.

ỲỲ **Árabe da Gávea**, Gávea Shopping Mall, R Marquês de São Vicente 52, **T** 021-22942439. *Map 5, D1, p254* A dull shopping centre setting belies the fact that this is the best Arabic restaurant in Rio, with particularly good falafel and lamb couscous.

Natural energy drinks

Rio may not be one of the world's great gourmet destinations, but there is nowhere better for fruit juices. The choice is staggering. Some bars have over 30 different juices to choose from - many from fruits that are unknown and unavailable outside of South America. Must tries include *cupuaçu*, a fragrant, pungent juice extracted from a relative of the cacao bean; *caju* made from the fruit of the cashew nut tree and *tapereba* - tangy, deliciously refreshing and made from an Amazon fruit related to the Brazil nut. If you are looking to top up your energy levels opt for an *açai* an *acerola* or a *camu camu*. *Açai* is a meal in itself - served thick, sweet, icy cold and dark maroon, and packed with electrolytes and vitamins. *Acerola*, which comes originally from the Yucatan, is a tropical cherry with a sharp, refreshing flavour and what was thought until recently to be the highest of all naturally occurring levels of vitamin C. This accolade is now accorded to *camu camu*, a light-orange fruit from the Amazon, which on average contains about 2g per 100g - 30 times as much (in parts per million) as an average orange. *Camu camu* is also a significant source of vitamin B, phosphorus, potassium and iron, together with the full complement of other minerals and amino acids which aid in the absorption of vitamin C.

Many of these juices are available as constituents of various non-alcoholic cocktails or *vitaminas*; made up with either water or milk, sugar and often *guaraná* powder - a naturally occurring stimulant made from a pounded Amazonian nut.

Les Artistes, R Marquês de São Vicente 75, Gávea, **T** 021-22394242. *Map 5, E1, p254* Another bar/restaurant most notable for the attractive and fashionable young crowd who come here, rather than for the food.

Búzios

There are many restaurants on and around Rua das Pedras and one of the charms of Búzios is browsing. The cheaper options tend to be off the main drag. There are plenty of beachside *barracas* all over the peninsula serving the usual beans, rice and chips combinations outside of the low season.

A few places on Praça Santos Dumont off Rua das Pedras offer sandwiches and self-service food, including the homely La Prima on Avenida Manuel Turíbio de Farias which doubles as a bakery. There's a small supermarket a couple of doors away.

Also see Casas Brancas page 123 (fine views and romantic dining) and Brigitta's page 124 (funky seafood bistro).

ŸŸŸŸ **Acquerello**, R das Pedras 130, **T** 022-26236576. Smart a/c seafood and Italian restaurant with a reasonable wine list. The best on the street.

ŸŸŸŸ **Satyricon**, Av José Bento Ribeiro Dantas 500, Praia da Armação (in front of Morro da Humaitá), **T** 022-26231595. Búzios's most illustrious restaurant specialising in Italian seafood. Decent wine list.

ŸŸ **Moqueca Capixaba**, R Manuel de Carvalho 116, Centro, **T** 022-26231155. Bahian seafood with (mostly seafood) dishes cooked in coconut or *dendê* oil.

Ÿ **Banana Land**, R Manuel Turíbio de Farias 50, **T** 022-26230855. Cheap and cheerful per-kilo buffet.

Ÿ **Chez Michou**, R das Pedras 90, Centro, **T** 022-26232169. An open-air bar with videos, music and dozens of choices of pancakes accompanied by ice cold beer. Always crowded.

Ÿ **Fashion café**, R das Pedras 151, **T** 022-26232697. Fast food and pizzas with a young crowd and a live band.

Itatiaia National Park

The hotels in the park all have restaurants. **Donati** and **Cabanas de Itatiaia** have the best, the latter with a view. Outside the park, **Via Park** (1441 Estrada Parque, in the village, 4 km before the park entrance, **T** 024-92687934) serves delicious trout with the usual Brazilian accompaniments, in super-generous portions.

Petrópolis and around

Fast-food outlets, *pastel* shops and *lanchonetes* are all found around the square in Petrópolis. There are cheap eats and a good café in the ABC supermarket in Teresópolis.

ŸŸŸŸ **Da Irene**, R Tenente Luís Meireles 1800, Teresópolis, **T** 021-27422901. Very popular upmarket Russian restaurant. Reservations necessary.

ŸŸ **Falconi**, R do Imperador 757, Petrópolis, **T** 024-22421252. Traditional restaurant with rustic elegance that has been serving Italian food since 1914. Good value, with pasta and pizza for US$3. Recommended.

ŸŸ **Taberna Alpina**, Duque de Caxias 131, Teresópolis, **T** 021-27420123. Excellent German cuisine.

Ÿ **Bar Gota d'Água**, Praça Baltasar da Silveira 16, Teresópolis. A little bar with simple fish dishes and *feijoada*.

¥ **Cantina Dom Giovanni**, R do Imperador 729, Petrópolis, **T** 024-22425588. A first-floor, simple, canteen- style Italian restaurant that is justifiably popular for self-service lunch and dinner.

¥ **Casa d'Ângelo**, R do Imperador 700, by Praça Dom Pedro II, Petrópolis, **T** 024-22420888. A traditional, long- standing tea house with self-service food. Doubles as a bar at night.

¥ **Pavelka**, R Washington Luiz, Petrópolis, **T** 024-22427990. Daily 0800-2100 (Fri until 0200). Locals in the know stock up at the deli with the German, Austrian and Czech specialities such as sausages and trout smoked on the premises, and tuck into the éclairs and millefeuilles fresh from the bakery in the little attached café. Recommended.

Ilha Grande

Aside from **Sito do Lobo** (guests only), food on the island is fairly basic: fish, chicken or meat with beans, rice and chips. There are plenty of different restaurants serving these exciting combinations in Abraão. We list the very few better options.

¥¥ **Fogão de Lenha**, R Projetada A, Abraão, **T** 024-33615097. Wood-fired pizzas and good *caipirinhas*.

¥¥ **Lua e Mar**, Abraão, on the waterfront, **T** 024-33615113. A few more adventurous fish-based options than the other restaurants. But only a few.

Paraty and around

The best restaurants in Paraty are in the historic part of town and are almost as good as any you will find in Rio or São Paulo. Watch out for surreptitious cover charges for live music, which are often very discreetly displayed. If you are looking for budget options, look outside the city centre. Paraty has some plates unique to the region, like *peixe à Parati* - local fish cooked with herbs, green bananas and served with *pirão*, a mixture of *manioc* flour and the sauce that the fish was cooked in. Also popular is the *filé de peixe ao molho de camarão* - fried fish fillet with a shrimp and tomato sauce. There is plenty of choice in Paraty and browsing is a good option. The less expensive restaurants, those offering *comida por quilo* (pay by weight), and the fast-food outlets are outside the historical centre, mainly on Avenida Roberto Silveira.

There are plenty of places to eat in Trindade, none of which are particularly bad nor particularly recommendable. Expect fish, beef or chicken with beans, rice, salad and chips; and the odd pizza.

TTTT **Copa de Ouro**, next to the Ouro, R Dr Pereira 145, historical centre, Paraty, **T** 024-33711311. Very good seafood and Brazilian dishes and a reasonable wine list. Recommended.

TTTT **Merlin O Mago**, (next to Coxixo), R do Comércio 376, historical centre, Paraty, **T** 024-33712157, www.paraty.com.br/merlin.htm. Franco-Brazilian cooking in an intimate dining room/bar, by a German cordon bleu-trained chef and illustrious photojournalist. Decent wine list. The best restaurant in town. Highly recommended.

TTT **Do Hiltinho**, R Mcal Deodoro 233, historical centre, Paraty, **T** 024-33712155. Decent seafood, local dishes.

TTT **Le Gite d'Indaitiba,** see Sleeping, page 131.

TT **Café Paraty**, R da Lapa and Comércio, historical centre, Paraty, **T** 024-33711464. Sandwiches, appetizers, light meals, also bar with live music nightly. A local landmark.

ŸŸ **Corto Maltese**, R do Comércio 130, Paraty, **T** 024-33711473. Pasta and the usual Italian fare.

ŸŸ **Dona Ondina**, R do Comércio 2, by the river, historical centre, Paraty, **T** 024-33711584. Closed Mon in Mar and Nov. Family restaurant with well-prepared simple food. Good value.

ŸŸ **Punto Di Vino**, R Mcal Deodoro 129, historical centre, Paraty, **T** 024-33711348. Wood-fired pizza and calzoni served with live music and a good selection of wine.

ŸŸ **Thai Brasil**, R Dona Geralda 345, historical centre, Paraty, **T** 024-33710127, www.thaibrasil.com.br. Beautiful restaurant ornamented with handicrafts and furnished with hand-painted chairs and tables. The cooking loosely resembles Thai without spices. Brazilians yelp in pain at the sight of a chilli.

Ÿ **Fish & Chips**, R do Comércio 95, Paraty, **T** 024-33712747. A British fish and chippie owned by an expat from Tunbridge Wells. Good…er fish and chips. And some veggie options.

Ÿ **Kontiki**, Ilha Duas Irmãs, **T** 024-99995999, www.paraty.com.br/kontiki.htm. *Daily 1000-1500 and Fri -Sat for dinner.* Wonderful setting on a tiny island 5 minutes from the pier where a small speedboat runs a (free) shuttle service, or you can take a boat taxi from Paraty. Ordinary food. Reservations recommended.

Ÿ **Sabor da Terra**, Av Roberto Silveira, next to Banco do Brasil, Paraty, **T** 024-33712447. *Until 2200.* Reliable, if not bargain-priced, self-service food.

Bars and clubs

Rio is as bacchanalian and bohemian as any city could ever be, but only if you get away from the obvious tourist areas and samba shows proffered by many of the hotels. By night, when there are no concerts on the beach, Copacabana is mostly tawdry and dangerous, and Ipanema mostly touristy and dull. But only a taxi-drive away in Leblon, Lapa and Gávea, Rio is alive and throbbing.

Leblon is mostly restaurant/bar based. People sit at tables, drink *chope* and eat tapas, before spilling out onto the streets and moving on to a club like Melt or Bom Bar. At the close of the week Lapa becomes one of the best places to go out in South America – a soup of people and musical styles as bizarre as it is wonderful. There is a night spot here for every taste – from down-at-heel Tom Waits to frenetic samba and Brazilian techno. Gávea's bars may be as grungy and simple as Lapa's are theatrical, but this is the trendiest spot to hang out in Rio on a Sunday and Monday if you are middle class, good looking and under 30. The streets are packed after 2300. See also Eating and drinking, pages 133-154.

Central Rio

Armazém 161, R do Lavradio 161, Lapa, **T** 021-25096879. *Closed Sun. Map 2, G7, p248* One of the recent flourishing of antique shop/bars on Lapa's principal nightlife street. It plays host to samba and *chorinho* bands and is busiest at the weekend.

Bar Luiz, R da Carioca 39, Centro, **T** 021-22626900. *Map 2, D8, p248* For 117 years this little bar has been at the centre of Rio life. Almost every Carioca you can name have at one time formed part of the lively throng which gathers here on weekday evenings, and most particularly on Fridays and Saturdays, to drink the famous *chope* and German tapas.

Café Cultural Sacrilégio, Av Mem de Sá 81, Lapa, **T** 021-39701461. *Closed Sun. Map 2, G7, p248* Live samba and *choro* shows in a bar divided into three distinct areas: a large dance hall decorated with naive art and sculptures; a veranda; and an open area at the back. The tapas and Kir are excellent.

Café Musical Carioca da Gema, Av Mem de Sá, 79, Lapa, **T** 021-22210043. *Closed Sun. Map 2, G7, p248* One of Lapa's best known and busiest samba bars, and one of the best starting points for a night out. Excellent bands with *chorinho* and old samba on Fridays and a livelier set on Saturdays. Come at 2100 before it gets too busy.

Caroline Café, R da Assembléia 13, Centro, **T** 021-25334725. *Closed Sun. Map 2, C10, p248* An offshoot of the popular *mauricinho* bar in the Jardim Botânico, and full of students and middle- class office workers. Live jazz on Wednesday, Djs on Thursday, and rock on Friday.

Casa da Mãe Joana, Av Gomes Freire 547, Centro, **T** 021-25319435. *Closed Sun-Mon. Map 2, F6, p248* Samba bar/restaurant in a crumbling colonial building that was inaugurated in 2001. Some of Rio's oldest samba and *chorinho* names play here; octogenarian bands who look like the Buena Vista Social Club of Rio and whose music is equally infectious. Decent bar food and *chope*.

Centro Cultural Carioca, R do Teatro 37, Praça Tiradentes, Centro, **T** 021-22526468. *Closed Sun.* *Map 2, D8, p248* Couples have been dancing samba here since the 1940s when the *praça* was at the heart of bohemian Rio; music here today tends towards traditional samba.

Club Six, R das Marrecas 38, Lapa (next to the viaduct), **T** 021-25103230. *Map 2, G9, p248* Huge pounding European/NYC dance club with a state-of-the-art sound system and three separate dance floors offering mostly hip hop and contemporary R&B.

Dama da Noite, R Gomes Freire 773, Lapa, **T** 021-22212072. *Closed Sun-Mon.* *Map 2, G7, p248* Large club taking up two storeys of a beautiful colonial house protected by Brazil's National Heritage Commission. Delicious crêpes, *chope* and live samba.

Mercado Moderno, R do Lavradio 130, Centro, **T** 021-22323499. *Closed Sun-Mon.* *Map 2, F7, p248* Another of Lapa's bizarrely captivating furniture shop, bar and samba club fusions, with beautiful people dancing frenetically to live samba and *chope*.

Rio Scenarium, R do Lavradio 20, Lapa, **T** 021-38525516, www.rioscenarium.com.br. *Closed Sun-Mon.* *Map 2, E6, p248* Three-storey samba club in a colonial building used as a move prop warehouse. Overflowing with joie de vivre and people dancing furiously to the bizarre backdrop of a 19th- century apothecary's shop or a line of mannequins wearing 1920s outfits. This is Rio at its Bohemian best. Buzzes with beautiful people of all ages on Fridays and Saturdays. Come after 2300.

The fall and rise of Lapa

In the belle époque, Lapa's colonial streets were the Bohemian heart of Rio – lined with little bars and dance halls which were the haunt of artists and intellectuals like Di Cavalcanti. But, after the war, they fell into decay and disrepute and only the dangerous walked here. For decades Lapa festered. And then in the 1980s a series of performance artists in love with the memory of the area braved Lapa, and the neighbourhood slowly began to revive. Others followed them and a small alternative community began to form. Art and antiques dealers moved in. And then came tango and samba clubs, bars and a handful of restaurants. Today, at least between Thursday and Sunday, Lapa is once more the heart of Bohemian Rio and many of its decaying colonial houses are now renovated and freshly painted. Enough, however, remain for Lapa to retain a slightly edgy, Havanesque feel. Come here for a great night out and a window on the panoply and polyphony of modern Rio. Arrive at around 2100 while it is still relatively quiet, take a streetside table under the arches at any one of the crumbling colonial cafés along Avenida Mem da Sá, order an absinthe and wait. Little by little characters from every walk of Rio life enter the living stage – down at heel *favela* couples drunk and stumbling, *patricinhas* dressed in Zoomp's ultra-expensive casual, capoeira artists, jugglers, old men in blazers with hula hoops round their necks, befuddled tourists, towering transvestites in lycra shorts the size of a glove. As their numbers increase to boiling point they become a throng, unable to keep apart from each other, moving in Brownian motion past the doors of numerous gradually waking clubs; past the thump and thud of techno, the staccato whir of *forró* and the hip swing of samba. Once the clubs have really got going, leave your table and join the throng – to dance to any music of your choice and become for a night... a Carioca.

What night where?

Monday Gávea, around Praça Santos Dumont with dancing pretty much limited to *Cozumel*, nearby in the Jardim Botânico. *Empório* in Ipanema has live music.
Tuesday *Devassa* in Leblon and *Bom Bar* down the road.
Wednesday *A Casa da Lua* in Ipanema and *Clan Café* in Cosme Velho have live music. Good dancing at *Bunker 94* in Copacabana.
Thursday Pretty much anywhere is busy, particularly Leblon and Lapa. *Melt* in Leblon has its busiest night.
Friday Lively anywhere. *Mistura Fina* (Lagoa), *Bar do Tom* (Leblon) and *Clan Café* (Cosme Velho) usually have an interesting live jazz, MPB or bossa nova and *Club Six* in Lapa has its busiest dance music night.
Saturday Much the same as Friday and the best night for Lapa and any of the samba clubs there, especially the *Rio Scenarium*, and for *Bom Bar* and the lounge clubs *Bardot* in Leblon and *Sítio Lounge* in Gávea. *Nuth* in Barra da Tijuca is always heaving.
Sunday Generally quiet, although Gávea is always busy and there are often live acts at *Melt* (Leblon). *00* (Gávea) has a gay night.

Semente, R Joaquim Silva 138, Lapa, **T** 021-22425165. *Map 2, H8, p248* Rustic little samba bar which throbs with life and where the likes of Marisa Monte and Beth Carvalho both drink *chope* and perform occasional extemporaneous concerts.

Symbol, R Almirante Barroso 139 F, Centro, **T** 021-25330292. *Closed Sun-Mon. Map 2, E11, p248* One of the new wave of dance clubs which are springing up all over Rio. Symbol's various restaurants and dance floors cover an area of nearly 1½ sq km, enabling clubbers to come for a night and stay for days should they wish to.

The Twenty Pounds Blues Bar, R Mem de Sá 82, Lapa, **T** 021-22925709. *Closed Sun-Tue. Map 2, G7, p248* A little, second-floor bar in a colonial building in the heart of Lapa. Live blues, rock, burgers, chips and hotdogs.

Santa Teresa

Simplesmente, R Paschoal Carlos Magno 115, Santa Teresa, **T** 021-25086007. *Closed Sun.* *Map 3, C1, p250* A popular samba club filled with students and 20-somethings at the weekend after 2200.

Pão de Açúcar, Botafogo, Urca

Casa de Matriz, R Henrique de Novaes 107, Botafogo, **T** 021-22661014, www.casadematriz.com.br. *Map 4, D3, p252* Atmospheric, grungy little club in a residential house; with a bar, Atari room, small cinema and two dance floors. Full of students.

Copacabana and Leme

Bip Bip, R Almirante Gonçalves 50, Copacabana, **T** 021-2679696. *Map 5, F11, p254* Simple *botequim* bar which attracts a crowd of jamming musicians every Tuesday.

Bunker 94, R Raul Pompéia 94, Copacabana, **T** 021-25210367, www.bunker94.com.br. *Map 5, G11, p254* European-style dance club where the likes of DJs Marky and Patife play; music varies from from rock during the week to techno and hard and progressive house on the weekends. Busy from Wednesday to Saturday from 0200. The queues have become a party in themselves.

Paddy Fla's, R Ronald de Carvalho 154, Copacabana, **T** 021-22448163, www.paddyfla.tripod.com/drinks. *Map 4, G7, p252*

The only Irish pub in Rio where you're likely to find any Irish residents or tourists. Guinness on draught and chicken korma.

Ipanema, Arpoador and Leblon

Academia da Cachaça, R Conde de Bernadotte 26G, Leblon, **T** 021-25292680; also at Av Armando Lombardi 800, Barra da Tijuca, www.academiadacachaca.com.br. *Map 5, F2, p254* Modest, bar with a polished concrete floor, formica tables and the best *cachaças* and *caipirinhas* in the state, together with a range of cheap Brazilian dishes. Attracts a young crowd. Good on Fridays.

Bar do Tom, R Adalberto Ferreira 32, Leblon, **T** 021-22744022. *Open only for concerts, usually every day, except Sun-Tue in summer. Map 5, F2, p254* A small bar venue played by important Brazilian names like Nana Caymmi, Emilio Santiago and Hermeto Pascoal.

Barril 1800, Av Vieira Souto 110, Ipanema, **T** 021-5230085, www.barril800.com.br. *Map 5, H9, p254* Very popular with tourists who gather to watch the sunset. Little else to recommend it.

BomBar, Av General San Martin 1011, Leblon, **T** 021-22492161. *Closed Sun. Map 5, H1, p254* A bar/club which dedicates itself to 'beer drinkers and hell raisers' and attracts a singles crowd in their 20s. Packed after 2300, especially on Tuesday and Saturday.

A Garota de Ipanema, R Vinícius de Moraes 49, Ipanema, **T** 021-25233787. *Map 5, H8, p254* The bar where composers Tom Jobim and Vinícius de Moraes used to sit as teenagers and watch the passers-by, especially the girls. One of them, a teenager called Heloísa Eneida Menezes Paes Pinto, used to walk past every day on her way to the beach, and she so transfixed him that he wrote the most famous of all bossa nova songs in homage to her; *'The Girl from*

Ipanema', after which the bar was eventually n amed. It is now mostly visited by foreign tourists who eat in the downstairs restaurant and drink to the sound of live bossa nova in the bar.

Devassa, Av General San Martin 1241, Leblon, **T** 021-25406087. *Map 5, H1, p254* A two-floor pub/restaurant/bar which is always heaving and which brews its own beer.

Melt, R Rita Ludolf 47, Leblon, **T** 021-22499309. *Map 5, H1, p254* Downstairs bar and upstairs sweaty club with occasional performances by the cream of Rio's new samba funk scene – usually on a Sunday. Busy any night and always heaving on Thursdays.

Empório, R Maria Quitéria 37, Ipanema, **T** 021-25221159. *Map 5, G6, p254* Spit and sawdust street bar which has very little to recommend it other than that it stays open until dawn and attracts hordes of 20- and 30-something Brazilians, especially on Mondays.

The Irish Pub, R Jangadeiros 14A, Ipanema, **T** 021-25133044. *Map 5, H1, p254* Similar to Shenanigans (see below) but with live music on Mondays. For something more genuinely Irish head for Paddy Fla's in Copacabana (see page 161).

Shenanigans, R Visconde de Pirajá 112, Ipanema, **T** 021-22675860. *Map 5, G9, p254* Irish theme pub showing US sports and serving Newcastle Brown Ale alongside Guinness and darts.

Vinícius, R Vinícius de Moraes 39, Ipanema, 2nd floor, **T** 021-22871497. *Map 5, H8, p254* Mirror image of the Garota de Ipanema (see above) with slightly better acts and food.

Bardot, R Dias Ferreira 24A, Leblon, **T** 021- 22745590. *Closed Sun-Tue. Map 5, G1, p254* Stylishly decorated bar/restaurant with superlative cocktails, DJs at the weekends and an attractive 30-40-something crowd. One of the few in Rio with a club lounge area.

A Casa da Lua, R Barão da Torre 240A, Ipanema, **T** 021-38133972. *Closed Mon-Tue.* *Map 5, G8, p254* Tiny and recently opened bar with respectable tapas and steaks and live music from MPB to rock and blues on Wednesdays and Fridays.

Jobi Botequim, Av Ataulfo de Paiva 1166, Leblon, **T** 021-22740547. *Map 5, G1, p254* Always buzzing. One of the city's most celebrated *botequims* and a Zona Sul institution. Sumptuous food, including *rissole de camarão com catupiry* (prawn and cream cheese rissole). Come to experience Rio as the Cariocas do.

Lord Jim Pub, R Paul Redfern 63, Ipanema, **T** 021-22593047. *Until 0300 most nights.* *Map 5, H4, p254* Mock-English pub with a red telephone box outside, Guinness, Newcastle Brown Ale, American fast food and Brazilian.

Gávea, Lagoa and Jardim Botânico

Braseiro da Gávea, Praça Santos Dumont 116, Gávea, **T** 021-22397494. *Map 5, D1, p254* Lively bar, always jam-packed with the young and beautiful. However, the décor is neither of these. Good after 2100 any night but best on Sundays and Mondays.

Caroline Café, R JJ Seabra 10, Jardim Botânico, **T** 021-25400705. *Map 5, A4, p254* Popular bar with Rio's young and good-looking middle classes, who come here to drink foreign beer and be seen. Kicks off after 2130. Live bands and DJs at weekends.

Clan Café, R Cosme Velho 564 (in front of the Corcovado train station), **T** 021-25582322. *Closed Sun-Mon.* *Map 4, north of A1, p252*

Great sit-down *choro* and samba club almost unknown to tourists, with live music and decent bar food.

Cozumel, Av Lineu de Paula Machado 696, Jardim Botânico, **T** 021-22942915. *Map 5, A4, p254* Mexican restaurant, which transforms into a club after about 2200. Free margaritas, tacky music and people, most of whom are looking not to go home alone.

Drink Café, Parque dos Patins, Av Borges de Medeiros 5, Lagoa, **T** 021-22394136. *Map 5, F4 p254* One of the best of the Lagoa Lakeside kiosks playing varied music from MPB to jazz and blues throughout the day and night in the summer. Important artists occasionally play here. Cheap beer and bar food.

Sítio Lounge, R Marquês de São Vicente 10, Gávea, **T** 021-22742226. *Map 5, west of E1, p254* Though decorated with antiques, this is one of very few lounge-style bars in Rio, with DJs on Thursdays and Saturdays, and a wealthy, cocktail-sipping crowd.

Mistura Fina, Av Borges de Medeiros 3207, Lagoa, **T** 021-25372844 *Map 5, F6, p254* Bar, restaurant and live-music venue. The downstairs restaurant piano bar has an excellent happy-hour programme with performances by important Carioca musicians. Upstairs is a smoky, intimate little club.

Rhapsody, Av Epitácio Pessoa 1104, Lagoa, **T** 021-22472104. *Map 5, F6, p254* Piano bar/restaurant with a Brazilian and Diana Krall-style crooning.

00 (Zero Zero), Av Padre Leonel Franca 240, Gávea, **T** 021-25408041. *Map 5, west of F1, p254* Mock-LA bar/restaurant/club with a small outdoor area. Currently the trendiest club in Rio for Brazil's equivalent of Sloanes. Lively and popular gay night on Sunday.

South of Leblon and Tijuca National Park

Pepe, Posto 2, Barra da Tijuca beach. *Map 1, H8, p246* Popular beach bar frequented by toned and tanned surfers.

Nuth, R Armando Lombardi 999, Barra da Tijuca. *Map 1, H8, p246* Barra's slickest club; very mock-Miami and frequented by a mixed crowd of rich kid surfers, footballers (Romario comes here) and women with surgically-enhanced beauty. The music is a mix of tacky Brazilian and Eurotrash with occasional samba funk live acts.

Búzios

In season Búzios nightlife is young, beautiful and buzzing. Out of season it is non-existent. The bulk of the bars and clubs are on Rua das Pedras. **GuapoLoco**, R das Pedras, **T** 022- 26232657, is a Mexican theme bar/restaurant with dancing, and Búzios's main club. **Privelege**, Av José Bento Ribeiro Dantas 550, R Orla Bardot, **T** 022-26230288, www.privilegenet.com.br, is one of Brazil's best European-style dance clubs with pumping techno, house and hip hop and five rooms including sushi bar and lounge. **Ta-ka-ta ka-ta**, R das Pedras 256, is strewn with motorbike parts and H aarleys.

Paraty

The best way to sample Paraty's nightlife is wander its handful of streets around the centre. **Bar Coupé**, Praça da Matriz, **T** 024-33711432, www.barcoupe.com, is a popular hang-out with outside seating, good bar-snacks and breakfast. **Bar Dinho**, Praça da Matriz at R da Matriz, **T** 024-33711790, has a good bar with live music at weekends. **Clube Bandeirantes**, is close to the centre and popular with local people for dancing, entry US$3-5. **Umoya**, R Comendador José Luiz, is a video bar/café, with live music at weekends.

Arts and entertainment

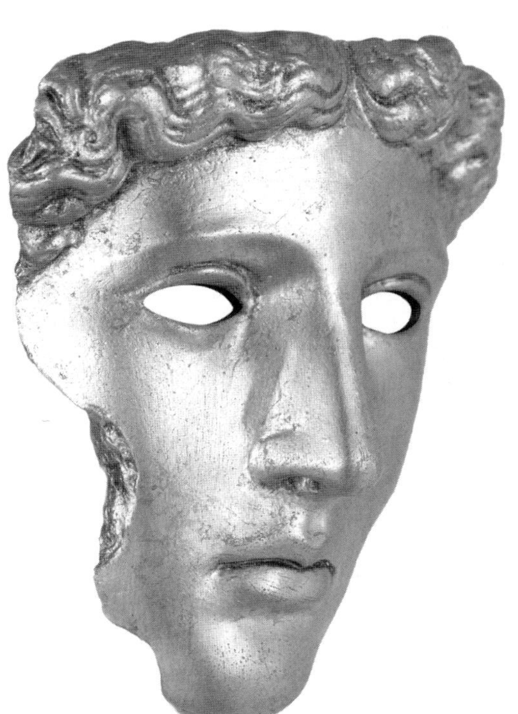

Rio is excellent for live music, with many venues hosting acts playing everything from bossa nova and samba to the new wave of funk and Brazilian rap spilling out from Brazil's vast underclass. There are various music festivals like the annual Rio de Janeiro art rock festival, national Samba Day on December 2nd and New Year's when there are impromptu and organized concerts on all the beaches.

The city has a number of orchestras and internationally respected dance companies who perform regularly in venues in the city centre. The city also hosts a biennial classical music festival showcasing Brazilian and Latin American composers and musicians. The next biennials are due in 2005 and 2007.

As well as a healthy spread of art cinemas and multiplexes, the city boasts one of the best film festivals in Latin America, which usually runs during September or October and showcases a wealth of art-house films from classics to the most recent offerings from Cannes, Venice and Sundance. Many of the latest Brazilian releases are premiered here.

Information on what's on where in Rio can be hard to come by. The Brazilian embassy in London has a useful calendar of events on their site, www.brazil.org.uk. The tourist office website, www.riotur.com.br, has a cultural calendar in English. The weekly *Veja* magazine (in Portuguese) includes an entertainment insert and always keep an eye out for posters advertising events.

Cinema

Nowhere can the disparity between foreign and Brazilian ideas about Rio be seen more clearly than in the city's few appearances on film. Rio has been mythologized in foreign films as exotic, sensual, eternally sunny and largely middle class. These views contrast greatly with Brazilian depictions which tend to be realist and focus on the daily struggle for survival by the poor majority of Cariocas whose samba, football and Carnival form the cultural backbone of the city.

There are cinemas serving subtitled Hollywood and major Brazilian releases in almost all the malls (see page 195). Many of the cultural centres also have cinemas and there are a few screens dedicated to art-house films. The normal seat price is around US$4, discounts on Wednesday and Thursday (students pay half price any day of the week). Other films are shown in the following theatres:

Centro Cultural do Banco do Brasil, R Primeiro de Março 66, Centro, **T** 021-28082020. *Mêtro Uruguaiana.* *Map 6, A3, p256* One of Rio's better arts centres with the best of the art-house films and exhibitions from fine art to photography.

Cinemateca do MAM, Infante Dom Henrique 85, Aterro do Flamengo, **T** 021-22102188. *Map 2, H11, p248* Cinema classics, art films and a good café with live music and views of Guanabara Bay.

Estaçao Ipanema, R Visconde de Pirajá 605, Ipanema. *Map 5, G6, p254* Less mainstream films from Europe, Brazil and the US.

Best

Films set in Rio

- *Black Orpheus* (1959) - the Orpheus myth retold through Carnival in a 1950s Rio *favela*.
- *Bus 174* (2002) - Shocking docu-film about the hijacking of a Rio bus, including real footage.
- *Central Station* (1998) - touching film set in Rio and the northeast.
- *City of God* (2002)- excellent film about gangster life in the *favelas*.
- *Flying down to Rio* (1933) - the film that brought Fred Astaire and Ginger Rogers together.

Music and dance

For further information about Brazilian music and dance genres, see Background, pages 230-231.

Live music

In summer there are free concerts by big-name national and local acts almost every night of the week on Ipanema, Leblon, Flamengo and Copacabana beaches, in Botafogo and at the marina in Glória. In summer, locals bring musical instruments and chairs onto Praia do Vermelha beach in Urca from around 2100 and Gilberto Gil and others frequently play free concerts in the *favelas* – most notably in Rocinha where Gil's wife runs a programme integrating music, art and social improvement. See www.veja-rio.com.br and www.samba-choro.com.br. Aside from these free concerts, the following formal venues have live music. See also Bars and clubs, pages 155-166.

ATL, Shopping Via Parque, Av Ayrton Senna 3000, Barra da Tijuca, **T** 021-3850535. *Map 1, H6, p256* Rio's biggest concert venue, inaugurated in the 1990s by Diana Ross. Plays host to the biggest Brazilian and international acts.

Villa-Lobos – Rio's greatest musical son

One of the many contradictory beauties of Brazil is that while the country as a whole is entrenchantly institutionalized and socially stratified, its best music has always burst forth spontaneously from the various roots of Brazil, and been loved by all. Heitor Villa-Lobos, the country's most distinguished composer once famously stated: 'one foot in the academy and you are changed for the worse'. He went on to change the academy; founding a system of education, still used today which fused classical training with a love and appreciation for popular and traditional musical forms.

Villa-Lobos began his musical career in Rio's cafés; at the turn of the 19th century he could be seen playing the cello in places like Bar Luiz in the city centre. He then secured a place in the Rio Symphony Orchestra where he played under Strauss's baton. By1923, he had won a government grant to study in Paris, a considerable amount of money at the time. Here he composed many of his most famous works. On his return to Brazil, Villa-Lobos founded the Conservatório Nacional de Canto Orfeónico and the Brazilian Academy of Music where he invented and instilled his much revered system of musical education.

Villa-Lobos was a magnetic personality and a Carioca through and through. He wore loud checked shirts, smoked a cigar and was famous for his anecdotes. His music, too, is idiosyncratic, anecdotal, visual and thoroughly Brazilian. *Bachianas Brasileiras* and *Little Caipira Train* are celebrations of daily Brazilian life. *Green Mansions* and *Saudades das Selvas Brasileiras* are dedications to the beauty of the natural landscape. He even wrote a series of *choros* – a musical style which fused Portugal and Africa and which would later produce samba. He died in November 1959, in his beloved Rio de Janeiro. His house is now a museum – see page 66.

Ballroom, R Humaitá 110, Humaitá, **T** 021-25377600, www.ballroom.com.br. *Daily.* *Map 1, F11, p246* A 1,200-seater venue with an eclectic repertoire showcasing cult Brazilian stars like Ed Motta, smaller established artists like Ivan Lins and contemporary and up-and-coming acts like Seu Jorge.

Canecão, Av Venceslau Brás 215, Botafogo, **T** 021-25431241, www.canecao.com.br. *Thu-Sun.* *Map 4, D7, p252* A 3,000-seat venue playing host to important Brazilian acts like João Bosco, Nação Zumbi, Toquinho, Gilberto Gil and Gal Costa.

Casa de Cultura da Universidade Estácio de Sá, Av Érico Veríssimo 359, Barra da Tijuca, **T** 021-24941023, www.casadecultura.estacio.br. *Map 1, H6, p246* Excellent cultural centre with a small concert hall played by up-and-coming names, a theatre (with performances for children) and arts cinema.

Garden Hall, Shopping Barra Garden, Av das Américas 3255, Barra da Tijuca, **T** 021-31513302, www.barragarden.com.br/shows.html. *Map 1, H6, p246* An eclectic programme ranging from kids' theatre to *choro* and samba groups.

Hipódromo Up, Praça Santos Dumont, 108, Gávea, **T** 021-22940095. *Daily.* *Map 1, F11, p* Small, intimate sit-down venue which has played host to distinguished names like Beth Carvalho and now has an eclectic menu including frequent live Samba and pagode.

Teatro Carlos Gomes, Praça Tiradentes, Centro, **T** 021-22328701. *Map 2, D7, p248* An attractive, semi-circular art-deco building, with a programme focusing on MPB and musicals, including the 2003 production of Chico Buarque's *Ópera do Malandro*.

Teatro João Caetanoe, Praça Tiradentes, Centro, **T** 021-22211223. *Map 2, D7, p248* An attractive 19th-century theatre

Best

Rio bars for live music

- **Rio Scenarium**, Lapa - samba, p158
- **Semente**, Lapa - samba and MPB, p160
- **Melt**, Leblon - Brazilian funk and MPB, p163
- **Clan Café**, Cosme Velho - *choro* and samba, p164
- **Mistura Fina**, Lagoa - jazz, bossa nova and samba, p165

playing host to *choro* and samba artists as well as well-respected Brazilian musicians like Sivuca and Egberto Gismonti.

Teatro Rival BR, R Álvaro Alvim 33, Centro, **T** 021-22404469. *Map 2, F9, p248* An eclectic programme of theatre, classical music and high-brow performers like Danilo Caymmi and Airto Moreira.

Toca do Vinicius, R Vinícius de Moraes, 129, Ipanema. *Map 5, G8, p254* Rio's leading bossa nova and *choro* record shop with live concerts from some of the finest past performers, like Carlos Lyra, every Sunday lunchtime in summer

Classical music and dance

Rio's classical music scene is good in parts. Since the move of the capital from Rio to Brasília in the 1960s and the increasing international popularity of bossa nova and Brazilian jazz, there has been little federal support for classical music in Brazil. The Opera Festival in Manuas has helped to raise the profile somewhat and Rio has a number of excellent orchestras, including the Symphony Orchestra and the Rio Philarmonic. The most celebrated operas are Villa-Lobos's *A Floresta do Amazonas*, written shortly before his death for the Brazilian opera star Bidu Sayão, and Antonio Carlos Gomes's Italianate 19th-century works *Fosca* and *O Guarani*.

The Theatro Municipal is home to Rio's ballet company. Sadly, like Brazilian football, ballet loses its greatest dancers to foreign companies. The company regularly perform in the USA and Europe and focus on dance expressions of Brazilian cultural themes like peace and urban violence on the streets of Rio.

Centro Cultural Banco do Brasil, R Primeiro de Março 66, Centro, **T** 021-38082020, www.ccbb.com.br. *Map 6, A3, p256* Varied national and international performances.

Sala Cecília Meireles, Largo da Lapa 47, Lapa, **T** 021-22243913. *Map 2, H9, p248* The city's most important small concert hall featuring traditional classics and chamber music.

Salão Leopoldo Miguez, Escola de Música de UFRJ, R do Passeio 98, Lapa, **T** 021-22401391. *Map 2, G9, p248* Built in 1922 and inspired by the Sala Gaveau in Paris, this important venue has excellent acoustics and holds concerts by distinguished performers.

Sala Maestro Armando Prazeres, Instituto Bennet, R Marquês de Abrantes 55, Flamengo, **T** 021-25260448. *Map 3, J5, p250* A varied programme featuring chamber music and soloists.

Teatro João Caetano, Praça Tiradentes, Centro, **T** 021-22211223. *Map 2, D7, p248* A varied programme including all kinds of music.

Theatro Municipal, Praça Floriano, Centro, **T** 021-22991633, www.theatromunicipal.rj.gov.br. *Map 2, F9, p248* An impressive neo-baroque building holding major concerts. Events are listed on the website. Ticket prices start at about US$10.

! Rio's samba schools are famous for their Carnival celebrations, but they are open all year and are particularly lively at weekends. See Festivals and events, page 182, for further details.

Learning to Brazilian dance

Dance is one of the world's great expanding art forms and pastimes, with salsa (little-known in Brazil) probably being the most popular Latin dance worldwide. Brazil has numerous dance styles which are perhaps even more beautiful and infectious than salsa and involve similar steps over music in 2/4 time. For more information, see www.dancadesalao.com. Many hostels organize dance classes.

Casa de Dança Carlinhos de Jesus, R Alvaro Ramos 11, Botafogo, **T** 021-25416186, www.carlinhosdejesus.com.br. *Map 4, E5, p252* One of the biggest schools teaching Brazilian dance and ballroom.

Dança Jaime Aroxa, R São Clemente 155, Botafogo, **T** 021-25398779, www.jaimearoxa.com.br. *Map 4, C4, p250* Short courses (in Portuguese) on samba, salsa, tango, bolero and waltz.

Escola de Dança de Salão Maria Antonieta, R do Catete 112, Catete (next to Catete Metrô station), **T** 021-25588589, www.dancadesalao.com/escolaantonieta. *Map 3, E5, p250* Evening classes in Brazilian dance, together with tango and salsa.

Theatre

There are about 40 theatres in Rio, presenting a variety of classical and modern performances. These are invariably in Portuguese. Seat prices start at about US$15; some children's theatre is free.

Teatro Espaço, The Puppet Show, R Dona Geralda 327, Paraty, **T** 024-33711575, ecparati@ax.apc.org. Wed, Sat 2100, US$12. This

! Little known to visitors but beloved to cultured Brazilans, SESC centres are spaces devoted to the arts, with fine art and photographic exhibitions, theatre, film and live music. See www.sescrj.com.br for information on forthcoming events.

Black experimental theatre

Abdias do Nascimento was a pioneer in social theatre and in the civil rights movement in Brazil. Born in 1914, his initial dreams of becoming a doctor or an accountant were thwarted by racism. He joined the army, but was expelled after getting into a brawl after being refused entry in a bar – for being black. Inspired by a theatre performance in Peru, he travelled to Buenos Aires to study dramatic arts, returning to Brazil two years later to find he had been sentenced to two years in prison for the bar brawl. He used his time to found a highly successful theatre company and trained himself as a director. Upon his release in 1944, he founded the Black Experimental Theatre Company. At first people laughed at him, but soon eminent white writers started to work for the company. One was Vinicius de Moraes, a poet/diplomat whose play Orfeu da Conçeicao would become a famous film, *Black Orpheus*. Abdias took the title role in the play. As the company grew in reputation, Abdias became a leading political figure in the black rights movement – for which he was exiled in 1968. He returned only in 1982 when he was elected to the Federal Chamber of Deputies.

world-famous puppet show should not be missed. The puppets mime stories, which are funny, sad, even shocking, with incredible realism. The series of short pieces (lasting 1 hour) are works of pure imagination and a moving commentary on the human condition.

Teatro Nelson Rodrigues, Caixa Cultural Centre, Av República do Chile 230, Centro, **T** 021-22628152. *Map 2, D7, p248* Considered to be one of the best stages for theatre and dance in the country.

Festivals and events

During the week of festivities marking the beginning of the traditional privations of Lent the city's poor put on the world's greatest fancy dress party – the themed pageant of Carnival which has become synonymous with Brazil. Activity focuses on the Sambódromo – a purpose-built mock street where the *blocos* parade – each representing a particular theme which often relates to Brazil's history or its current political preoccupations. You have to know what's going on where to enjoy Carnival. Outside the parade and the other organized events – like the masked balls held behind the doors of sweaty clubs and scheduled events like the gay parade in Ipanema – the streets of Rio can be eerily quiet during Carnival week. Rio's New Year's Eve party is the largest in the world and attracts far bigger crowds than Carnival. It also takes place in the city's public spaces. Millions gather on the beaches to see the spectacular fireworks cascade off the skyscrapers and some of Brazil's best bands play free concerts. The Brazilian holiday season links the two – a time replete with spontaneous parties and free concerts.

★ Carnival

Carnival in Rio is as spectacular as its reputation suggests – a riot of colour, flamboyance and artistry unrivalled in the Americas. On the Friday before Shrove Tuesday, the mayor of Rio hands the keys of the city to *Rei Momo*, the Lord of Misrule, signifying the start of a five-day party. Imagination runs riot, social barriers are broken and the main avenues, full of people wearing fancy dress, are colourfully lit. Areas throughout the city, such as the Terreirão de Samba in Praça Onze, are used for shows, music and dancing. And while things can be ghostly quiet in the southern beach zones, spectacularly dressed Carnival groups throng around the Sambódromo (see below), strutting, drumming and singing in preparation for their parade.

Carnival parades

Unlike Salvador, which is still a wild street party, Rio's Carnival is a designated parade. The numerous samba schools in Rio are divided into two leagues before they parade through the Sambódromo. The *Grupo Especial* parade on Sunday and Monday while the *Grupos de Acesso A* and *B* parade on Saturday and Friday respectively. There is also a *mirins* parade (younger members of the established schools) on Tuesday. Judging takes place on Wednesday afternoon and the winners of the various groups parade again on the following Saturday.

Every school comprises 2,500-6,000 participants divided into wings (*alas*) each with a different costume and parading on beautifully-designed floats (*carros alegóricos*). Each school chooses a theme (*enredo*) and composes a song (*samba*) that is a poetic, rhythmic and catchy expression of the theme. A percussion wing (*bateria*) maintains a reverberating beat that must keep the entire school, and the audience, dancing throughout the parade.

Schools are given between 65 and 80 minutes and lose points for failing to keep within this time. Judges award points to each school for components of their procession, such as costume, music and design, and make deductions for lack of energy, enthusiasm or discipline. The winners of the *Grupos de Acesso* are promoted to the next highest group while the losers, including those of the *Grupo Especial*, are relegated to the next lowest group. Competition is intense and the winners gain a monetary prize funded by the entrance fees.

Oscar Niemeyer's Sambódromo and the Carnival Museum

The Carnival parades are the culmination of months of intense activity by community groups, mostly in the city's poorest districts. To understand the traditions of the schools, the meanings of the different parts of the parade and Carnival as a whole, visit the **Museu do Carnaval** (*entrance in R Frei Caneca,* ***T*** *021-5026996, Mon-Fri 1100-1700, free*) in the Sambódromo; although small, it has lots of photographs and the English-speaking staff are very informative. The **Sambódromo** (*R Marquês de Sapucai, Cidade Nova*), is 600 m long with seating for 43,000 people. Designed by Oscar Niemeyer and built in 1983-84, it handles sporting events, conferences and concerts during the rest of the year.

Fancy-dress balls

Rio's *bailes* (fancy-dress balls) range from the sophisticated to the wild. The majority of clubs and hotels host at least one. The **Copacabana Palace Hotel**'s is elegant and expensive, while the **Scala Club** has wild parties. It is not necessary to wear fancy dress; just join in, although the clubs are hot and crowded so don't overdress. The most famous are the **Red & Black Ball** (Friday) and the **Gay Ball** (Tuesday) which are both televised. Venues for these vary.

Tickets

The Sambódromo parades start at 1900 and last about 12 hours; gates open at 1800. There are *cadeiras* (seats) at ground level, *arquibancadas* (terraces) and *camarotes* (boxes). Seats and boxes reserved for tourists have the best view, sectors 4, 7 and 11 are preferred (they house the judging points); 6 and 13 are least favoured (being at the end when dancers might be tired) but have more space. The terraces, while uncomfortable, house the most fervent fans and are the best place to soak up the atmosphere, but it's too crowded to take pictures. Tickets start at US$40 for *arquibancadas* and are sold at travel agencies as well as the **Maracanã Stadium** box office. Tickets should be bought as far as possible in advance – they are usually sold out before Carnival weekend, but touts outside can generally sell you tickets at inflated prices; if you are offered one of these, check its date. Tickets for the champions' parade on the Saturday following Carnival are much cheaper. Many tour companies offer Rio trips which include Carnival, with tickets at rather inflated prices. The nearest Metrô is Praça Onze and this can be an enjoyable ride in the company of costumed samba school members. You can follow the participants to the *concentração*, the assembly and formation on Avenida Presidente Vargas, and mingle with them while they queue to enter the Sambódromo. Ask if you can take photos.

Sleeping and security

Visitors wishing to attend the Carnival are advised to reserve accommodation well in advance. Virtually all hotels raise their prices during Carnival, although it is usually possible to find a room. Your property should be safe inside the Sambódromo, but the crowds outside can attract pickpockets; as ever, don't brandish your camera, and only take the money you need for fares and refreshments (food and drink are sold in the Sambódromo). It gets hot! Wear as little as possible (shorts and a T-shirt).

Taking part: joining a Carnival *bloco* or *banda*

Bandas and *blocos* (organized Carnival groups) can be found in all neighbourhoods, and some of the most popular and entertaining are **Cordão do Bola Preta** (*meets Sat 0900, R 13 de Maio 13,*

Centro), **Simpatia é Quase Amor** (*meets Sun 1600, Praça General Osório, Ipanema*) and the transvestite **Banda da Ipanema** (*meets Tue and Sat 1600, Praça General Osório, Ipanema*). It is necessary to join a *bloco* in advance to receive their distinctive T-shirts, but anyone can join in with the *bandas*.

Most samba schools will accept a number of foreigners and you will be charged upwards of US$125 for your costume; your money helps to fund poorer members of the school. You should be in Rio for at least two weeks before Carnival. It is essential to attend fittings and rehearsals on time, to show respect for your section leaders and to enter into the competitive spirit of the event. For those with the energy and the dedication, it will be an unforgettable experience.

Rehearsals

Ensaios are held at the schools' *quadras* from October onwards and are well worth seeing. It is wise to go by taxi, as most schools are based in poorer districts.

Samba schools and parties

Samba schools hold parties throughout the year, especially at the weekends; these are well worth visiting. Try contacting the following: **Acadêmicos de Salgueiro**, R Silva Teles 104, Andaraí, **T** 021-22385564; **Beija Flor de Nilópolis**, Pracinha Wallace Paes Leme 1025, Nilópolis, **T** 021-27912866; **Imperatriz Leopoldinense**, R Prof Lacê 235, Ramos, **T** 021-22708037; **Mocidade**, Independente de Padre Miguel, R Coronel Tamarindo 38, Padre Miguel, **T** 021-33325823; **Portela**, R Clara Nunes 81, Madureira, **T** 021-33900471; **Primeira Estação de Mangueira**, R Visconde de Niterói 1072, Mangueira, **T** 021- 25674637; **Unidos da Viradouro**, Av do Contorno 16, Niterói, **T** 021-27177540.

Useful information

Carnival week comprises an enormous range of official and unofficial contests and events which reach a peak on the Tuesday.

Riotur's guide booklet and website gives concise information on these in English. The entertainment sections of newspapers and magazines such as *O Globo*, *Jornal do Brasil*, *Manchete* and *Veja Rio* are worth checking. *Liga Independente das Escolas de Samba do Rio de Janeiro*, Felipe Ferreira's Rio Carnival guide, has good explanations of the competition, rules, the schools, a map and other practical details.

Other festivals

January

São Sebastião (20 January) The patron saint of Rio's festival is celebrated with an evening procession. This leaves from Capuchinhos church, Tijuca (in the Zona Norte – not to be confused with Barra da Tijuca), and arrives at the cathedral of São Sebastião. On the same evening, an Umbanda festival is celebrated at the Caboclo Monument in Santa Teresa.

February

Presente de Yemanjá (2 February) An Afro-Brazilian ceremony with flowers and gifts being thrown into the bay after a maritime procession from Praça 15 de Novembro.

Carmen Miranda's birthday (9 February) An exhibition and film show at the museum in Flamengo (see page 60).

Carnival Rio's most famous festival, see page 179 for details. Those looking for something alternative, might like to try Carnival in Paraty, where hundreds of people cover their bodies in black mud and run through the streets yelling like prehistoric creatures (anyone can join in).

March

Foundation Day (1 March) Celebrated with a Mass in the Igreja de São Sebastião.

April

Semana Santa (ending Easter Sunday in March/April) Celebrated with religious processions and folk songs in many cities and towns.

Tiradentes Day (21 April) Civic ceremonies are held in front of the Palácio Tiradentes in Central Rio (see page 33).

May

Labour Day (1 May) Celebrated with cultural and sporting events throughout Rio.

Festa do Divino Espírito Santo (Whitsun) (late May/early June) Celebrated throughout Rio state, but particularly in Paraty.

June

Festas Juninas A series of saint's day festivals which take place throughout Brazil in June, and which have come to be a celebration of *caipira* (or country yokel) life. Girls dress up in billowng skirts and bonnets, couples dance *forró* and even more ultra-sweet cakes and desserts are eaten than usual. In Rio things kick off with the festival of **Santo Antônio** (13 June), when the main event is a Mass, followed by celebrations at the Convento do Santo Antônio and the Largo da Carioca. There is normally some kind of festival somewhere every weekend, reaching full fruition at the festival of

São João on the night of 23-24 June, a major event throughout the country, marked by huge bonfires, even more *forró*, *quadrilha* dancing and Brazilian mulled rum or *quentão* (made with *cachaça* and sugar, spiced with ginger and cinnamon and served hot). The *Festas Juninas* close with the festival of **São Pedro** on 29 June, with boat processions celebrating Peter as the patron saint of fishermen.

July

Semana de Santa Rita (mid-July) Notable in Paraty for its traditional foods, shows, exhibitions and dances.

August

Festival da Pinga (over a weekend in August, Paraty) A three-day festival in honour of blessed cane spirit of Paraty. There is a *cachaça* (distilled liquor made from sugar cane) fair at which local distilleries display their products.

September

Semana da Nossa Senhora dos Remédios (around 8 September) Processions and religious events take place in Paraty.

Rio Film Festival Latin America's premier arts film festival showcasing numerous new Brazilian films alongside choice items from Mumbai, Sundance, Cannes, Berlin, Venice, et al.

October

Nossa Senhora da Penha pilgrimage (12 October) Devotees ascend the steps of this church in the northern suburb of Penha on their knees to pay homage to and petition Our Lady. There are great views from the *balustrade* (see page 87).

Bienal de Música Contemporânea Brasileira Rio's leading classical music festival showcasing leading Brazilian composers and next due in 2005 and 2007.

December

Yemanjá (31 December) Dedicated to the Orixá goddess of the sea, a once African deity which became as Brazilian as capoeira after centuries of evolution in Bahia. Devotees dress in white and gather on Copacabana, Ipanema and Leblon beaches, singing and dancing around open fires and making offerings. The elected Queen of the Sea is rowed along the seashore. At midnight small boats are launched as offerings to Yemanjá. The religious event is dwarfed, however, by **Reveillon** (see below) and many followers of Yemanjá are now making their offerings on 29 or 30 December and at Barra da Tijuca or Recreio dos Bandeirantes to avoid the crowds and noise.

★ **Reveillon** (New Year) By far the biggest street party in Rio, and one of the world's largest gatherings. Several million people pack the sand on Copacabana, dancing to the numerous live bands (which almost always include Jorge Ben) and watching the fireworks spill in waterfalls from the beachfront skyscrapers and shoot into the air from barges out at sea. It is most crowded in front of the Copacabana Palace Hotel. Another good place to see the fireworks is in front of Le Meridien, famous for its fireworks' waterfall at about 10 minutes past midnight.

Shopping

To buy decent souvenirs in Rio you need to go for the upper-price bracket and look to fashion, beachwear, expensive jewellery or designer items for the home. Brazilian beachwear is without doubt the best in the world: confident, elegant, beautifully cut and in wonderful fabrics, and Rio is the place to buy it. All the best brands are from here with the exception of the most famous, Rosa Chá, who are from São Paulo but have a shop in the Fashion Mall. Brazilian high fashion, shoes and household goods are equally as beautiful as the best of Europe or North America at a fraction of the price. They are beginning to get a name for themselves abroad so now is an excellent time to buy. The best buys at the bottom end of the market include Havaiana flip flops, which retail at just over a tenth the price of Europe (and which are an essential beach item), coffee, guaraná powder and CDs. Brazil has one of the largest recording industries in the world and an enormous wealth and diversity of music in its own unique traditions.

Arts and crafts

Artíndia, Museu do Índio (see page 65), R das Palmeiras 55, Botafogo, **T** 021-22868899. *Mon-Fri 0930-1730, Sat-Sun 1300-1700.* *Map 4, C3, p252* Indigenous art from all over Brazil including ceramics, feather *coronas*, masks and carved wooden and stone objects.

Casa de Artesanato do Estado do Rio de Janeiro, R Real Grandeza 293, Botafogo, **T** 021-22867300, www.rioartesanato.com.br. *Mon-Fri 0900-1700.* *Map 4, E3, p252* Arts and crafts from all over Rio state and courses on how to produce them.

Jeito Brasileiro, R Ererê 11A (next to the Corcovado rail terminal), Cosme Velho, **T** 021-22057636. *Mon-Fri 0900-1800, Sat 0900-1600, Sun 0900-1300.* *Map 4, north of A1, p252* Arts, crafts, jewellery and leather items from all over the country, including objects and art made by the Camucim people.

O Sol, R Corcovado 213, Jardim Botânico, **T** 021-22945099, www.artesanato.sol.com.br. *Mon-Fri 0900-1800, Sat 0900-1300.* *Map 5, A3, p254* An NGO promoting arts and crafts from all over the country, with proceeds going to help traditional and indigenous communities. One of the best collections in Rio.

Raiz Forte Produtos da Terra, Av Ataulfo de Paiva 1160, Leblon, **T** 021-22590744. *Mon-Fri 0900-2000, Sat-Sun 0900-1800.* *Map 5, G1, p254* Sacred, traditional and tribal arts and crafts, musical instruments and other objects from all over the country.

Beachwear

Blue Man, Fórum da Ipanema, R Visconde de Pirajá, Ipanema, **T** 021-22474905; also at São Conrado Fashion Mall, **T** 021-

31399986. *Map 5, G5, p254* Bright, young, super-confident and in a range of different fabrics from denim to tassly lycra.

Bum Bum, R Visconde de Pirajá 351, Ipanema, **T** 021-22879951; also at R das Pedras, Búzios, www.bumbum. com.br. *Map 5, G7, p254* Ultra-sexy, bright bikinis and *sungas* for the tanned and toned.

Farm, R das Pedras, Búzios. Elegant and cool beachwear and light clothes for women.

Lenny, São Conrado Fashion Mall, R Visconde de Pirajá 351, Ipanema, **T** 021-22879951; also at R das Pedras, Búzios, www.lenny.com.br. *Map 1, G9, p246* Lenny Niemeyer is widely regarded as Brazil's most sophisticated bikini designer; understated, beautifully cut one pieces and bikinis in unusual prints.

Rosa Chá, São Conrado Fashion Mall, R Visconde de Pirajá 547, Ipanema, **T** 021-33221849, www.rosacha.com.br. *Map 1, G9, p246* The shop of Brazil and the world's most famous beachwear designer, Amir Slama. The bikinis of choice for the likes of Naomi Campbell.

Salinas, São Conrado Fashion Mall, R Visconde de Pirajá 547, Ipanema, **T** 021-22740644; also at R das Pedras, Búzios. *Map 1, G9, p246* Together with Rosa Chá, the most highly regarded Brazilian bikinis on the international scene – small, exquisitely made with great attention to detail.

Bookshops

Livraria Antiquário, R 7 de Setembro 207, Centro, **T** 021-22214746. *Map 2, D7, p248* Cheap second-hand books with a handful of non-Portuguese titles. There are many other second-hand bookshops on Avenida Marechal Floriano and in the city centre.

Livraria Kosmos, R do Rosário 155, Centro, **T** 021-22248616, www.kosmos.com.br. *Mon-Fri 1000-1800.* *Map 2, C8, p248* Rare and antique books; with an online search and purchase facility.

Livraria da Travessa, Many branches throughout town, including R Primeiro de Março 66, Centro **T** 021-38082066; Av Rio Branco 44, Centro, **T** 021-22538949; R Visconde de Pirajá 462, Ipanema, **T** 021-22538949; and R Visconde de Pirajá 572, Ipanema, **T** 021-32059002, www.travessa.com.br. All kinds of books including art, photography, local interest, international titles, CDs and magazines, tasteful cards and postcards.

Livraria Leonardo da Vinci, Av Rio Branco 185, Centro, **T** 021-2533223; also at R Conde de Bernadotte 26, Leblon, www.leonardodavinci.com.br. *Map 2, E9, p248* Well-established, serious bookshop with an excellent range of titles. Voted the best bookshop in Rio by the *Jornal do Brasil* newspaper.

Livraria Renovar, R Visconde de Pirajá 273, Ipanema, **T** 021-22874080, www.editorarenovar.com.br. *Mon-Fri 1000-1900.* *Map 5, G7, p254* Law books upstairs and a selection of interesting intellectual books downstairs, including titles on Rio art and architecture. Nice little a/c café for browsing with a coffee.

Design and homeware

Inter Studio Arquitetura e Design, R Visconde de Pirajá 595F, Ipanema, **T** 021-25111237. *Mon-Fri 1000-1900, Sat 1000-1400.* *Map 5, G5, p254* Wooden, ceramic, horn, glass and metal objects and small sculptures by various Brazilian designers.

Contemporâneo Moda and Design, R Visconde de Pirajá 437, Ipanema, **T** 021-22876204. *Mon-Sat 0900-2000.* *Map 5, G6, p254* Many of the best fashion labels including Alexandre Herchovitch and Fause Hauten alongside homeware designers such as the Campana Brothers and Filomena Blum.

Rio Design Center, Av Ataulfo de Paiva 270, Leblon, **T** 021-32069100; also at Av das Américas 7770, Barra da Tijuca, **T** 021-24619999, www.riodesign.com.br. *Mon-Fri 1000-2000, Sat 1000-2000, Sun 1500-2100.* *Map 5, G3, p254* All manner of homeware, interior decoration and design miscellany from Brazillian and international names.

Fashion

Alice Capella, R das Pedras, Búzios. Very sexy sophisticated dresses, skirts and tops. This is their only shop in Brazil.

Alice Tapajós, São Conrado Fashion Mall, São Conrado, **T** 021-33220833. *Map 1, G9, p246* Casual, feminine and sensual women's wear from a designer with an international name who has been famous on the Rio fashion scene for more than 25 years.

Andrea Saletto, R Nascimento Silva 244, Ipanema, **T** 021-25225858; also at São Conrado Fashion Mall. *Map 5, G7, p254* One of the most sophisticated women's labels in elegant and low- profile classic cuts in light and tropical fabrics like cotton, linen and silk.

Carlos Tufvesson, R Nascimento Silva 304, Ipanema, **T** 021-25239200, www.carlostufvesson.com. *Mon-Fri 1000-1900, Sat 1000-1400.* *Map 5, G6, p254* Beautiful handmade evening wear in lush fabrics from one of the bright young things of the Rio fashion world.

Clube Chocolate, São Conrado Fashion Mall, São Conrado, **T** 021-33220937; also at Rio Sul Shopping Centre. *Map 1, G9, p246* One of the most coveted women's labels within Brazil alongside high fashion names from Europe (such as Prada) in a smart shop selling design books and miscellany. Great café.

Frankie Amaury, São Conrado Fashion Mall, São Conrado, **T** 021-33220937. *Map 1, G9, p246* Stylish leather jackets for both sexes.

Gilson Martins, R Visconde de Pirajá 462B, **T** 021-22276178. *Map 5, G6, p254* Funky handbags in all sort of shapes and sizes – from Sugar Loaf mountain to footballs.

Maria Bonita, R Aníbal de Mendonça 135, Ipanema, **T** 021-25405354; also at Rio Sul and Barra Shopping Centres. *Map 5, G5, p254* Impeccably cut, elegantly simple, sophisticated women's wear in high-quality fabrics from one of the oldest labels in Rio.

Tenda, R das Pedras, Búzios. A little boutique with many Brazilian designers, including the supermodels's bikini choice – Rosa Chá.

Jewellery

Antonio Bernardo, R Garcia d'Ávila 121, Ipanema, **T** 021-25127204. *Map 5, G5, p254* Other branches at R Visconde de Pirajá 351 and São Conrado Fashion Mall, www.antoniobernardo.com. *Mon-Fri 1000-2000.* Brazil's foremost jeweller, who has been making beautifully understated jewellery with contemporary designs for nearly 30 years. Internationally acclaimed but available only in Brazil and Miami.

Markets

Babilônia Feira Hype, Jockey Club, R Jardim Botânico 971, **T** 021-22670066, www.babiloniahype.com.br. *Sat-Sun. Map 5, D2, p254* Quirky, hippy and second-grade art, fashion and home decoration to the backdrop of street musicians and belly dancers.

Feira Cultural da Fotografia & Imagem, Museu da República garden, R do Catete 153, Catete, **T** 021-25586350. *Last Sun of every month.* *Map 3, E5, p250* Photographers free-for-all with exhibitions, workshops, slide shows, and equipment and work for sale.

Feira Nordestina, Centro Luiz Gonzaga de Tradições Nordestinas, Campo de São Cristóvão, São Cristóvão, **T** 021-38609976, www.feiradesaocristovao.com.br. *Fri-Sun 1000-2300.* *Map 1, D10, p246* 32 sq km of handicrafts, food stalls, performance arts, live bands and suchlike devoted entirely to the culture of northeastern Brazil.

Hippy Fair, Praça General Osório, Ipanema. *Sun 0900-1800* *Map 5, G9, p254*; also **Hippy Fair II**, *Map 2, C11, p248* Praça 15 de Novembro, Centro. *Tue, Fri 0800-1800.* Poor quality artisan products chocolate-box art, bric-a- brac and the occasional real find - look out for the favela houses and lion's heads made out of rope.

Lapa Antiques Fair, R do Lavradio, Lapa. *Sat 0900-1600.* *Map 2, G7, p248* Rio's most entertaining market, filled with colourful characters, weird and wonderful bric-a-brac from old gramophones to 1940s cars and people dancing tango in the streets.

SEBRAE Artisan Market, Shopping Casino Atlântico, Av Atlântica 4240, Copacabana, **T** 021-25272380. *Sat 1100-1900.* *Map 4, G8, p252* Small artisan and jewellery market with everything from perfumed soaps to hippy seed jewellery and sand paintings.

Music

Modern Sound Música Equipamentos, R Barata Ribeiro 502D, Copacabana, **T** 021-25485005. *Map 4, H5, p252* A large selection of Brazilian music, jazz and classical.

Toca do Vinicius, R Vinicius de Moraes 129, **T** 021-2475227, www.tocadovinicius.com.br. *Map 5, G8, p254* A haven for *choro*, samba and bossa nova lovers, with CDs, books, memorabilia and Sunday lunchtime concerts from the likes of Carlos Lyra.

Photography

Processing film and having prints made from digital images in Brazil is good value. Print film is about the same price as in Europe or the USA. Slide film is far more expensive and can be difficult to find. Camera equipement can be twice as expensive as in the US and half as much again as in the UK.

Flash Studio, R Visconde de Pirajá 156, Ipanema, **T** 021-25222518. *Map 5, G9, p254* Expensive but high quality and cheaper than the equivalent in Europe or the USA.

Mecánica de Precisão, R da Conceição 31, shop 202. *Map 2, C7, p248* Camera repair service.

Shoes and bags

Lenny and Companía, R Garcia d'Avila 56, Ipanema, **T** 021-25122170; also at São Conrado Fashion Mall, São Conrado, **T** 021-24221283. *Map 5, G5, p254* Beautiful Italian inspired-shoes and bags.

Victor Hugo, Victor Hugo Visconde de Pirajá 507, Ipanema, **T** 021-22599699, www.victorhugo.com.br. *Map 5, G5, p254* Brazil's answer to Louis Vuitton and equally as stylish.

Shopping centres

Barra Garden, Av das Américas 3255, Barra da Tijuca, **T** 021-31513367, www.barragarden.com.br. *Mon-Sat 1000-2200, Sun*

1500-2100. Map 1, H6, p256 Medium-sized general shopping centre with a day spa and concert hall but no cinema.

Botafogo Praia Shopping, Praia de Botafogo 400, Botafogo, **T** 021-25599880, www.botafogopraia.com.br. *Mon-Sat 1000-2200, Sun 1500-2100. Map 4, A6, p252* Six floors of general shops and restaurants with one of the most modern cinemas in Rio.

Gávea Shopping, R Marquês de São Vicente 52, Gávea, **T** 021-22749896, www.shoppinggavea.com.br. *Mon-Sat 1000-2200, Sun 1500-2100. Map 5, D1, p254* Mid- to upper-range fashion, a couple of reasonable bookshops, restaurants, cafés and cinemas.

Gávea Trade Center, R Marquês de São Vicente 124, Gávea, **T** 021-22395217, www.gaveatrade.com.br. *Mon-Fri 1000-2200, Sat 1000-2100. Map 5, E0, p254* A good selection of mid-range shops.

Barra Shopping & New York City Center, Av das Américas 5000, Barra da Tijuca, **T** 021-24324980, www.nycc.com.br. *Mon-Fri 1000-2200, Sun 1500-2200. Map 1, H6, p246* Large shopping centre and adjacent entertainment complex, lots of surf shops and one of the city's best multiplex cinemas.

São Conrado Fashion Mall, Estrada da Gávea 899, São Conrado, **T** 021-30830000. *Daily 1000-2200. Map 1, G9, p246* The most upmarket shopping centre in Rio, with many of the country's better designers and a string of the standard top-end international labels either in their own shops or stores like **Chocolate**. Four cinemas and a decent restaurant and café (both in the Chocolate boutique).

Rio Sul Shopping Center, R Lauro Müller 116, Botafogo, **T** 021-25457279. *Mon-Sat, 1000-2200, Sun 1500-2100. Map 4, E7, p252* Large, mid-range shopping centre with a few upper-end labels and a decent cinema.

Sports

Two sports dominate Rio de Janeiro life – football (*futebol*) and volleyball (*vôlei*). Both are played on the city's beaches with astonishing skill and dexterity, and both are afforded quasi-religious status. Questioning whether Brazil are the best in the world at either is just about the worst offence a foreigner can commit, short of mistaking Ayrton Senna for an Argentinian.

Another sport you are likely to come across, when wandering through the streets of Rio, is capoeira. This is the most spectacular of all martial arts with huge, muscular men stripped to the waist and spinning around each other with impossible speed and accuracy in front of a clapping, circular crowd. It is the only sport to have originated in the Americas. Almost all of Brazil's hostels offer capoeira classes and many hotels will be able to recommend an instructor.

Aside from these there are plenty of other sporting activities on offer in the city, from diving to surfing, rock climbing, sea kayaking and hang-gliding. See also tours, page 26.

Cycling

Rio Bikers, R Domingos Ferreira 81, Urca, **T** 021-22745872. Bike hire and road bike tours. See also tours, page 27.

Diving

The Atlantic coast of Rio de Janeiro state has some of the best diving in the country. The best sites are around Arraial do Cabo and Búzios where cold and warm currents meet just off the coast; marine life is abundant and there is a high concentration of wrecks. Expect to see schools of tropical and subtropical reef fish like batfish and butterfly fish; dolphins are frequent visitors. The best visibility is between November and May, between 8 and 15 m. Water temperature is always below 20°C. All the agencies listed below are PADI members.

Mar Azul, R das Pedras 275, Centro, Búzios, **T** 022-26234354. Organize dives all around Búzios and Arraial do Cabo – a short drive away.

Ocean Centro de Mergulho, Pousada Sankay, Ilha Grande, **T** 021-25577037. Diving and snorkelling around Ilha Grande and the islands in the bay.

Diver's Quest, R Maria Angelica 171, shop 110, Jardim Botânico, **T** 021-22862513. Courses up to instructor level and trips throughout Brazil.

Football

The most important games, including most of the internationals, are held in the world's largest football stadium, **Maracanã** (see page 85). Most hotels and hostels will be able to tell you when

'Todo o mundo tenta mas so Brasil e penta' (The whole world tries but only Brazil has won five times.)

For those who don't know, Brazil have won the World Cup five times, most recently in 2002. Many of Brazil's football heroes were, and are, Cariocas. Leônidas da Silva, known to Brazilians as 'Homen Borracha', invented the bicycle kick and was the first player to put Brazilian football on the map with a series of stunning goals in the 1938 World Cup in France. Although Brazil didn't win the cup, Leônidas was voted player of the tournament and received a hero's welcome on his return. Until that point, football had been a white Brazilian's game; Leônidas's fame made him an icon for the poor and marginalized black community and the *favelas* went football crazy. Many of Brazil's stars have come from poor, lower to middle-class backgrounds: Garrincha, the inventor of the banana shot, was born a cripple but won two World Cup winner's medals; Jairzinho, Brazil's greatest ever winger; and most recently Romário and Ronaldo, who still live in the city.

Rio's football teams have a pedigree to equal the city's players. *Flamengo* (with red and black hoops), *Botafogo* (with a white star on a black background), *Fluminense* (tricolour stripes) and *Vasco da Gama* (white with a diagonal black stripe) have long and distinguished histories and numerous national and international trophies to their names. The football season begins in mid-January, with the hotly contested *Rio de Janeiro-São Paulo* tournament; the final is held in early March. Next comes the *Campeonato Carioca* (the state championships). Carioca teams also contest the *Copa do Brasil*, the pan-continental *Copa Libertadores da América* and, at the end of the season, the *Campeonato Brasileiro* national championship, which begins in August and has its final in December.

there is an important game. Many offer tours which are far more expensive than a do-it-yourself trip. Turn up a good three hours before the game to see all the samba and pre-game activity.

For information on games and championships contact the **Confederação Brasileira de Futebol**, R da Alfândega 70, Centro, **T** 021 25095937, http://cbfnews.aol.com.br.

Golf

Gávea Golf Club, Estrada da Gávea 800, São Conrado, **T** 021-33224141, www.gaveagolfclub.com.br. Beautiful setting, par 68, 18 holes, four of which run along the beach.

Itanhangá Golf Club, Estrada da Barra, Barra da Tijuca, **T** 021-24942507, www.itanhanga.com.br. 18-hole and nine-hole courses, visiting cards available from Av Rio Branco 26, 16th floor.

Petrópolis Country Club, Nogueira, **T** 024-22212169. Nine holes, wide fairways, approachable club.

Teresópolis Golf Club, Av Presidente Roosevelt 2222, Teresópolis, **T** 021-27421691, closed Monday. 18 holes, illuminated for night play.

Hang-gliding

Just Fly, T/F 021-22680565, www.justfly.com.br. US$80 for tandem flights with licensed instructors from Pedra Bonita out over the southern beaches. Views are spectacular. There are flights all year but the best thermals occur between September and December. The best time of day is between 1000 and 1500.

Rio by Jeep, T 021-96938800, www.riobyjeep.com. Tandem flight tours above Rio from Pedra Bonita with licensed instructors.

Rio's surf beaches

BB Beach Break; **PB** Point Break; **RB** Reef Break; **SB** Shore Break; **R&L** Right and Left. Wave heights are given in feet.

Rio de Janeiro city

Ipanema: hollow, not much shape, BB, R&L, 1-5 ft.
Copacabana: posto 5, needs a big swell, water can be dirty, SB, R&L.
Arpoador: breaks next to the rocks, gets good, the beach is illuminated making night surfing possible, BB, L, 1-8 ft.
Canto de Leblon: big swell, gets good, a wave breaks next to the rocks, PB, R&L.
Leblon: hollow next to the breakwater, BB, R&L, 1-5 ft.
São Conrado: BB, R&L, 1-5 ft.
Barra da Tijuca: 18 km-long beach with sand banks, closes out when big, BB, R&L, 1-5 ft.

West of Barra da Tijuca

Follow Avenida Estrado da Cunabara, a continuation of Av Lucio Coasta, the main coastal road that runs from the Zona Sul to Barra.
Recreio dos Bandeirantes: the next beach after Barra, breaks by a rock a few metres from shore, can handle some size when other spots close out, BB, R&L, 2-8 ft.
Macumba: next beach after Recreio, BB, R&L, 1-4 ft.
Prainha: next beach after Macumba, wild and good, BB, R&L, 1-8 ft.
Grumari: next beach after Prainha, just round the headland, BB, R&L, 1-7 ft.
Barra da Guaratiba: around the headland from Prainha, river mouth, perfect and powerful waves in the right conditions, BB, L, 2-5 ft.
Ilha Grande: *Lopes Mendes*: two-hour walk from Abraão; Aventureiro: 4 km from Provetá village in the Biological Reserve; permission is required from Ibama (see page 28) to surf the Leste and Sul beaches. BB, R&L, 1-4 ft.

Rio de Janeiro state, east of Niterói

The following beaches are all east of Rio along Estrada Amaral Peixoto, the coastal road which leaves Niterói to the southeast and hugs the Atlantic all the way to Búzios. Look out for signs to Inoã and Maricá.

Niterói: Itaipu: BB, R&L, 1-5ft; Itacoatiara: BB, R&L, 1-6 ft,

Maricá, 60 km east of Rio, the first of the surf beaches, mostly pounding SBs.

Ponta Negra: 15 km beyond Maricá, BB, R&L, 1-6 ft

Jacone: 12 km beyond Ponta Negra, breaks on submerged rocks outside the shore break, powerful, short and shallow, R&L, RB, 1-5 ft

Saquarema: one of the larger towns between Niterói and Búzios, 11 km beyond Jacone, the best surfing spot in the state. Cold, open seas with consistent crashing waves of up to 10 ft. Frequent national and state championships are held here. Two beaches: *Vila* next to the rocks in town, BB, L, 1-8ft and *Itaúna*, 2 km north of the town. When big it breaks L behind the rocks and can be heavy, BB, R&L, 1-12 ft.

Massambaba: a long stretch of deserted beach between Saquerama and Arraial de Cabo, BB, R&L, 1-6 ft.

Arraial do Cabo: little beach resort 66 km beyond Saquarema, on the point south of Cabo Frio where the coast turns to the east and the northernmost point with a big, head-on swell. Several beaches, including Praia Grande; at the eastern end of Massambaba beach, 2 km out of Arraial town, BB, R&L, 1-6 ft.

Cabo Frio: resort town just south of Búzios, 15 minutes' walk north of town; naturist beach, cold water, BB, R&L, 1-5 ft. Fogete, 4 km south of town, BB, R&L, 1-5 ft. Pero, 7 km north of town, BB, R&L, 1-5 ft.

Búzios: Geribá, 3½ km south of the centre, BB, R&L, 1-5 ft. Brava, 2 km east, BB, R&L, 1-5 ft.

Horse racing

Jockey Club Racecourse, Praça Santos Dumont 131, Gávea, **T** 021-22591596. Meetings are on Monday and Thursday evenings, and at the weekend at 1400. Long trousers required, a table may be booked. Take any bus marked 'via Jóquei'. Betting is by tote only, entrance US$1-2.

Horse riding

Hípico Brasileiro, Av Borges de Medeiros 2448, Jardim Botânico, **T** 021-25278090. The premier stadium and training centre for horse riding (including Olympic and modern pentathlon) in Rio. Beautifully situated under the gaze of the Corcovado Christ and next to the Lagoa.

Parachuting

Barra Jumping, Aeroporto de Jacarepaguá, Av Ayrton Senna 2541, **T** 021-33252494, www.barrajumping.com.br. Tandem flights from one of the few agencies with accreditation from the Associação Brasileira de Vôo Livre.

Paragliding

From Leblon beach with Señor Ruy Marra, a Brazilian paragliding champion (US$75), **T** 021-33222286, or find him at the beach most days in high season.

Rock climbing and hiking

ECA, Av Erasmo Braga 217, room 305, **T** 021-22426857. Spectacular beginner and intermediate climbs on Sugar Loaf and Rio's other inselbergs with a personal guide US$100 per day. The owner, Ralph, speaks English.

Rio Hiking, R Coelho Neto 70/401, Laranjeiras, **T** 021- 97210594, www.riohiking.com.br. A full range of adventure tours including rock climbs on Sugar Loaf, a range of medium and long walks in the Tijuca National Park and around the Pedra da Gávea. Full-day tours are around $40. Excellent English.

Clube Excursionista Carioca, R Hilário Gouveia 71, Room 206, **T** 021-22551348. A climbing club that meets every Wednesday and Friday. Recommended for enthusiasts.

Sailing

For information on yachting in Rio, contact **Federação Brasileira de Vela e Motor**, R Alcindo Guanabara 15, Centro, **T** 021-22203738; or the **Federação de Vela**, Praça Mahatma Gandhi 2, 12th floor, **T** 021-22208785.

Surfing

Brazilians took up surfing in the 1930s and from the outset women were surfing alongside men. The country has several representatives in the world's top 50 surfers for both sexes, and there are almost as many surfers in Brazil as there are beach volleyball players. Rio does not have the breaks that can be found further south on Santa Catarina island, but there is decent, though not outstanding, surf on the city's ocean beaches as well as to the south and the north of the metropolitan area, in Rio de Janeiro state. Swells are largest between June and October, with waves up to 12 feet . Water temperature drops to 18°C so you will need a wetsuit. Surf schools include:

Escola de Surf Rico, Av Sernambetiba, Posto 4, in front of the Hotel Sheraton Barra, Barra da Tijuca, **T** 021-33283016.

Escolinha de Surf Paula Dolabella, Av Vierira Souto, Ipanema, in front of R Maria Quitéria, **T** 021-22592320.

Swimming

Rio's bay beaches are a disgrace and what was once the world's most beautiful natural harbour is now filthy. Stay away from the water anywhere north of Copacabana. Even Copacabana is now too dirty for swimming. And whilst Arpoador, Ipanema and Leblon are by no means pristine, they are clean enough for swimming. The cleanest beaches in the metropolitan area are in Niterói, Barra da Tijuca or Recreio dos Bandeirantes. There is often a strong undertow on all these beaches; children and weak swimmers should be very careful. There are better beaches within Rio state, at Búzios (see page 94), Paraty (see page 107) and Ilha Grande (see page 103).

Volleyball

Brazil's men and women have consistently been in the top three in world rankings over the past few years in court volleyball, and in the top two for beach volleyball, which is played with fewer players and fewer clothes on almost every beach in Rio. The first beach volleyball world championships were held on Ipanema in 1987. It is possible to watch or participate in a game on Copacabana between Rua Paula Freitas and Hilário de Gouveia, in front of the Rio Internacional Hotel, and on Ipanema and Leblon, in front of Postos 10 and 11.

Gay and lesbian

Being gay in Brazil is difficult for many – this is still a macho Latin culture, particularly outside the main cities. While Carnaval may look outrageously camp to foreigners, it's not a gay event, rather a celebration of samba in which the dressing-up has been taken to another dimension. Gay life in Brazil is inseparable from the economic realities of this wonderful, but economically disadvantaged, nation and this manifests itself in sexual tourism, AIDS and poor but street-smart guys picking up foreigners in the hope of a passport to somewhere better.

By European standards, Rio's clubs and bars are tame and unimpressive with bad music and small venues – a cheaper copy of the decadence now available to the pink pound or pink dollar at home. *Le Boy* and *La Girl* in Copacabana are examples of both. If you want to dance you're better looking out for the one-off club nights in Lapa or elsewhere. These are not fixed occurences – buy Rio's Globo newspaper for daily listings or visit a website like www.riogayguide.com (a predictable guide in English) or www.cenacarioca.com.br and others in Portuguese.

The main gay beach is in Ipanema – look for the rainbow flags – and apart from the views out to sea and the islands beyond, the landscape on the beach is equally awe-inspiring. When you're beached-out, late afternoon or early evening, take a short stroll up Rua Farme de Ameado and look out for Bofetada at number 87 on the left; a nice authentic bar open to the street and great for a first *Caipirinha* with *Bolinhos de Bacalhau*. It attracts a mix of the Ipanema beach crowd and is friendly, tip the waiters.

Saunas are plentiful in Rio as elsewhere but those that cater for tourists come with the full complement of rent-boys and tricks to part you from your money. If you indulge, protect yourself and be savvy!

Gay cafés, bars and restaurants

Blue Angel, R Júlio de Castilhos 15B, Copacabana, **T** 021-25132501. *Map 5, G11, p254* A combination of gay and lesbian cultural and social centre and restaurant bar, with food and beer alongside live music, DJs, theatrical performances, cinema (with screenings of Carmen Miranda and Edith Piaf classics) and transvestite cabarets. Gay night Wednesday.

Bofetada, R Farme de Amoedo 87A, Ipanema, **T** 021-22271676. *Map 5, G8, p254* Bar and café, good for people-watching. Mixed environment, also popular with students. Gay night Sunday.

Fork, R Teixeira de Melo 30, Ipanema, **T** 021-22879300. *Map 5, H9, p254* Little bar restaurant which serves as a popular meeting point for the upper-middle-class Zona Sul gay scene. The menu comprises simple comfort food - pasta, generous sandwiches (roast beef with Dijon mustard, tomato and watercress) and a variety of desserts.

Maxim's Café, Av Atlântica 1850, Copacabana, **T** 021-22557444. *Map 4, H6, p252* Located in a gay-friendly area; transvestites and hustlers are part of the scene.

Nightclubs

The Copa, R Aires Saldanha 13A, Copacabana, **T** 021-22567412. *Map 5, E12, p254* 1960s-style lounge-bar with reasonable cocktails and good looking staff. Three dance floors, live Djs. Gay nights Tuesday and Wednesday.

Dama de Ferro, R Vinicius de Moraes 288, Ipanema, **T** 021-22472330. *Map 5, F8, p254* Predictable bar/club with lounge and dance floor, uninspiring music. Gay night Friday.

Galeria Café, R Teixeira de Melo 31, Ipanema, **T** 021-25233250, *Map 5, H9, p254* Another predictable bar/club with uninspiring music. Live DJs and dance parties. Gay night Thursday.

Incontrus (Inc.), Praça Serzedelo Correa15, Copacabana, **T** 021-25496498. *Map 4, south of H5, p252* Recently renovated and the only gay bar/club open every night of the week. Drag-shows during the week after 0100. Best on Sunday.

La Girl, R Raul Pompéia 102, Copacabana, T21-22478342. *Map 5, G11, p254* Tacky, small lesbian club with lousy music – but it's pretty much the only one Rio has. Gay night Monday.

Le Boy, R Raul Rompéia 102, Copacabana, **T** 021-25134993. *Map 5, G11, p254* Popular gay club open Tuesday to Sunday, and Monday during summer. Capacity for 1,100 people, go-go boys, drag-shows on weekdays, and special attractions or guest Djs. Gay nights Tuesday and Saturday.

Zero Zero (**00**) R Padre Leonel França 240, Gávea, **T** 021-25408041. *Map 5, E0, p254* One of the city's trendiest, mock-LA bars. Plays hip hop and house. Gay night Sunday.

Kids

Brazilians love children and make a great deal of fuss over them. Expect your little one to be the most popular member of the family by far, and to be greeted at every turn with countless coos and exclamations of 'Que bonitinho!!' or 'Que fofo!!'; which are roughly translated as 'How sweet/ cute/gorgeous'. Kids are welcome everywhere at any time. Most restaurants have high chairs available. Some shops even have pushchairs. And most children love Rio – especially on the cable car up the Sugar Loaf, a helicopter around Corcovado and at the beach (though beware of the strong rip currents when swimming). There is a designated toddler play area at the beach in Leblon – the Baixo Baby, which is kitted out with all manner of free toys. Most of the museums are rather stuffy for kids and have few interactive displays.

Attractions

Espaço Cultural da Marinha, Av Alfredo Agache on the waterfront, **T** 021-21046025. *Map 2, B10, p248* Popular with kids for its museum of underwater archaeology and navigation. See page 53 for further details.

Jardim Zoológico, Av Dom Pedro II, Quinta da Boa Vista, São Cristovão, **T** 021-25692024. *Tue-Sun 1000-1600, $2. From central Rio, take the Metrô to São Cristovão and follow signs to the Quinta da Boa Vista Par (a 5-min walk). Map 1, D10, p246* The zoo is in the northeast corner of the park. A smart modern zoo with a collection of 2100 animals almost all of whom are kept in modern, spacious enclosures. Only the Asian elephant and larger carnivores look forlorn. The zoo has an important captive breeding programme for golden and golden -headed lion tamarins, spectacled bears and yellow-throated capuchin monkeys. The aviary is impressive. Children can enjoy a ride in a little train throughout the park.

Museu do Indio, R das Palmeiras 55, **T** 021-22868899. *Map 4, C3, p252* Kids here can daub themselves in body paint and stick on transfers and there are *malocas* (indigenous long houses) through which they can romp and crawl. See page 65, for further details.

Planetario, R Padre Leonel França 240, Gávea. **T** 021-22740096. *Map 5, E0, p254* Small planetarium with shows for children and adults, giving guided observations of the stars. See page 74 for further details.

Rio Water Planet, Estrada dos Bandeirantes 24000, Recreio dos Bandeirantes, **T** 021 24289000, www.riowaterplanet.com. *Sat-Sun 1000-1700, $12. Take a bus to Recreio dos Bandeirantes and a taxi from there. Public transport is poor. Map 1, G1, p246* Large water park with shows and events sitting at the base of one of Rio's

Best

Kids' activities in Rio

- Taking the tram ride from Santa Teresa, p 62.
- Visiting the Museu do Indio, p65.
- Playing on the beach at Ipanema, p70.
- Going up the cog railway to Corcovado, p77.
- Taking the ferry to Niterói, p91.

spectacular boulder mountains. The rides, which include white water toboggans, slides and wave machines, are sculpted into the natural landscape.

Santa Teresa tram, *station next to the Cathedral or from Cinelândia.* *Map 2, F8, p248* The tram speeds across the Arcos de Lapa aquaduct and up through the winding, cobbled streets for a fantastic view of Rio.

Terra Encantada theme park , Av Ayrton Senna 2800, Barra da Tijuca, next to Via Parque Shopping Mall, **T** 021-4219444, www.terra-encantada.com.br. High season (Jan and July 8-Aug 1st): Tue-Sat 1400-2200, Sun 1200-2200 (last ride at 2100). Low season: Thu-Sat 1400-2100 , Sun 1200-2100, $8. *Any bus passing along the main road from the Zona Sul to Barra will leave you here. The theme park is next to the Via Parque Shopping Mall.* *Map 1, G5, p246* A 300,000 sq m theme park in Barra with attractions based on Brazil's diverse cultural heritage: indigenous, African and European. These include roller coasters, river rapids, a cinema and shows. Rides close at 2200. There are bars, restaurants and nightspots on the main street.

Wet'n' Wild Rio, Av das Americas 22000, **T** 021-4289300. *Daily Sep-May 1000-1900, $10. Take a bus to Recreio dos Bandeirantes and a taxi from there. Public transport is poor.* *Map 1, H0, 246* US style water theme park with loads of long slides, rides and other such fun.

Directory

Airline offices

Aerolineas Argentinas, Antonio Carlos Jobim Airport, **T** 021-22103121; **Air Canada**, Av Amte Barroso 63, **T** 021-22205343; **Air France**, Av Presidente Antonio Carlos 58, **T** 021-25323642; **Alitalia**, Av Presidente Antonio Carlos 58, **T** 021-25242544; **American Airlines**, Av Pres Wilson 165, **T** 021-25329367, and in the Copacabana Palace Hotel (see page 115); **Avianca**, Av Pres Wilson 165, **T** 021-22404413; **British Airways**, Antonio Carlos Jobim Int Airport, **T** 021-33983888; **Continental Airlines**, R da Assembleia 10, **T** 021-25311142; **Delta Air Lines**, R Ouvidor 161, **T** 021- 25067552; **Iberia**, Av Pres Antonio Carlos 51, **T** 021-22821336; **KLM**, Av Rio Branco 311, **T** 021-25247744; **Lan Chile**, R da Assembleia 92, **T** 021-22209722; **Lufthansa**, Av Rio Branco 156, **T** 021-36875000; **Pluna**, Antonio Carlos Jobim Int Airport, **T** 021-33982454; **United Airlines**, Av Pres Antonio Carlos 51, Centro, **T** 021-38041200; **Varig**, Av Rio Branco 277, Centro, **T** 021-22203821, also at R Visconde de Piraja 351, Ipanema; **VASP**, R Sta Luzia 735-B, **T** 021-38148079, also at R Visconde de Piraja 444, Inpanema.

Banks and ATMs

Banks are open weekdays from 1000-1600 and closed on weekends and public holidays. Visa and American Express are the most widely used. Cash points (ATMs) can be found almost everywhere, but are usually closed after 2200, although the machines at both airports run for 24 hours. The most reliable banks for international Visa cards are **Banco 24 horas** and **Bradesco**. Traveller's cheques can be exchanged in most banks but expect to wait at least 30 minutes.

Bicycle hire

Although there are no designated bike hire companies, most of Rio's hostels and backpacker guesthouses rent out bikes to their guests, including the Copacabana Palace Hotel on Avenida Atlântica.

Car hire

There are many other agencies on Av Princesa Isabel, Copacabana. **Avis**, Galeão international airport, **T** 021-33985060, Santos Dumont airport, **T** 021-38147378, Av Princesa Isabel 150A and B, Copacabana, **T** 021-25438481; **Hertz**, international airport, **T** 021-3984338, Av Princesa Isabel 273-A, Copacabana, **T** 021-22757440; **Interlocadora**, international airport, **T** 021-33983181; **Localiza**, international airport and Santos Dumont Airport, **T** 0800-992000, Av Princesa Isabel 150, Copacabana, **T** 021-22753340; **Nobre**, Av Princesa Isabel 7, Copacabana, **T** 021-25414646; **Telecar**, R Figueiredo Magalhães 701, Copacabana, **T** 021-22356778.

Credit card lines

For emergencies: **American Express, T 011-2470966**; Credicard, **T** 0800-784411; **Diners Club**, **T** 0800-784444; **MasterCard**, **T** 000811-8870533; **Thomas Cook Visa**, **T** 000811-7840553; **Visa**, **T** 000811-9335589.

Cultural institutions

American Library, União Cultural Brasil-Estados Unidos, R Col Oscar Porto 208. **Centro Brasileiro Britânico**, R Ferriera de Araújo 741, Pinheiros, **T** 021-30390567. **Centro Cultural Fiesp**, Av Paulista 1313, Tue-Sun 0900-1900, has foreign newspapers and magazines. **Goethe-Instituto**, R Lisboa 974, Mon-Thu 1400-2030.

Dentists

Amílcar Werneck de Carvalho Vianna, Av Pres Wilson 165, suite 811. English speaking. **Dr Mauro Suartz**, R Visconde de Pirajá 414, room 509, **T** 021 22876745. Speaks English, helpful.

Disabled

Rio de Janeiro is not ideal for disabled people and facilities are restricted to four- and five-star hotels. Few taxis have disabled access;

there are especially reserved disabled seats on the Metrô and buses, but access is through turnstiles which are difficult for wheelchairs.

Electricity

Most plugs in Rio city are 220 volts. Outside Rio city they are often 110 volts – ask in your hotel. Transformers (*transformadores*) are readily available. Outlets are usually standard US two-pin type.

Embassies and consulates

Argentina, Praia de Botafogo 228, **T** 021-25531646, 1100-1600; **Australia**, Av Presidente Wilson, **T** 021-38244624; **Austria**, Av Atlântica 3804, **T** 021-25222286; **Canada**, R Lauro Müller 116, **T** 021-25433004; **Denmark**, Praia do Flamengo 66, **T** 021-25586050; **France**, Av Pres Antônio Carlos 58, **T** 021-22101272; **Germany**, R Pres Carlos de Campos 417, **T** 021-25536777; **Greece**, Praia do Flamengo 344, **T** 021-25526799; **Netherlands**, Praia de Botafogo 242, **T** 021- 25529028; **Paraguay**, Praia de Botafogo 242, **T** 021-25532294; **Sweden/Finland/Norway**, Praia do Flamengo 344, **T** 021-25535505; **UK**, Praia do Flamengo 284, T 021-25533223, Metrô Flamengo; **Uruguay**, Praia de Botafogo 242, **T** 021-25536030; **USA**, Av Pres Wilson 147, **T** 021- 22927117.

Emergency numbers

Police T 190 (see also under 'Police'); **ambulance T** 193 or **T** 021-2371234; **fire service T** 193; **operator T** 107.

Immigration

Federal Police, Praça Mauá (passport section), entrance in Av Venezuela, **T** 021-22912142. To renew a 90-day visa, US$12.50.

Internet/email

Throughout the city: **@point**, Barra Shopping, Av das Americas 4666, Barra da Tijuca. Several places in Rio Sul Shopping Center, Botafogo. Many on Av NS de Copacabana and R Visconde de Pirajá,

Ipanema. **Phone Serv**, Av N S de Copacabana 454, loja B. **Tudo é Fácil**, three branches in Copacabana: R Xavier da Silveira 19; Av Prado Júnior 78 and R Barata Ribeiro 396.

Language schools

AmeriSpan, T 1-800-879-6640 (USA), www.amerispan.com, have several language schools worldwide and across Brazil and can arrange volunteer and internship placements. Other language schools in Rio include **Cursos da UNE** (União Nacional de Estudantes), R Catete 243. **Instituto Brasil-Estados Unidos**, Av Copacabana 690, 5th floor. **IVM Português Prático**, R do Catete 310, recommended.

Launderettes

Fénix, R do Catete 214, loja 20, Catete; **Lavanderia**, Visconde de Pirajá 631A, Ipanema, **T** 021-22948142; **Laundromat** at Av NS de Copacabana 1216.

Left luggage

At the **Rodaviária Novo Rio**, Av Rodrigues Alves, Centro, **T** 021-22915151, and at both **Antonio Carlos Jombim International Airport, T** 021-33984526, and **Santos Dumont Airport T** 021-2102457.

Libraries

Biblioteca Nacional, Av Rio Branco 219, Centro, **T** 021-2628255.

Media

Balcão, an advertising newspaper, US$2, twice weekly, offers apartments in and around Rio, language lessons, discounted tickets, items for sale and advertises shops. There are similar advertisements in the classified sections of dailies *O Globo* and *Jornal do Brasil*; both have entertainments pages too; *O Globo* has a travel section on Thursday; the *Jornal do Brasil* has a 'what's-on' magazine on Friday, as does *Veja*, a weekly news magazine. Riotur's fortnightly booklet lists main attractions; *Rio This Month* (less reliable) is free from hotels. TurisRio's free magazine about the State of Rio de Janeiro is interesting and can be found in the larger hotel receptions.

Medical services

Hospital Miguel Couto, Mário Ribeiro 117, Gávea, **T** 021-22746050, has a free casualty ward. **Hospital Municipal Rocha Maia**, R Gen Severiano 91, Botafogo, **T** 021-22952295, near Rio Sul Shopping Centre, free, but there may be queues, a good public hospital for minor injuries and ailments. **Hospital Municipal São Pedro de Alcântara** (Santa Casa), Av Dom Pedro de Alcântara, Paraty, **T** 022-33711623. **Saúde de Portos**, Praça Mcal Âncora, **T** 021-22408628, Mon-Fri 1000-1100, 1500-1800, for vaccinations, international vaccination book and ID required. **Policlínica**, Av Nilo Peçanha 38, recommended for diagnosis and investigation.

Police

The **Tourist Police**, Av Afrânio de Melo Franco, Leblon, **T** 021-25115112, publish a sensible advice leaflet, available from hotels and consulates; consulates also issue safety guidelines. Tourist police officers are helpful, efficient and multilingual; they patrol all the main tourist areas and if you have any problems, contact them first.

Post offices

Central Post Office, R 1 de Março 64, corner of R do Rosário, Centro, there are many others throughout the city. **Poste restante** is at the Correios, Av Nossa Senhora de Copacabana 540 and all large post offices. **Federal Express**, Av Calógeras 23 (near Santa Luzia church) **T** 021-22628565, is reliable; airmail usually takes about a week to Europe or the USA.

Public holidays

1 January, **New Year**; 21 April, **Tiradentes**; 1 May, **Labour Day**; June, **Corpus Christi**; 7 September, **Independence Day**; 12 October, **Nossa Senhora Aparecida**; 2 November, **All Souls' Day**; 15 November, **Proclamation of the Republic**; and 25 December, **Christmas**. Other religious or traditional holidays, including **Good Friday** and, usually, 1 November, **All Saints' Day** and 24 December, **Christmas Eve**, are fixed each year.

Religious services

Church of England/American Episcopalian: R Real Grandeza 99, Botafogo. **First Church of Christ Scientist**: Av Mcal Câmara 271. **International Baptist Church**, R Desembargador Alfredo Russel 146, Leblon. **Masonic Temple**: R da Matriz 76, Botafogo. **Roman Catholic**: Chapel of Our Lady of Mercy, R Visconde de Caravelas 48, Botafogo. **Synagogue**: Associação Religiosa Israelita, R Gen Severiano 170, Botafogo. **Union Church**, R Parque da Lagoa de Marapendi, Barra da Tijuca.

Students

Student Travel Bureau, Av Nilo Peçanha 50, SL 2417, Centro, **T/F** 021 25442627, and R Visconde de Pirajá 550, Ipanema, **T** 021 25128577, www.stb.com.br, has details of travel, discounts and cultural exchanges for ISIC holders.

Taxi firms

Radio taxis include: **Cootramo, T** 021-25605442, **Coopertramo, T** 021-22602022, **Centro de Táx, T** 021-25932598, **Transcoopass, T** 021-25604888. Luxury cabs are allowed to charge higher rates. For taxi tours the following have been recommended: **Inácio de Oliveira, T** 021-22254110, is a reliable taxi driver for excursions, he only speaks Portuguese. **Grimalde, T** 021-22679812, talkative daytime and evening tours, English and Italian spoken, negotiate a price.

Telephone

International operator, 000 111; **domestic operator**, 101. The IDD for Brazil is +55 followed by 21 for Rio. Public phones are operated by phone cards – dial the number of the network operator of the phone box prior to the local code to make a call (for instance 021 for Telefonica, 031 for Telemar or 015 for Embratel). To dial internationally: 00 followed by 21 or 15 and then the relevant country code. International telephone booths are blue. Telephone numbers often change – if in doubt, phone 102 for **Auxilio á Lista**, which is the current daily updated directory of telephone numbers. Local and long distance calls can be made from public phones; buy phone cards from the newspaper stand by the tourist information centre.

Time

Rio is GMT -2, and GMT -4 from April to October.

Toilets

There are very few public toilets in Rio de Janeiro, but shopping centres, many bars and restaurants (eg McDonalds) offer facilities. Just ask for the *banheiro*.

Transport enquiries

Transport enquires are best put to the tourist office as most phone attendants for transport companies in Rio do not speak English.

Useful addresses

Check out www.addresses.com.br for a comprehensive guide to addresses in the city.

Background

A sprint through history

4000 BC	Indigenous peoples living in hunter-gatherer communities settle around Guanabara Bay.These people may have been Tupi-Guaraní speakers.
1500	Portuguese explorer Pedro Alvares Cabral stumbles across Brazil while looking for a back door to India.
1502	Gaspar de Lemos arrives in Guanabara Bay. Mistaking it for the mouth of a great river, he names it January River and builds a small fort to officially claim it for Portugal. Convicts are left behind to 'mingle with the native inhabitants and learn their language'.
1505	After mistreatment of the native Tamoio people and their women, the convicts are killed or driven away, the fort destroyed and Rio is almost forgotten.
1555	France sends a ship of Calvinists to Rio under the captaincy of Nicholas de Villegagnon. They build a fort in the Bay, treat theTamoio far better than the Portuguese and succeed in forging a military alliance with their giant chief Cunhambebe.
1567	After a 10-year war against the French and their allies, the Portuguese win a decisive battle on Flamengo beach and reclaim Rio. General Mem de Sá establishes the city of São Sebastião do Rio de Janeiro in what is now the central business district. The Jesuit Manoel de Nóbrega establishes a Jesuit college and subjugates the local indigenous people completely.
1575	The last of the Rio de Janeiro Tamoio people are massacred and their women and children separated from each other and sold as slaves.

1585	The city's population is 3,850, of which 750 were Portuguese,100 African and the majority enslaved Indians. The city begins to take shape around the Jesuit monastery on the Morro de São Januário.
1586	The Benedictines begin to build the Mosteiro de São Bento which still stands today.
1600	For almost a century Rio languishes as a small settlement surrounded by sugar plantations and is largely controlled by Jesuits.
1701	Gold is discovered in the inland state of Minas Gerais. Gold prospectors pour across the Atlantic from Portugal and Rio begins to grow as a city.
1763	Coffee replaces gold as Brazil's principal export and Rio replaces Salvador as colonial Brazil's capital.
1807	Napoleon Bonaparte threatens to attack Portugal. Under the protection of British, the entire Portuguese Royal Family abandon their subjects and flee for Brazil.
1808	The British exact a high price for their help. Under the Treaty of Methuen, Portugal's ports were 'opened to friendly nations', meaning Britain. An estimated £200 million sterling in gold leaves Brazil for England by the end of the century and the Imperial government has to borrow money from British banks to buy British goods. And so begins a huge national debt which has crippled the country to this day.
1815	Napoleon is defeated at Waterloo and King João returns to Lisbon in order to prevent a revolution in Portugal. He leaves his son, Pedro, as Regent of Brazil.

1822	Realizing that Portugal is weak and in no position to prevent Brazil's independence, Pedro pronounces his famous cry "Independence or death... by the blood that flows in my veins and upon my honour, I swear to God to free Brazil." Imperial Brazil is born; but there is little social change.
1831	Dissatisfaction with Dom Pedro I and the Portuguese lead to the *garrafada* bottle-throwing riot in Rio. Dom Pedro abdicates to return to Portugal and assume the throne there. His five-year-old son, Dom Pedro II becomes the new Emperor.
1888	Abolition of slavery. Freed slaves continue to be exploited by plantation owners and in the cities; *favelas* begin to form on the hills of Rio.
1889	On 15 November, a bloodless military coup deposes the monarchy and institutes a federal system.
1900-1905	Poor sanitation in the slums leads to outbreaks of bubonic plague and yellow fever. Whole areas of the colonial city are razed to the ground and replaced with North American-style broad avenues.
1937	President Getúlio Vargas suspends the constitution and proclaims a new dictatorial state, Estado Nôvo, which lasts until 1945.
1960	Under President Jucelino Kubitschek, the nation's capital is transferred to Brasília. São Paulo begins to overtake Rio as Brazil's cultural and economic centre.
1964	A military coup gives power to the armed forces. In the first years the authoritarian regime (which is to

last for 21 years), achieves spectacular economic growth for the middle classes. But the gulf between rich and poor is widening by the day and Rio's *favelas* are mushrooming.

1970s	As power shifts to São Paulo and Brasília, Rio becomes seen as a leisure town for the rich and a centre for Brazil's music and entertainment scene.
1989	Brazil enjoys its first elections for almost 30 years. But the new president, Fernando Collor, freezes bank accounts and steals millions for his own private use. He is impeached and expelled from office.
1989-1992	Gun crime and drug trafficking rise steadily, as does police brutality. Numerous kidnappings by gangs from the *favelas* and muggings at gunpoint by crack-addicted nine year olds eventually result in a police clampdown, leading to the notorious street children massacres of the early 1990s.
1992	Rio hosts a world environmental summit. Much of the money pledged to the rainforest and indigenous peoples disappears and government officials get rich.
2002	Ex-union leader Luís Inácio da Silva, popularly known as Lula, is elected president. He pledges to give all Brazilians three meals a day before he leaves office.
2004	Deputy Governor of Rio Luiz Paulo Conde announces plans to build a wall around two of the largest *favelas*. His plans are widely criticized by human rights groups, including Amnesty International.

Art and architecture

BC-1502	Although there were sophisticated tribal civilizations like the Omagua, their cities were built of perishable materials. Examples of ceramics and ceremonial pieces can be seen in the Museu do Índio.
16th-17th century	Brazil's first important buildings were ecclesiastical. Most were Mannerist, based on a reinterpretation and embellishment of classicism. The Church of Ordem Terceira do Carmo and the Mosteiro de São Bento are two of Rio's best examples. The former preserves one of the finest gilt baroque naves in Latin America.
18th century	Italian baroque, imported into Portugal in the 17th century, was developed under Pombal after the Lisbon earthquake. The style is characterized by imposing churches with domes and towers (church of Nossa Senhora da Candelária). Fine art in Rio during this period was still largely ecclesiastical and dominated by the baroque sculpture of the Portuguese Francisco Xavier de Brito (church of São Francisco de Penitência), and the more sober work from the Mineiro son of a black slave, Valentim Fonseca e Silva or Mestre Valentim (church of São Francisco de Paula and many others).
19th century	King João VI invited a French artistic mission to Rio to introduce the latest European architectural and artistic trends. All new government buildings were built in the neoclassical style, such as the Palácio de Itamaraty and the Museu Histórico Nacional. French painters inspired a whole generation of secular Brazilian painters, including Vítor Meireles and Pedro Américo.

Early 20th century	Belle époque France and Victorian England's love for architectural fusion was copied in Rio and the result was the so-called *arquitetura eclética*. This comprises a mish-mash of styles from neoclassical to English mock-Tudor and Rhineland Gothic revival. The Theatro Municipal and Museu Nacional de Belas Artes are good, stolid examples. This period also saw the razing to the ground of much of colonial Rio. Influenced by the ideas of modernism and a strong desire to free themselves from subservience to Europe, a group of young, intellectual artists conceived a movement known as *Antropofagia* or 'cannibalism' which sought to 'kill and devour' international art and re-express it as Brazilian.
Mid to late 20th century	Modernist architecture was introduced to Brazil by Le Corbusier who designed the Ministry of Education along with Lúcio Costa and Oscar Niemeyer. These two went on to become Brazil's most influential architects. Niemeyer buildings include the Sambódromo and the Museu de Arte Moderna in Niterói.
21st century	The stars of public postmodern, post-Niemeyer Brazilian architecture are mostly not from Rio. Contemporary Brazilian fine art remains socially conscious. The conceptual work of artists like Cildo Meireles, Jac Lierner and Tunga consists of icons designed to draw attention to political and environemental issues, whilst the painter Siron Franco addresses the destruction of the rainforest as well as the darker aspects of the Brazilian psyche from sexual fetishism to political corruption.

Music

Axé

As popular as samba but twice as fast and twice as frenetic. Daniela Mercury (*Feijão Com Arroz*) is the most famous name. Chiclete com Banana are currently the biggest band in Brazil, whilst Band Beijo's *Ao Vivo* captures the raw energy of live axé like no other.

Bossa nova

A slowed-down version of samba garnished with chord progressions inspired by 1950s US jazz. There are three great bossa nova names – João Gilberto, Tom Jobim (*Família Jobim*) and Vinícius de Moraes. Go for a compilation CD.

Brazilian jazz fusion

The most famous of all Brazilian fusion tracks is Deodato's *Also Spracht Zarathustra* on his CD *Prelude*. Airto Moreira's *Identity* is a great CD, as is Flora Purim's *Flight*. Other classics include Egberto Gismonti and Delia Fischer's *Antônio*. Altogether more off the wall is eccentric, multi-instrumentalist Hermeto Pascoal.

Choro

Ragtime Rio-style, a fusion of Africa and Europe born out of the abolition of the slave trade. Its most legendary figure is flautist Pixinguinha; for something less gramophone, try violinist Raphael Rabello.

Electronica and club music

World-famous DJs like Marky and Patife frequently play in Rio. More interesting is DJ Dolores, who fuses traditional Brazilian and international sounds and who won the BBC World Music Awards in 2004. Bebel Gilberto (daughter of João), the most famous name in electronica, is less typical; more New York than Brazil. For something homegrown check out Suba and Fernanda Porto.

Forró

A less frenetic dance rhythm from the northeast, forró was invented at 'for all' (*forró*) barn dances thrown for Brazilian railway workers by their English bosses. It is a beach-bar dance with yokely lyrics, powered by a pulsating drum and accordion. It is danced far closer than anything you will find in Hispanic America. Traditional names are Luiz Gonzaga and Sivuca. Also look out for Mastruz com Leite or Mel Com Terra.

Frevo

A fast 2/4 instrumental style which evolved from the polka. Many Brazilian singers and bands have sung some frevo, but Claudionor Germano e Expedito Baracho are two of the few who specialize.

Mangue beat

A fusion of electronic sounds, Brazilian rhythms and rap, headed by the charismatic and short-lived Chico Science, whose legacy is continued today by the likes of Otto (*Sem Gravidade*) and DJ Dolores.

Miscellaneous

Marlui Miranda (*Todos os Sons*), a musicologist and jazz musician has done more than any living person to show the world the complexity and beauty of indigenous Amazon music. Master percussionist Naná Vasconcelos defies categorization – orchestral, folkloric, technically awe-inspiring and completely original.

Música Popular Brasileira (MPB)

A group of Bahian musicians known as the **tropicalistas** embraced electric instruments and fused bossa and jazz to produce a new set of Brazilian sounds which included everyone from Milton Nascimento (*Clube da Esquina*), to Gil, Caetano, Jorge Ben, Djavan (*Bicho Solto*), Almir Satir, Zé Ramalho, Elis Regina (*Elis and Tom*) and Chico Buraque. More modern names include silky-voiced Marisa Monte and eccentric Bahian percussionist Carlinhos Brown (*Alfagamabetizado*).

Rap brasileiro

It would be a mistake to think that Brazilian hip-hop is a pale imitation of the US version. It is funkier, more melodic and more socially aware. It is strongly influenced by Brazilian musical genres and spontaneous northeastern **repentista** street poetry.

Samba

The most famous of the country's dance rhythms sounds wonderfully happy but is invariably bittersweet: rhythms filled with joy and optimism and lyrics as sad as a lament. Samba came to Rio from Angola and reached its full fruition in the Rio Carnaval of the 1930s. Offshoots include **samba canção**, a sit-down, more harmonically sophisticated form of guitar samba, and **pagode** which is the opposite. For carnival samba, buy a compilation of the best songs from this year's Rio Carnaval, while for pagode, look out for Beth Carvalho or Zeca Pagodinho. Perhaps the greatest names in samba canção are João Bosco (*Galos De Briga* and *Caça À Raposa*) and Baden Powell (*Nosso Baden*). Other names to look out for are Nelson Gonçalves and Paulinho da Viola.

Samba rock

Sounds like neither rock nor samba, but is funky, irresistibly danceable and very popular in Rio. Its godfather, Jorge Ben, wrote one of the country's most famous songs *Mas Que Nada*. He plays free concerts over New Year on Copacabana beach. Many of his best songs are on *Brazilian Hits and Funky Classics*. Other names to look out for are Seu Jorge, Ivo Mereilles and jazz-funksters Acid X – all Cariocas. *Favela Chic* is an excellent compilation.

Tropicalismo

This group of Bahians includes some of Brazil's best-known international names – Gilberto Gil (*Refazenda*), Caetano Veloso (*Bicho*), Tom Zé, Maria Bethânia and Gal Costa. *Doces Bárbaros* is a compilation with Caetano, Gil, Gal Costa and Maria Bethânia.

Books

Fiction

Torres, Antonio, *Blues for a Lost Childhood*. (1989), Readers International. An idealistic Brazilian journalist leaves his rural town for Rio only to be crushed by the realities of the city.

Non-fiction

Bellos, Alex, *Futebol: The Brazilian Way of Life*. (2003), Bloomsbury. A loving look at the beautiful game, its history, its players, supporters and its legendary feats.

Castro, Ruy, *Rio de Janeiro*. (2004), Bloomsbury. An anecdotal history and profile of Rio de Janeiro written by a Carioca.

Fausto, Boris, *A Concise History of Brazil*. (1999), Cambridge University Press. Dry as dust but the only readily available, reliable history of the country available in English.

Gosling, Priscilla Ann, *How to be a Carioca*. (1992), Luso-Brazilian Books. A funny and illuminating look at the idosyncrasies of Cariocas.

Harvey, Robert, *Liberators*. (2002), Constable and Robinson. A wonderful romp through the liberation of South America with a colourful section on imperial Brazil. How all history should be written.

Hemming, John, *Red Gold*. (2004), Pan. The little-known history of Brazil's indigenous people is alternatively shocking and inspiring. This wonderful, scholarly and beautifully written account is as readable and exciting as Prescott's *Conquest of Peru* and will, in time, rank alongside it. A must for anyone with an interest in Brazil.

McGowan, Chris, *The Brazilian Sound: Samba, Bossa Nova and the Popular Music of Brazil*. (1998), Ricardo Pessanha, Temple University Press. An encyclopaedic survey of Brazilian popular music with interviews from many of the key players.

Page, Josephe A, *The Brazilians*. (1995), Da Capo Press. One of the few popular books on Brazil which really gets under the country's skin. With excellent chapters on Carnival, football and Rio.

Travel

Fawcett, Percy, *Exploration Fawcett*, (2001), Weidenfeld & Nicholson. The diaries of the intrepid explorer who disappeared in Matto Grosso in the 1920s and whose decriptions of the table-top mountains there inspired Conan Doyle to write *The Lost World*.

Fleming, Peter, *Brazilian Adventure*, (1998) Pimlico. The sparkling, delightfully humorous account of a 1930s expedition in search of Colonel Percy Fawcett.

Robb, Peter, A Death in Brazil, (2004) Bloomsbury. A poetic odyssey through Brazil's history, culture and landscape.

Glossary

avenida avenue
barraca stall or hut
estrada road
fazenda ranch or farm
ladeira slope
largo plaza
Paulista person from São Paulo
praça square
rodoviária bus station
bairro suburb
Carioca person from Rio
favela slum
igreja church
lanchonete snack bar
morro hill
pousada hotel
praia beach
Umbanda Afro-Brazilian religion

Language

The official language in Brazil is Portuguese, some English is spoken in Rio but usually only in tourist establishments.

Greetings and courtesies

hello *oi*
good morning/afternoon/night *boa dia/tarde/boa noite*
goodbye *adeus/tchau*
please *por favor/faz favor*
yes/no *sim/não*
thank you (very much) *(muito) obrigado/a*
how are you? *como vai você tudo bem?/tudo bom?*
I am fine *vou bem/tudo bem*
excuse me *com licença*
I don't understand *não entendo*
please speak slowly *fale devagar por favor*
what is your name? *qual é seu nome?*
my name is... *o meu nome é...*
go away! *vai embora!*

Getting around

on the left/right *à esquerda/à direita*
straight on *direto*
bus station *a rodoviária*
bus *o ônibus*
bus stop *a parada*
train *a trem*
airport *o aeroport*
first/second class *primeira/segunda clase*
train station *a ferroviária*
combined bus and train station *a rodoferroviária*
ticket *o passagem/o bilhete*

Questions and requests

where is? *onde está/onde fica?*
why? *por que?*
how much does it cost? *quanto custa?/quanto é?*
how do I get to...? *para chegar a...?*
when? *quando?*
I want to go to... *quero ir para...*
when does the bus leave/arrive? *a que hor sai/chega o ônibus?*

Accommodation

room *quarto*
single/double room *(quarto de) solteiro/(quarto para) casal*
room with two beds *quarto com duas camas*
with private bathroom *quarto com banheiro*
hot/cold water *água quente/fria*
sheet(s) *o lençol (os lençóis)*
blankets *as mantas*
pillow *o travesseiro*
clean/dirty towels *as toalhas limpas/sujas*
toilet paper *o papel higiêico*

Eating out

breakfast *o caféde manh*
lunch *o almoço*
dinner/supper *o jantar*
meal *a refeição*
drink *a bebida*
without meat *sem carne*

Food and drink

beer *cerveja*
bread *pão*
chicken *frango/galinha*
bife *beef*
cheese *queijo*
coffee *café*

egg *ovo*
fruit juice *suco*
milk *leite*
pork *porco*
rice *arroz*
soft drink *refrigerante*
tea *chá*
fish *peixe*
ice cream *sorvete*
mineral water *água mineral*
potato *batata*
salad *salada*
sugar *açúcar*
wine *vinho*

Health

chemist *a farmacia*
doctor *o coutor/a doutora*
(for) pain *(para) dor*
stomach *o esômago (a barriga)*
head *a cabeça*
fever/sweat *a febre/o suor higiênicas*
diarrhoea *a diarréia*
condoms *as camisinhas/os preservativos*

Days and months

Monday *segunda feira*, Tuesday *terça feira*, Wednesday *quarta feira*, Thursday *quinta feira*, Friday *sexta feira*, Saturday *sábado*, Sunday *domingo*.
January *janeiro*, February *fevereiro*, March *março*, April *abril*, May *maio*, June *junho*, July *julho*, August *agosto*, September *setembro*, October *outubro*, November *novembro*, December *dezembro*.

Numbers

one *um/uma*, two *dois/duas*, three *três, four* *quatro*, five *cinco*, six *seis* (or *meia* half, ie half-dozen), seven *sete*, eight *oito*, nine *nove*, 10 *dez*, 11 *onze*, 12 *doze*, 13 *treze*, 14 *catorze*, 15 *quinze*, 16 *dezesseis*, 17 *dezessete*, 18 *dezoito*, 19 *dezenove*, 20 *vinte*, 21 *vente e um*, 30 *trinta*, 40 *cuarenta*, 50 *cinqüe*, 60 *sessenta*, 70 *setenta*, 80 *oitenta*, 90 *noventa*, 100 *cem/cento*, 1,000 *mil*.

Index

Credits

Footprint credits

Editor: Nicola Jones
Map editor: Sarah Sorensen
Picture editor: Robert Lunn

Publisher: Patrick Dawson
Series created by: Rachel Fielding
In-house cartography: Claire Benison, Kevin Feeney, Robert Lunn, Angus Dawson
Proof-reading: Elizabeth Barrick, Davina Rungasamy
Editorial: Felicity Laughton, Laura Dixon
Design: Mytton Williams
Maps: Footprint Handbooks Ltd

Photography credits

Front cover: Alamy (Carnival parade)
Inside: Powerstock, Alamy, Naturepl, Alex Robinson
Generic images: John Matchett
Back cover: Powerstock (Museu de Arte Contemporânea, Niterói)

Print

Manufactured in Italy by LegoPrint

Footprint feedback

We try as hard as we can to make each Footprint guide as up to date as possible but, of course, things always change. If you want to let us know about your experiences – good, bad or ugly – then, don't delay, go to www.footprintbooks.com and send in your comments.

® Footprint Handbooks and the Footprint mark are a registered trademark of Footprint Handbooks Ltd

Publishing information

Footprint Rio de Janeiro
1st edition
Text and maps

ISBN 1 904777 25 2
CIP DATA: a catalogue record for this book is available from the British Library

Published by Footprint
6 Riverside Court
Lower Bristol Road
Bath, BA2 3DZ, UK
T +44 (0)1225 469141
F +44 (0)1225 469461
discover@footprintbooks.com
www.footprintbooks.com

Distributed in the USA by
Publishers Group West

Every effort has been made to ensure that the facts in this pocket Handbook are accurate. However, the authors and publishers cannot accept responsibility for any loss, injury or incovenience sustained by any traveller as a result of information or advice contained in this guide.

Alice and Kevan Prior and David Smith are the British owners of this delightful, small hotel overlooking one of Búzios' most attractive beaches, the Praia de João Fernandes. The spacious individual bungalows, with sea views from their balconies, are all equipped with air-conditioning, satellite TV, mini-bar and individual safe. They are set in beautiful tropical gardens adjacent to the guest lounge, breakfast room and swimming pool.

POUSADA HIBISCUS BEACH, RUA 1, N° 22, QUADRA C,
PRAIA DE JOÃO FERNANDES, BÚZIOS, R.J., BRAZIL

Phone: (55) 22-2623 6221 (Brazil)
E-mail: info@hibiscusbeach.com.br
Website: www.hibiscusbeach.com

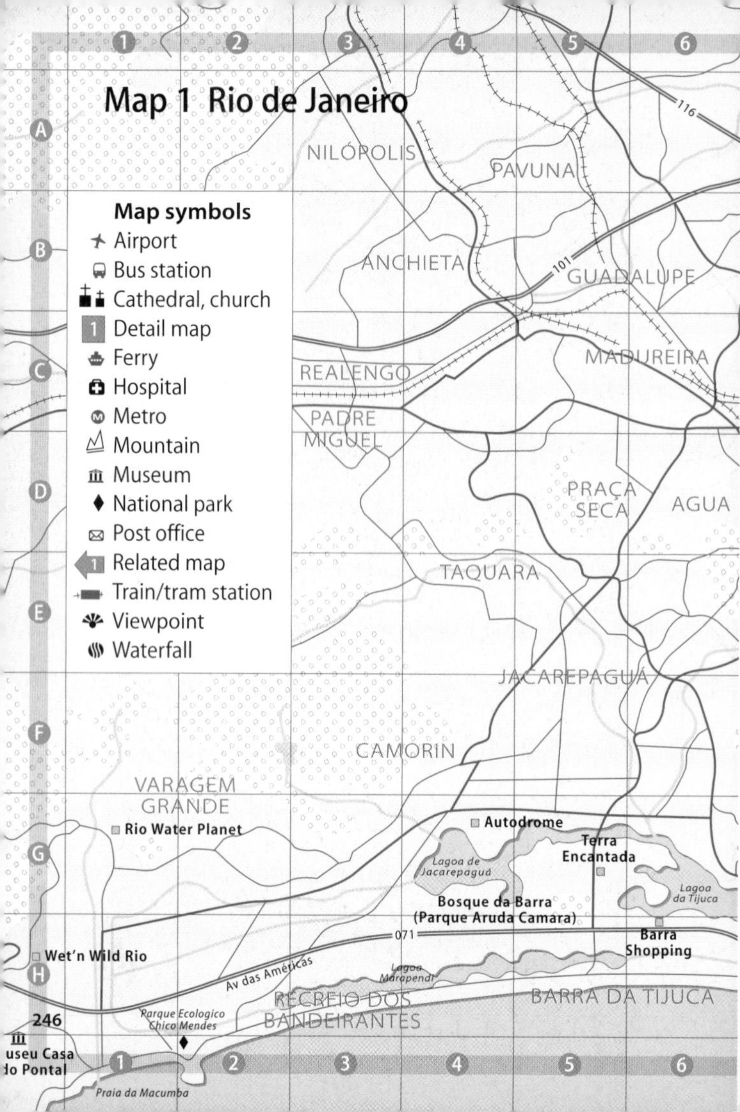
Map 1 Rio de Janeiro
Map symbols
Airport
Bus station
Cathedral, church
Detail map
Ferry
Hospital
Metro
Mountain
Museum
National park
Post office
Related map
Train/tram station
Viewpoint
Waterfall
NILÓPOLIS
PAVUNA
ANCHIETA
GUADALUPE
REALENGO
MADUREIRA
PADRE MIGUEL
PRAÇA SECA
AGUA
TAQUARA
JACAREPAGUÁ
CAMORIN
VARAGEM GRANDE
Rio Water Planet
Autodrome
Terra Encantada
Lagoa de Jacarepaguá
Lagoa da Tijuca
Bosque da Barra (Parque Aruda Camara)
071
Barra Shopping
Wet'n Wild Rio
Av das Américas
Lagoa Marapendi
RECREIO DOS BANDEIRANTES
BARRA DA TIJUCA
246
Parque Ecologico Chico Mendes
useu Casa do Pontal
Praia da Macumba
116
101
A
B
C
D
E
F
G
H
1
2
3
4
5
6

FREGUESIA
Ilha do Governador
VICÁRIO GERAL
Antônio Carlos Jobim (Galeão)
MONERÓ
040
RIBEIRA
PENHA
Av Brasil
IRAJA
COSMOS
RAMOS
Ilha do Fundão
Baía de Guanabara
INHAÚMA
101
Rio-Niterói Bridge
PILARES
Ilha Pombeba
Ilha de Santa Bárbara
Ilha das Enxadas
JACARÉ
SÃO CRISTOVÃO
Ilha das Cobras
SANTA
MÉIER
Quinta da Boa Vista
Rodoviaria Novo Rio
Ilha Fiscal
Jardim Zoológico
Museu Nacional
CENTRO
Santos Dumont
Maracanã Stadium
GRAJAÚ
GLÓRIA
USINA
TIJUCA
FLAMENGO
Parque Nacional da Tijuca
Bom Retiro
Pico da Tijuca
Major Archer's House
Mayrink Chapel
Pão de Açúcar
Paulo e Virginia Grotto
ALTO DA BOA VISTA
Corcovado Christ
Túnel Rebouças
Cascatinha Taunay
BOTAFOGO
LAGOA
Museu Açude
Vista Chinesa
Institute Moreira Salles
Lagoa Rodrigo de Freitas
COPACABANA
Mesa do Imperador
ITANHANGÁ
Planetario
VILA CANOA
GÁVEA
IPANEMA
Pedra Bonita
ROCINHA
Morro Dois Irmãos
Pedra da Gávea
São Conrado Fashion Mall
JOÁ
SÃO CONRADO
Atlantic Ocean
N
0 km 1
0 miles 1

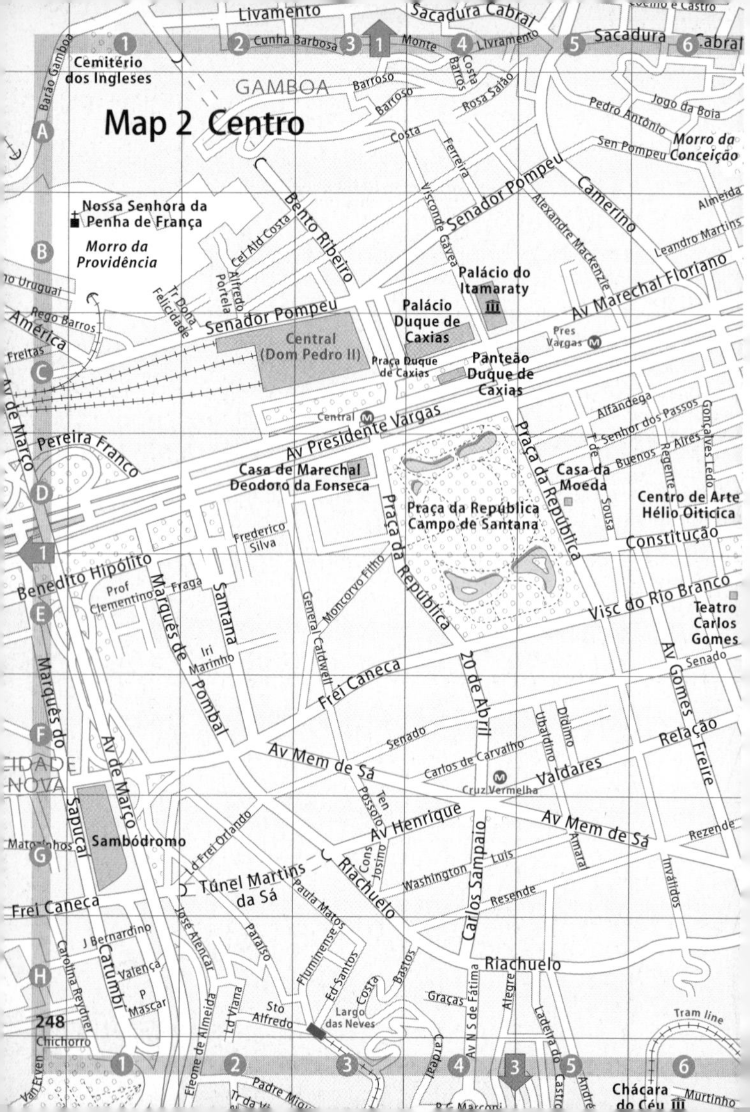
Map 2 Centro
Livamento
Sacadura Cabral
Cunha Barbosa
Monte
Livramento
Sacadura
Cabral
Costa Barros
Cemitério dos Ingleses
GAMBOA
Barroso
Rosa Saião
Barão Gamboa
Pedro Antônio
Jogo da Boia
Sen Pompeu
Morro da Conceição
Costa
Ferreira
Senador Pompeu
Camerino
Almeida
Leandro Martins
Nossa Senhora da Penha de França
Morro da Providência
Bento Ribeiro
Cel Ald Costa
Alfredo Portela
Tr Dona Felicidade
Visconde Gávea
Alexandre Mackenzie
Palácio do Itamaraty
Av Marechal Floriano
Rego Barros
América
Freitas
Senador Pompeu
Central (Dom Pedro II)
Palácio Duque de Caxias
Pres Vargas
Praça Duque de Caxias
Panteão Duque de Caxias
Av de Março
Central
Av Presidente Vargas
Alfândega
Senhor dos Passos
Gonçalves Ledo
Pereira Franco
Casa de Marechal Deodoro da Fonseca
Praça da República
Casa da Moeda
Buenos Aires
Regente
Tr de Sousa
Centro de Arte Hélio Oiticica
Praça da República Campo de Santana
Frederico Silva
Constituição
Benedito Hipólito
Prof Clementino
Fraga
Marquês de Pombal
Santana
Moncorvo Filho
General Caldwell
Visc do Rio Branco
Teatro Carlos Gomes
Iri Marinho
Frei Caneca
20 de Abril
Av Gomes Freire
Senado
Marquês do Sapucaí
Av de Março
Ubaldino
Didimo
Relação
Av Mem de Sá
Carlos de Carvalho
Valdares
CIDADE NOVA
Cruz Vermelha
Ten Possolo
Av Henrique
Av Mem de Sá
Rezende
Ld Frei Orlando
Sambódromo
Cons Josino
Amaral
Inválidos
Túnel Martins da Sá
Riachuelo
Luis
Washington
Paula Matos
Resende
Carlos Sampaio
Frei Caneca
José Alencar
J Bernardino
Paraíso
Catumbi
Fluminense
Valença
Ed Santos
Bastos
Riachuelo
Costa
P Mascar
Carolina Reydner
Ld Viana
Sto Alfredo
Largo das Neves
Graças
Av N S de Fátima
Alegre
Ladeira do Castro
Tram line
Chichorro
Eleone de Almeida
Cardeal
Van Erven
Padre Miguel
Chácara do Céu
Murtinho
A
B
C
D
E
F
G
H
1
2
3
4
5
6

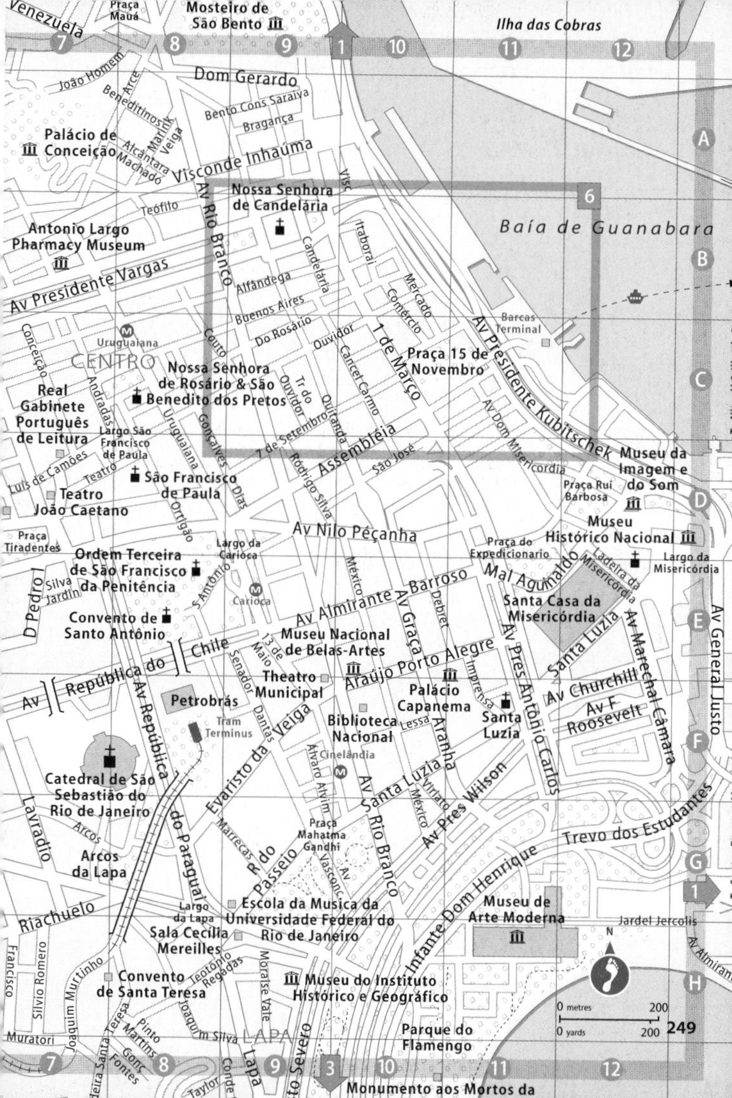
Mosteiro de
São Bento
Praça
Mauá
Venezuela
Ilha das Cobras
7
8
9
1
10
11
12
Dom Gerardo
João Homem
Arce
Beneditinos
Bento Cons Saraiva
Bragança
Marlink
Veiga
Palácio de
Conceição
Alcântara
Machado
Visconde Inhaúma
Nossa Senhora
de Candelária
6
A
Teófilo
Antonio Largo
Pharmacy Museum
Av Rio Branco
Baía de Guanabara
B
Itaboraí
Candelária
Av Presidente Vargas
Alfândega
Mercado
Comércio
Buenos Aires
Do Rosário
Barcas
Terminal
Uruguaiana
Couto
Ouvidor
1 de Março
Conceição
CENTRO
Nossa Senhora
de Rosário & São
Benedito dos Pretos
Praça 15 de
Novembro
Av Presidente Kubitschek
C
Real
Gabinete
Português
de Leitura
Andradas
Tr do
Ouvidor
Cancel Carmo
Quitanda
Av Dom
Misericórdia
Largo São
Francisco
de Paula
Uruguaiana
Gonçalves Dias
7 de Setembro
Assembléia
Museu da
Imagem e
do Som
Luís de Camões
Teatro
São Francisco
de Paula
Rodrigo Silva
São José
Praça Rui
Barbosa
Teatro
João Caetano
Ortigão
D
Av Nilo Peçanha
Museu
Histórico Nacional
Praça
Tiradentes
Largo da
Carioca
Praça do
Expedicionario
Ordem Terceira
de São Francisco
da Penitência
Mal Aguinaldo
Ladeira da
Misericórdia
Largo da
Misericórdia
Silva
Jardin
S Antônio
México
Av Almirante Barroso
Carioca
Debret
Santa Casa da
Misericórdia
D Pedro I
Convento de
Santo Antônio
Av Graça
Av Pres Antônio Carlos
Santa Luzia
Av Marechal Câmara
E
Av General Justo
Av Chile
13 de
Maio
Museu Nacional
de Belas-Artes
Araújo Porto Alegre
Imprensa
Av República do Chile
Senador
Dantas
Theatro
Municipal
Palácio
Capanema
Av Churchill
Av F
Roosevelt
Av República
Petrobrás
Evaristo da Veiga
Biblioteca
Nacional
Lessa
Aranha
Santa
Luzia
Tram
Terminus
Cinelândia
F
Álvaro Alvim
Av Rio Branco
Av Santa Luzia
Catedral de São
Sebastião do
Rio de Janeiro
Viriato
México
Av Pres Wilson
Lavradio
do Paraguai
Praça
Mahatma
Gandhi
Trevo dos Estudantes
Arcos
Marrecas
Arcos
da Lapa
R do
Passeio
Vasconc.
Av
Infante Dom Henrique
G
Riachuelo
Largo
da Lapa
Escola da Musica da
Universidade Federal do
Rio de Janeiro
Museu de
Arte Moderna
Jardel Jercolis
Sala Cecília
Mereilles
Francisco
Silvio Romero
Joaquim Murtinho
Convento
de Santa Teresa
Teotônio
Regadas
Moraise Vale
Museu do Instituto
Histórico e Geográfico
Av Almirante
H
Joaquim Silva
Pinto
Martins
Parque do
Flamengo
0 metres 200
0 yards 200
Muratori
Ladeira Santa Teresa
Gonç
Fontes
LAPA
Lapa
Conde
Taylor
Senador
3
Monumento aos Mortos da

Map 3 Glória, Santa Teresa & Flamengo
Chácara do Céu
Parque das Ruínas
Convento de Santa Teresa
Museu do Instituto Histórico e Geográfico
Parque do Flamengo
Monumento aos Mortos da Segunda Guerra Mundial
Enseada da Glória
Nossa Senhora da Glória do Outeiro
Museu da República
Parque do Catete
Museu do Folclore Edison Carneiro
SANTA TERESA
LAPA
GLÓRIA
CATETE
Av Augusto Severo
Av Beira Mar
Av Infante Dom Henrique
Praça Paris
Glória
Catete
Lapa
Conde Lages
Visc Paranaguá
Joaquim Silva
Pinto Martins
Gonç Fontes
Joaquim Murtinho
Muratori
Tram line
Curvelo
Largo do Guimarães
Dias de Barros
Hermenegildo de Barros
Teresópolis
Almirante Alexandrino
Bno dos Santos
Tr M Lebrão
Mendes
Benjamin Constant
Santa Cristina
Fialho
A Belo
Santo Amaro
Ladeira da Glória
Lad De Nossa Senhora
Russel
Ld Russel
Goitacazes
Br Guaratiba
Orl
Rangel
Pedro Américo
V Part Ms Mota
Andrade Pertence
Carlos de Sá
Silveira Martins
Bento Lisboa
Ferreira Viana
Correia Dutra
Artur Bernardes
Buarque
Bastos
Tavares
Cruzeiro Sul
Fca de Andrade
Aprazível
Leo Fróis
Áurea
Teresinha
Fon Guimarães
Triunfo
C Brandt
Castro
Monte
Sebastião Leme
R G Marconi
Cardeal
Ladeira do
André Cavalcanti
Túnel Santa Barbára

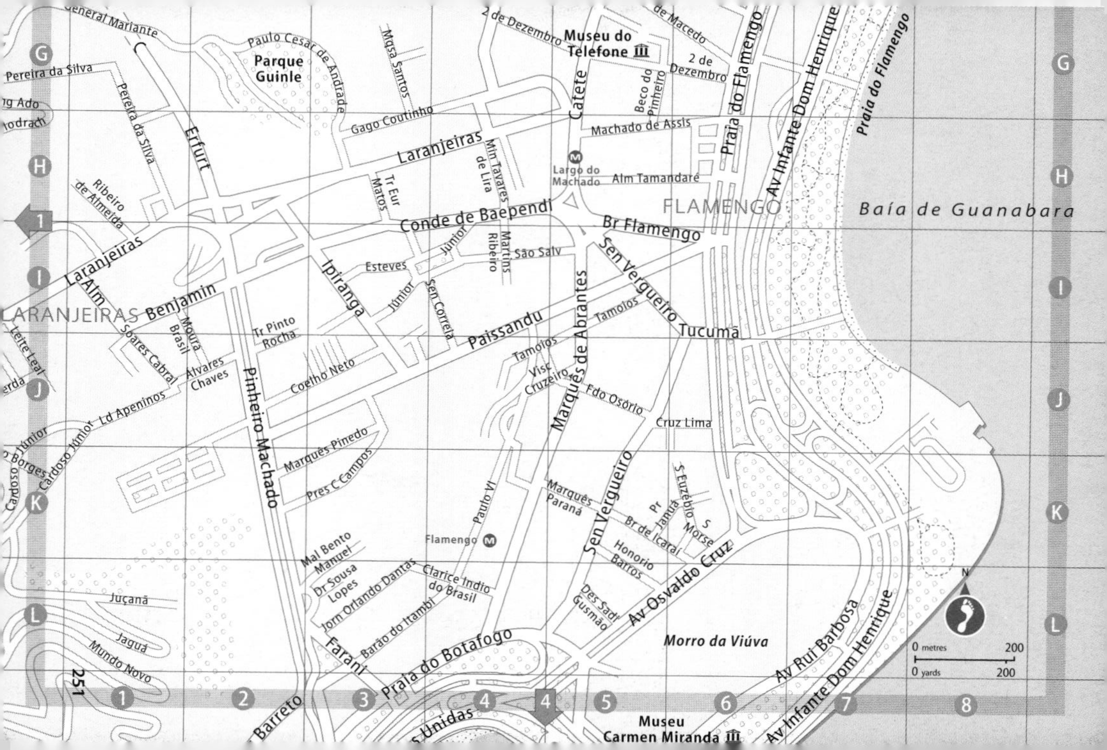

Baía de Guanabara
Praia do Flamengo
FLAMENGO
LARANJEIRAS
Museu do Telefone
Parque Guinle
Museu Carmen Miranda
Morro da Viúva
Largo do Machado
Flamengo
Av Infante Dom Henrique
Praia do Flamengo
Catete
Laranjeiras
Conde de Baependi
Br Flamengo
Sen Vergueiro
Tucumã
Marquês de Abrantes
Paissandu
Pinheiro Machado
Ipiranga
Erfurt
Benjamin
Alm
Av Osvaldo Cruz
Av Rui Barbosa
Praia do Botafogo
Farani
Barreto
Unidas
Machado de Assis
Alm Tamandaré
Gago Coutinho
Mqsa Santos
Paulo Cesar de Andrade
General Mariante
Pereira da Silva
2 de Dezembro
de Macedo
Beco do Pinheiro
Min Tavares de Lira
Tr Eur Matos
Martins Ribeiro
São Salv
Esteves
Júnior
Sen Correia
Tamoios
Visc Cruzeiro
Fdo Osório
Cruz Lima
Marquês Paraná
S Euzébio
Pr Januá
S Morse
Br de Icaraí
Honorio Barros
Des Sadi Gusmão
Paulo VI
Clarice Indio do Brasil
Jorn Orlando Dantas
Barão do Itambi
Mal Bento Manuel
Dr Sousa Lopes
Marquês Pinedo
Pres C Campos
Coelho Neto
Tr Pinto Rocha
Moura Brasil
Alvares Chaves
Soares Cabral
Ld Apeninos
Cardoso Júnior
Borges
Cardoso
Leite Leal
Ribeiro de Almeida
Juçanã
Jaguá
Mundo Novo
0 metres 200
0 yards 200
N
G H I J K L
1 2 3 4 5 6 7 8

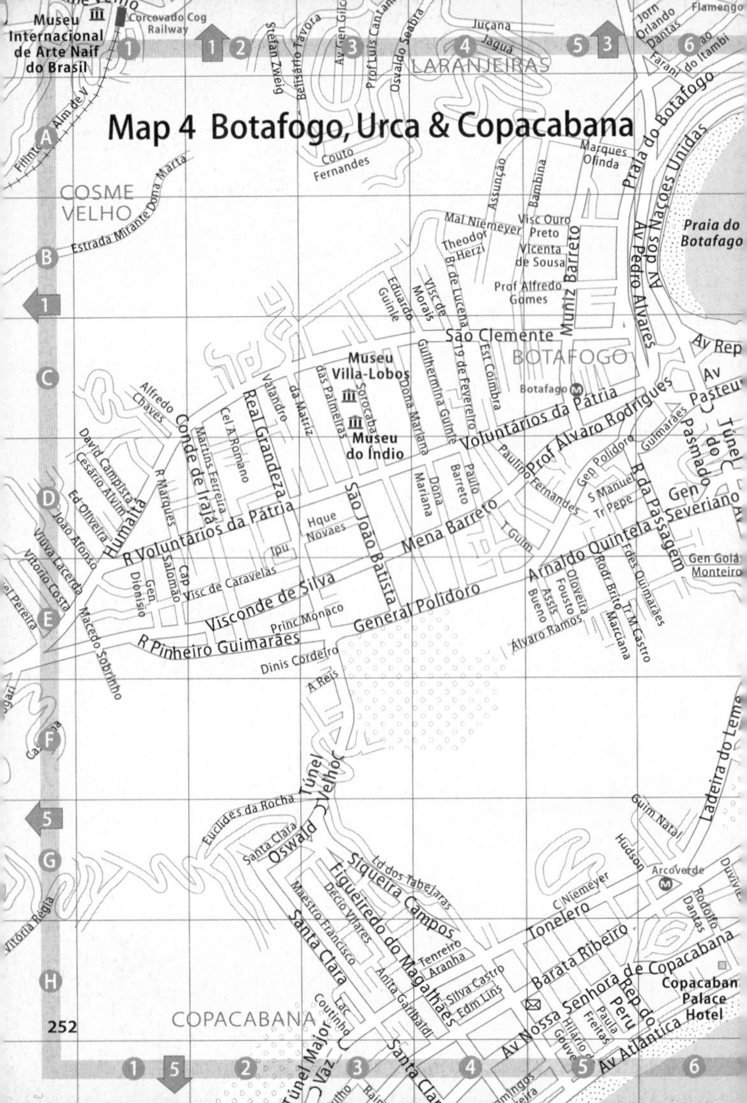

Map 4 Botafogo, Urca & Copacabana
Museu Internacional de Arte Naif do Brasil
Corcovado Cog Railway
COSME VELHO
LARANJEIRAS
BOTAFOGO
COPACABANA
Praia do Botafogo
Museu Villa-Lobos
Museu do Índio
Copacabana Palace Hotel
Botafogo
Arcoverde
Estrada Mirante Dona Marta
Alm de V
Filinto
Stefan Zweig
Belisário Távora
Av Gen Glicério
Prof Luís Cantanhede
Osvaldo Seabra
Juçana
Jaguá
Jorn Orlando Dantas
Flamengo
Farani
Couto Fernandes
Marques Olinda
Praia do Botafogo
Av dos Nações Unidas
Assunção
Bambina
Mal Niemeyer
Visc Ouro Preto
Theodor Herzl
Vicenta de Sousa
Prof Alfredo Gomes
Muniz Barreto
Av Pedro Alvares
Eduardo Guinle
Visc de Morais
Br de Lucena
São Clemente
19 de Fevereiro
Est Colômbia
Guilhermina Guinle
Dona Mariana
Sorocaba
das Palmeiras
da Matriz
Valandro
Real Grandeza
Cel A Romano
Martins Ferreira
Conde de Irajá
Alfredo Chaves
R Marques
Voluntários da Pátria
R Voluntários da Pátria
Prof Álvaro Rodrigues
Av Pasteur
Túnel do Pasmado
Guimarães
Gen Polidoro
S Manuel
Tr Pepe
R da Passagem
Gen Severiano
Paulino Fernandes
Paulo Barreto
Dona Mariana
São João Batista
Hque Novaes
Ipu
Mena Barreto
T Gulm
Arnaldo Quintela
Gen Golás Monteiro
Humaitá
David Campista
Cesário Alvim
Ed Oliveira
João Afonso
Viúva Lacerda
Vitório Costa
Macedo Sobrinho
Gen Dionísio
Salomão
Cap
Visc de Caravelas
Visconde de Silva
Princ Monaco
General Polidoro
R Pinheiro Guimarães
Dinis Cordeiro
A Reis
Oliveira
Fousto
Assis
Bueno
Rodr Brito
Marciana
Fdes Guimarães
Tr M Castro
Álvaro Ramos
Túnel Velho
Euclides da Rocha
Santa Clara
Oswald
Ld dos Tabajaras
Siqueira Campos
Figueiredo do Magalhães
Décio Vilares
Maestro Francisco
Tenreiro Aranha
Silva Castro
Edm Lins
Anita Garibaldi
Coutinho
Túnel Major Vaz
Tonelero
C Niemeyer
Barata Ribeiro
Av Nossa Senhora de Copacabana
Rep do Peru
Paula Freitas
Hilário de Gouveia
Av Atlântica
Ladeira do Leme
Guim Natal
Hudson
Rodolfo Dantas
Duvivier
Vitória Régia

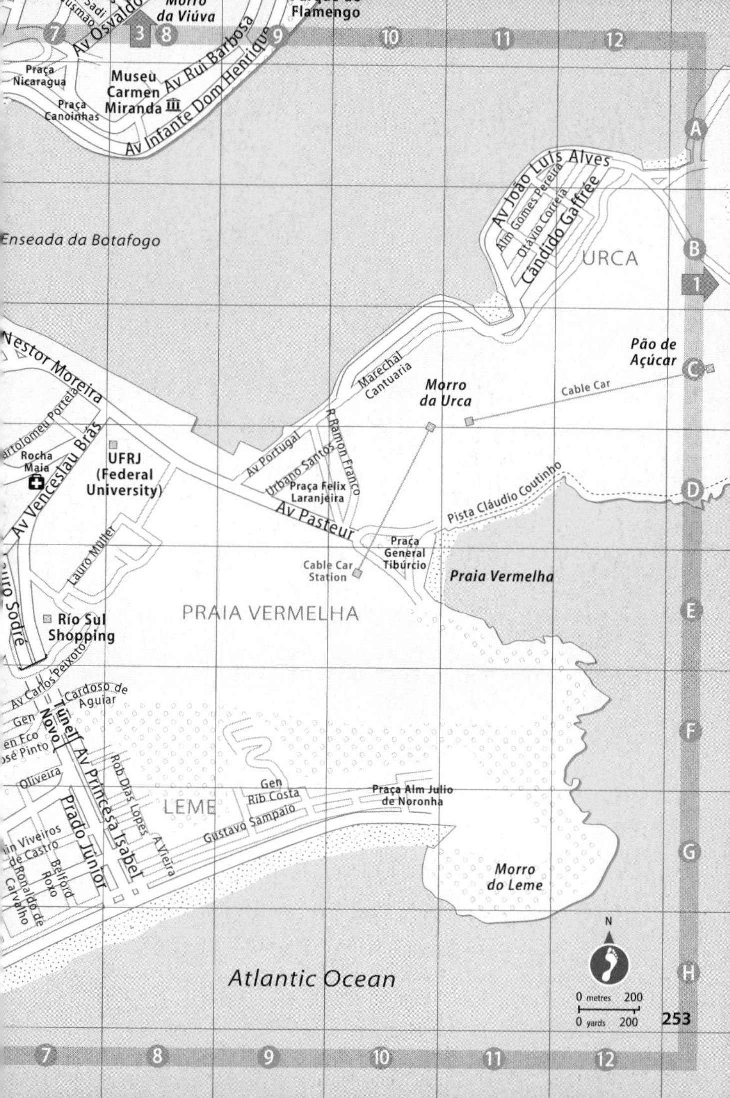

Morro da Viúva
Parque do Flamengo
Av Osvaldo
Av Rui Barbosa
Av Infante Dom Henrique
Praça Nicaragua
Museu Carmen Miranda
Praça Canoinhas
Enseada da Botafogo
Av João Luís Alves
Alm Gomes Pereira
Otávio Correia
Cândido Gaffrée
URCA
Pão de Açúcar
Cable Car
Morro da Urca
Marechal Cantuaria
Nestor Moreira
Bartolomeu Portela
Rocha Maia
Av Venceslau Brás
UFRJ (Federal University)
Av Portugal
Urbano Santos
R Ramon Franco
Praça Felix Laranjeira
Av Pasteur
Pista Cláudio Coutinho
Praça General Tibúrcio
Cable Car Station
Praia Vermelha
Lauro Muller
PRAIA VERMELHA
Rio Sul Shopping
Av Carlos Peixoto
Cardoso de Aguiar
Túnel Novo
Av Princesa Isabel
Prado Júnior
Rob Dias Lopes
Oliveira
Gen Rib Costa
Praça Alm Julio de Noronha
LEME
Gustavo Sampaio
A Vieira
Belford Roxo
Ronaldo de Carvalho
Viveiros de Castro
Morro do Leme
Atlantic Ocean
N
0 metres 200
0 yards 200
A
B
C
D
E
F
G
H
7
8
9
10
11
12
1
3

Map 5 Ipanema, Leblon & Lagoa
1
2
3
4
5
6
A
B
C
D
E
F
G
H
Sara Vilela
Visc Itaúna
Sen Simonsen
Parque Lage
Jardim Botânico
Inglês de Souza
Quintas
Peri
Eng Pena Chaves
R Cdr de Af Celso
R Ab Ramos
Tasso Fragoso
Gen
LAGOA
R Fernando Magalhães
R Dr G Esteves
Estela
Carminhoa
Abreu Fialho
A Ribeiro
M Jovimiano
JARDIM BOTÂNICO
Lopez Quintas
Visc Graça
Av Lineu de Paula Machado
Pacheco Leão
Jardim Botânico
Museu Botânico
Gen Garzon
Av Borges de Medeiros
Ilha Piraqué
Vila Hípica
R Particular
Lagoa Rodrigo de Freitas
Major Rubens
do Jequitibá
dos Oitis
Praça Santos Dumont
Gávea Shopping
Jóquei Clube
Parque Brigadeiro Faria Lima
Marquês de São Vicente
das Acácias
Gen Rabelo
Artur Araipe
Prof Man Ferreira
Av Rodrigo Otávio
Av Bartolomeu Mitre
Miguel Couto
Mário Ribeiro
Ilha dos Caiçaras
Gilberto Cardoso
Adalberto Ferreira
Fadel Fadel
Praça Milton Campos
Av Afrânio de Melo Franco
Félix Pacheco
Cap César Andrade
Des A Russel
Cde Bernadotte
Humberto de Campos
Av Epitácio Pessoa
Av Henrique Dumont
Itiquira
Leôncio Correia
Codajás
Av Visc de Albuquerque
General Venâncio Flores
João Barros
Prof A Ramos
LEBLON
Prof A M Teixeira
Barão da Torre
Garcia d'Ávila
Av Ataulfo de Pavia
Av General San Martin
Alm Pereira
Paul Redfern
Aníbal de Mendonça
Dias Ferreira
General Artigas
Rainha Guilhermina
Arist Espínola
Rita Ludolf
Jer Monteiro
Gen Urquiza
João Lira
Linhares
José
Durão
Carlos Góis
Guilhem
Almirante
O Goeldi
Av Delfim Moreira
Praia do Leblon
Praia do Ipanema
Atlantic Ocean
Av Niemeyer

COPACABANA
IPANEMA
ARPOADOR
Parque da Catacumba
Casa de Cultura Laura Alvim
Forte de Copacabana
Praia do Arpoador
Praça Gen Alcio Souto
Praça José Mariano Filho
Praça NS da Paz
Av Epitácio Pessoa
Prof Abelardo Lobo
Hilaire
da Fonte da Saudade
Dinis Cordeiro
A Reis
Túnel Velho
Oswald
Euclides da Rocha
Santa Clara
Siqueira Campos
Figueiredo do Magalhães
Ld dos Tabajaras
Décio Villares
Maestro Francisco
Tenreiro Aranha
Anita Garibaldi
Silva Castro
Edm Lins
Lac Coutinho
Túnel Major Vaz
S de Julho
Raimundo Correia
Dias de Rocha
Domingos Ferreira
Av Henrique Dodsworth
Pompeu Loureiro
Barata Ribeiro
Constante Ramos
Leopoldo Miguez
Barão de Ipanema
Bolivar
Xavier da Silveira
Miguel Lemos
Aires de Saldanha
Djalma Ulrich
Alm Goçalves
Túnel Pref Sá Fr Alvim
St Roman
Sá Ferreira
R Sousa Lima
Bulhões Carvalho
R Raul Pompéia
Francisco Sá
Júlio de Castilhos
Cons Lafaiete
R Gomes Carneiro
Canning
Av Rainha Elizabeth
R Joaquim Nabuco
Francisco Otaviano
Alberto de Campos
Vinicius de Moraes
Barão da Torre
Farme de Amoedo
Teixeira de Melo
Alm Guillobel
Sacope
Vitória Regia
Azevedo
Casurina
Cus Serrão
Frei Leandro
0 metres 200
0 yards 200

Map 6 Around Praça 15 de Novembro

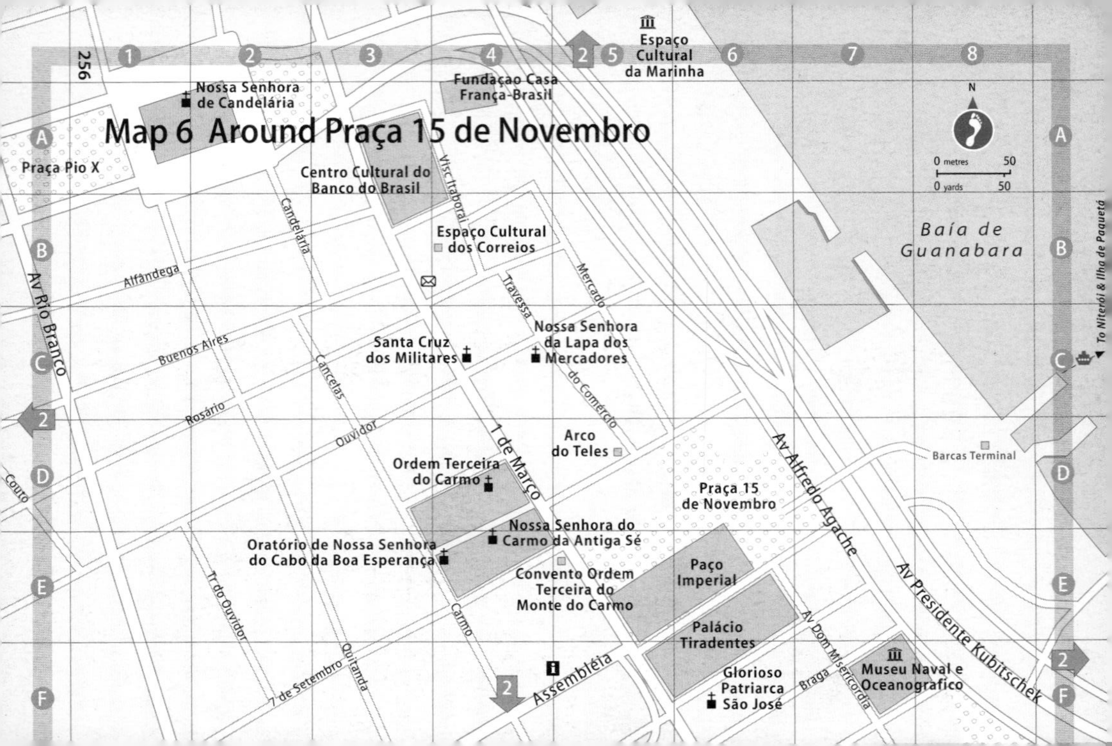